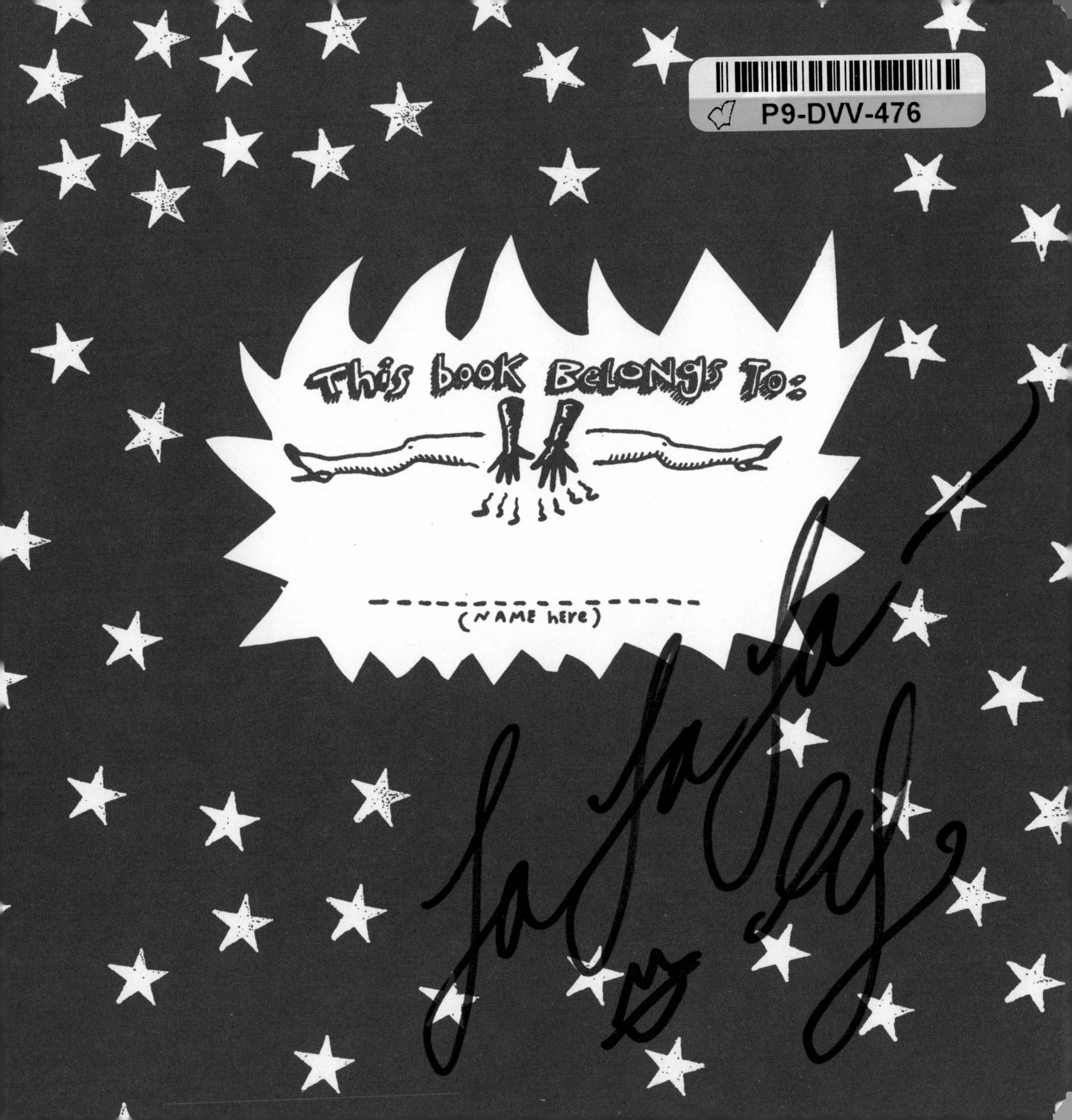
This book Belongs to:
(NAME here)

Lap Dancing for Mommy

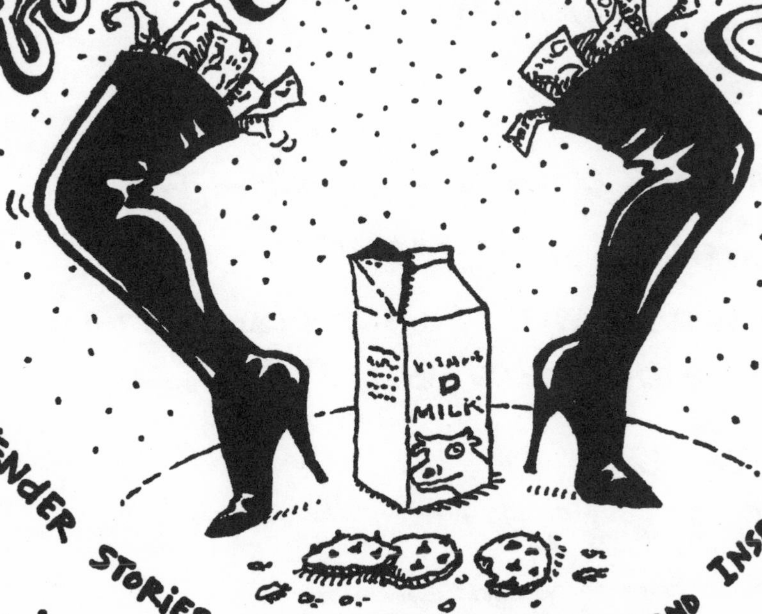
D
MILK

Tender Stories of Disgust, Blame and Inspiration

by Erika Lopez

Seal Press
Seattle

Seal Press
3131 Western Avenue/Suite 410
Seattle, WA ···· 98121
sealprss @ scn. org

Library of Congress Cataloging-in-Publication Data
LOPEZ, ERIKA
LAP DANCING FOR Mommy / by ERIKA LOPEZ
1. Title
PN 6727. L6B L36 1997   741.5'973-dc21   97-7304

ISBN → 1-878067-96-6

PRINTED in Canada
First Printing, JUNE 1997
10 9 8 7 6 5 4 3 2 1

Distributed to the trade by Publishers Group West
In Canada → Publishers Group West Canada, Toronto
In Europe + The U.K. → AiRLIFT BOOK COMPANY, London

COVER ART/DESIGN by ERIKA LOPEZ
COVER LAYOUT by TRINA STAHL
COVER Photo by MAX-IMAGE, SF

*

Thanks to all the PEOPLE
who've made it so we can
take FOR GRANTED the
FreedOM to BE who we
are, SAY WHAT WE WANT
and sit where we want.

and thanks to KRIS Kovick
FOR Giving me the courage
to bE as tASteless as I want.

*

Table of Contents

Phallusies

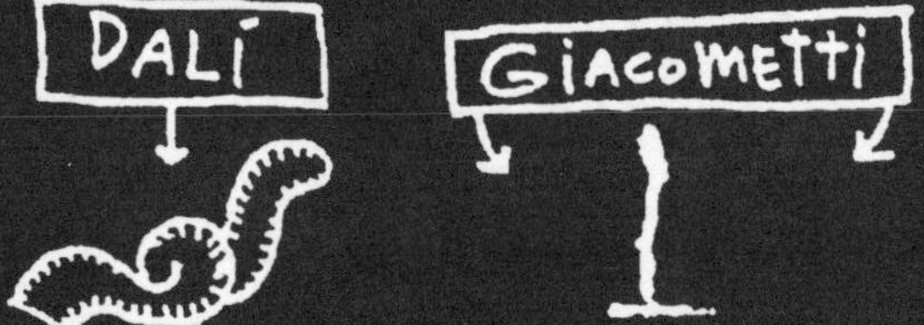
DALI
GIACOMETTI

THE FAKE PENIS EXHIBITION

(an ONGOING EXHIBITION throughout the book)

Leaning Tower of Penis OR A HUSSIER RATING

The IDEA FOR this COLLECTION OF FAKE PENISES CAME FROM MY SEARCH FOR THE ULTIMATE SEXUAL EXPERIENCE by MYSELF. THE ONLY FAKE PENISES I'VE SEEN OFFERED, are the PIG-COLORED ONES, Big Black RUBBER ONES, Penguin ONES, Dolphin shaped ones, + ONES looking Like Kings. I wanted something MORE. Something cooler, At least. I even Went to Stockholm, thinking I'D FiND SMooth, MODERN WOOD IKEA-TYPE PENISES, but I didn't. I'D been under the false IMPRESSION that I could COLLECT FAKE Penises throughout EUROPE the way others collect Matchbook covers + hotel towels. Like, Would touristy SPANISH ones be RED + Black?

DISAPPOINTEDLY RETURNING to the U.S. W/LIVER DAMAGE, A U2 T-SHIRT, + A WEDGE OF CHEESE, I KNEW I'D have to take Matters into My own hands.

But 1/2 way into PLANNING a COLLECTION OF FAKE PENISES, I thought of Judy Chicago + My Mother. Two women from the generation that loved its VAGINAS. Was I kicking DIRT in the face of EVERYthing they fought FOR, + CELEBRATing MY INTERNALIZED Misogyny by SURROUNDING MYSELF w/PENISES + Devoting A whole Lot of TIME to Making THEM? What happened to ALL that CUNT POSITIVE thinking?

I couldn't deny THE FACT THAT EVEN THOUGH I WANTED THE FREEDOM to HAVE hairy LEGS + go BRALESS, I also LOVED RECEIVING flowers, Gifts, + HEADBOARD-CRASHING PENETRATION W/MY KNEES at my shoulders... TO INDULGE IN THE POWERLESS FEELING THAT MADE ME FEEL like this guy WOULD PAY MY RENT + fix my CAR FOREVER.

AND THEN I SUDDENLY REALIZED I JUST MIGHT BE SAVING MY OWN LIFE BY FUCKING MYSELF FOR A WHILE.

SERIAL KILLER Penis

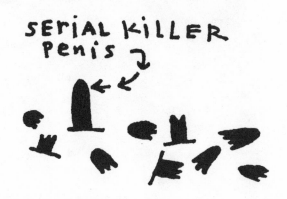

Pia
Sweden

(my *** first cartoon that wasn't on some CRAPPY NAPKIN.)

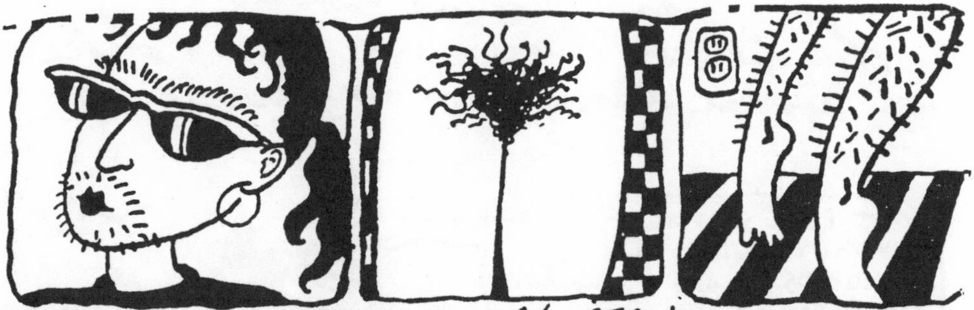

BEING 1/2 PUERTO RICAN + 1/2 Regular-WHITE-GIRL HAS LEFT **PIA SWEDEN** a very hairy woman WHO DOESN'T KNOW HOW TO SPEAK Spanish.

LIKE ALMOST EVERY OTHER SMALL FRAGILE girl, HER REALISTIC IDOLS WERE: FARRAH FAWCETT IN THAT SITTING-IN-FRONT-OF-A-BLANKET POSTER; AND THAT LITTLE BLONDE GIRL W/BANGS ON "NO MORE TEARS" Spray-on CONDITIONER (MADE BY Johnson + Johnson). THESE were the queens of **THE HAIRLESS BLOND PEOPLE** AND SHE LOVED THEM. So WHEN Pia WAS YOUNG (AND EVEN NOW, SOMETIMES) SHE'D PUT ON A TURTLENECK, THEN TAKE IT OFF & LEAVE IT ON HER HEAD. This would ENABLE the arms and body to CASCADE DOWN HER young BACK IN A LONG BLUE fall, SIMULATING JOHNSON + JOHNSON'S "NO MORE TEARS" GIRL,

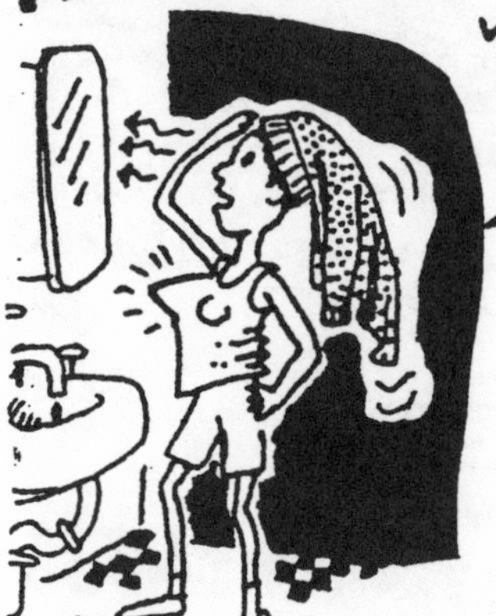

as if she were riding on a white horse on the beach (woosh, woosh)... Like an honest tampon commercial:

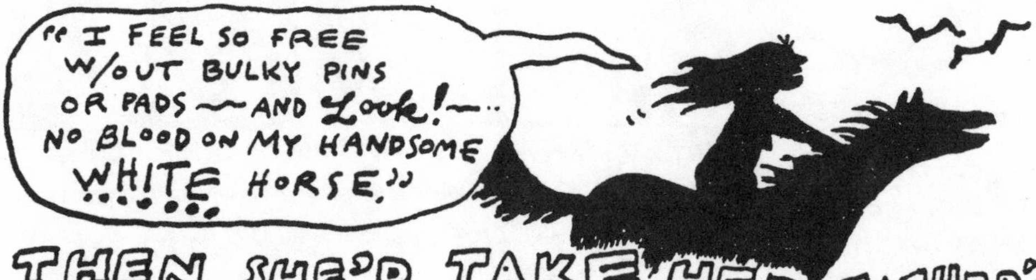
"I FEEL SO FREE W/OUT BULKY PINS OR PADS — AND Look! — NO BLOOD ON MY HANDSOME WHITE HORSE."

THEN SHE'D TAKE HER FATHER'S "L'LEGGS" EGG + split it in half and put BOTH halves UNDER HER COTTON RIBBED SEXY under-SHIRT.

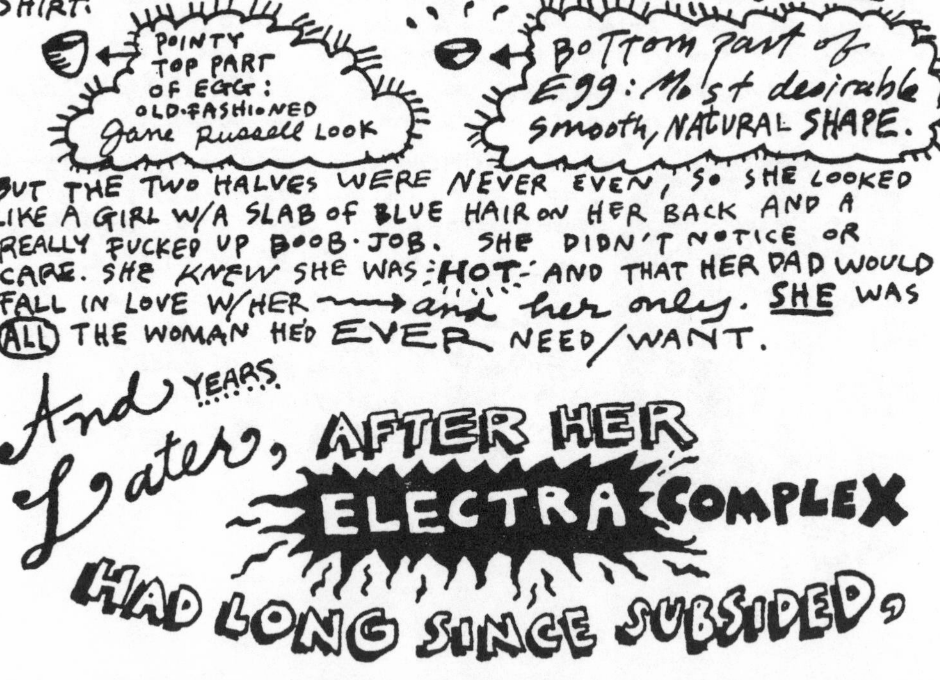
POINTY TOP PART OF EGG: OLD-FASHIONED Jane Russell LOOK
BOTTOM part of EGG: Most desirable smooth, NATURAL SHAPE.

BUT THE TWO HALVES WERE NEVER EVEN, SO SHE LOOKED LIKE A GIRL W/A SLAB OF BLUE HAIR ON HER BACK AND A REALLY FUCKED UP BOOB-JOB. SHE DIDN'T NOTICE OR CARE. SHE KNEW SHE WAS HOT AND THAT HER DAD WOULD FALL IN LOVE W/HER → and her only. SHE WAS ALL THE WOMAN HE'D EVER NEED/WANT.

And YEARS Later, AFTER HER ELECTRA COMPLEX HAD LONG SINCE SUBSIDED,

SHE BEGAN THE IMPOSSIBLE SEARCH → *looking for a pleasurable way of* REMOVING FUR.

One day...

SHE BOUGHT A PAIR OF BIRKENSTOCKS, AND *all of* A SUDDEN SHE DIDN'T EVEN *care if* SHE LOOKED SEXY: **SHE WAS COMFORTABLE.**

SHE LET THE HAIR ON HER LEGS GROW *real long*, SHE ATE TOFU & SUBSCRIBED TO THE UTNE *Reader*. *Then* SHE STARTED GOING BRALESS.

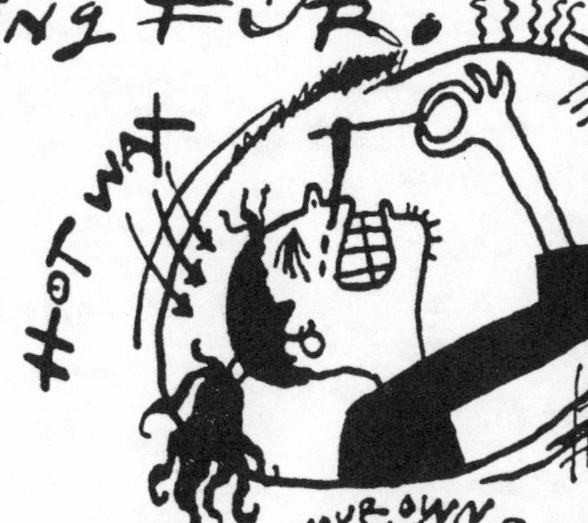
HOT WAX

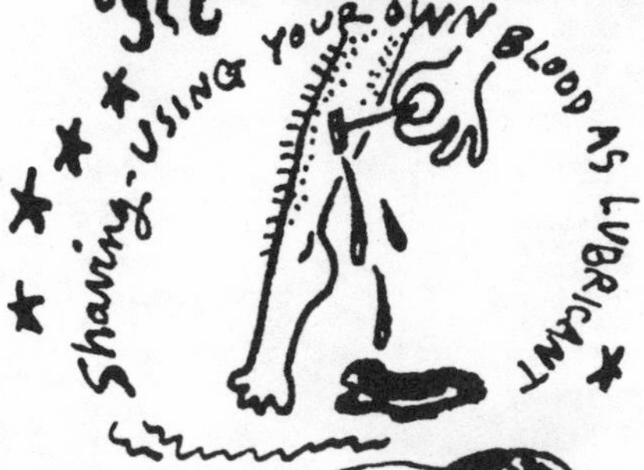
Shaving - USING YOUR OWN BLOOD AS LUBRICANT

The next MORNING SHE *looked in the mirror* AND DECIDED SHE MUST BE A LESBIAN, SO SHE PACKED HER BAGS + MOVED TO PROVINCETOWN BECAUSE SAN FRANCISCO WAS TOO EXPENSIVE.

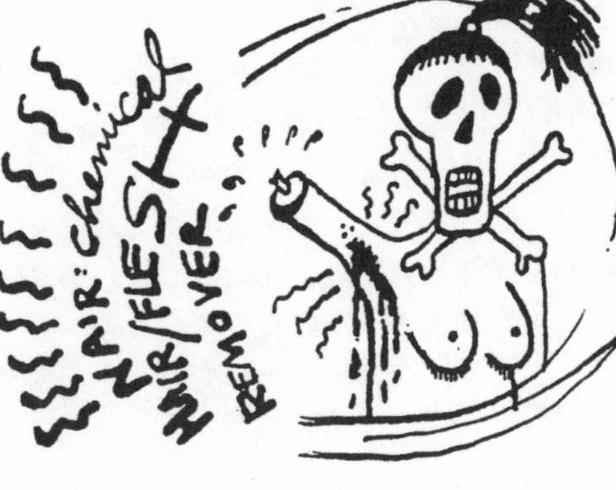
HAIR: chemical
HAIR/FLESH
REMOVER

Once she arrived in "poo town", she went to the library to check out a copy of *LESBIAN NATION* where its Author says if you want to TRULY LOVE yourself and your sisters, you have to sleep w/them FIRST. (IT WAS WRITTEN in the 70s.)

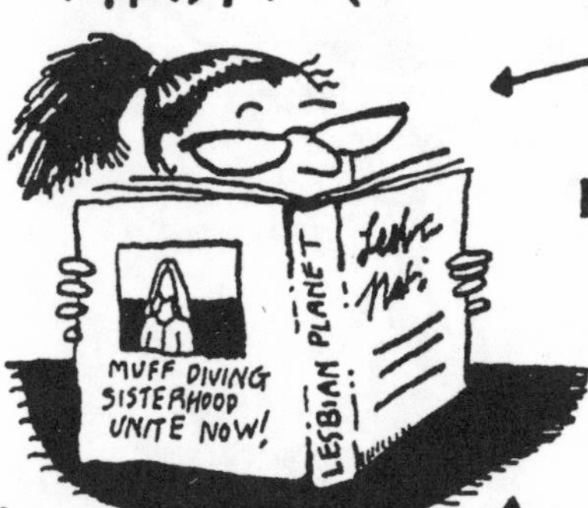

MUFF DIVING SISTERHOOD UNITE NOW!
LESBIAN PLANET

"OKAY. Now I'll be gay. It'll be great — like having a best friend + sleeping w/her. BUT IT'LL BE HARD GIVING ONE OF MY FRIENDS A FUCK ME LOOK W/OUT CRACKIN' UP. BUT I'LL get over it. They probably cover a situation like that in LESBIAN NATION."

"AND HOW WILL I KNOW IF someone else is a LESBIAN? Is there a sign? If so, I DON'T know it and I'll miss it... I'll still be alone, lonely, w/out love * maybe I'll hum Holly Near and Cris Williamson songs in public so that OTHER lesbians will hear me and think that I'm one of them because I know all the words to 'THE CHANGER + THE CHANGED'...."

"*If that doesn't work, I'll talk about how cool women tennis players are.* AND THE SEX. I'LL FEEL LIKE A VIRGIN AGAIN. HOW WILL I KNOW WHAT TO DO? I KNOW! *I will* RENT LESBIAN PORN FILMS FROM SPRUCE ST. VIDEO AND STUDY THEM. BUT *wait.... what* if SOMEONE I *know* is THERE RENTING '*my Fair Lady*' AND THEY SEE ME? THEN THEY'LL POLITELY SMILE, AND WHEN THEY LEAVE, THEY'LL TELL *everyone* I'M GAY. I'LL LOSE MY JOB, MALE WAITERS WILL HATE WAITING ON ME (THEY'LL THINK I WON'T TIP), MY FRIENDS WON'T HUG ME, PEOPLE WILL CLOSELY OBSERVE *my mannerisms* AND MY CATHOLIC DAD *won't speak to me. My mom will because* SHE'S ALREADY *gay.* BUT WHAT IF I'M NOT *even sure* I'm LESBIAN MATERIAL AND I *change my mind back* BUT I'M OUT *of* THE CLOSET *anyway*? THAT WOULD TRULY SUCK.

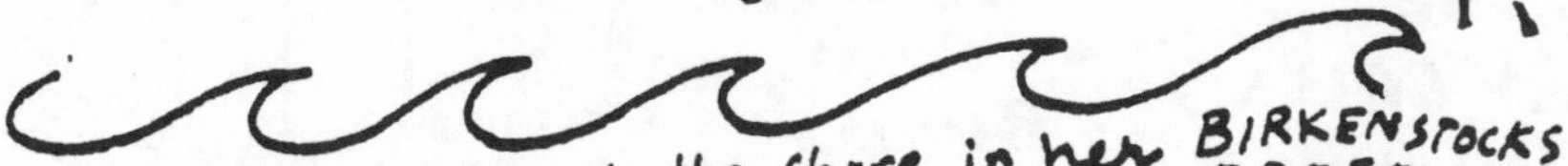

(so Pia Sweden decided to go to the shore in her BIRKENSTOCKS AND BE PROFOUND)

"I WILL GO TO THE SHORE NOW. I NEED TO Relax... put my mind on OTHER THINGS. I WILL COMMUNE w/ nature & CENTER my soul AT The womb of the earth, HERE AT THE OCEAN THAT GIVETH FORTH PLANET LIFE. I WILL THINK ABOUT THE QUALITY OF MY OWN LIFE. I WILL BE AMAZED AT THE Sheer BEAUTY

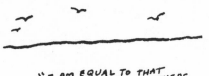

"I AM EQUAL TO THAT SHATTERED CRAB OVER THERE IN THE SAND"

OF THE OCEAN AND MARVEL AT JUST how INSIGNIFICANT I AM. I AM A FLY PERCHED ON THE EDGE OF AN ORANGE, SCRATCHED UP TUPPERWARE CUP FROM 1973. My mind wanders.

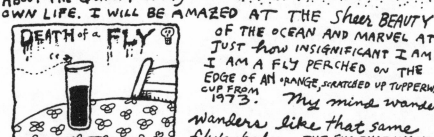

DEATH of a FLY

wanders like that same fly's body... THE FLY THAT WANTED TO BE GREAT AND TASTE THE CHERRY KOOL-AID in that scarred Tupperware cup, BUT DROWNED instead. Never to RETURN To her fly family again. I NOW TURN TO THOUGHTS of THE SKIN-SLOUGHING EFFECTS of WET sand ON MY FEET. I GO to work on my heels... AWAY, BAD CALLUS, away. AND I THINK THAT THE NEXT person I sleep w/ would Remark to his or herself →

POTENTIAL LUXURY FEET OF LOVE

"WOW. WHAT SOFT AND SILKY FEET PIA-THE-BABE HAS. SHE IS JUST like A DELICATE (BUT) ASSERTIVE FLOWER. JUST LIKE A COSMO GIRL. NOW I LOVE HER only, AND I WILL NEVER EVEN THINK of Leaving HER... flower THAT SHE iS."

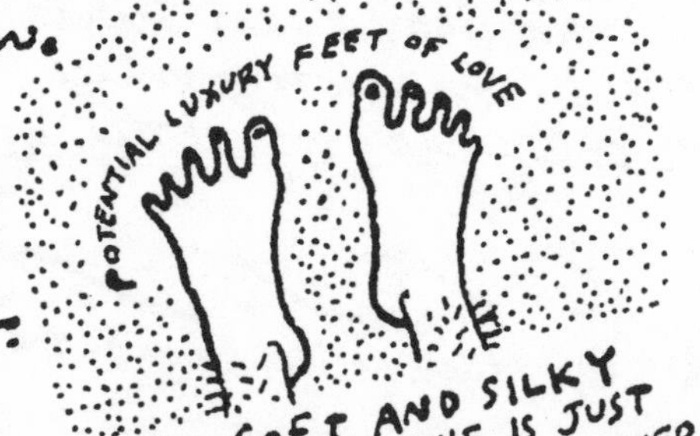

COSMOPOLITAN

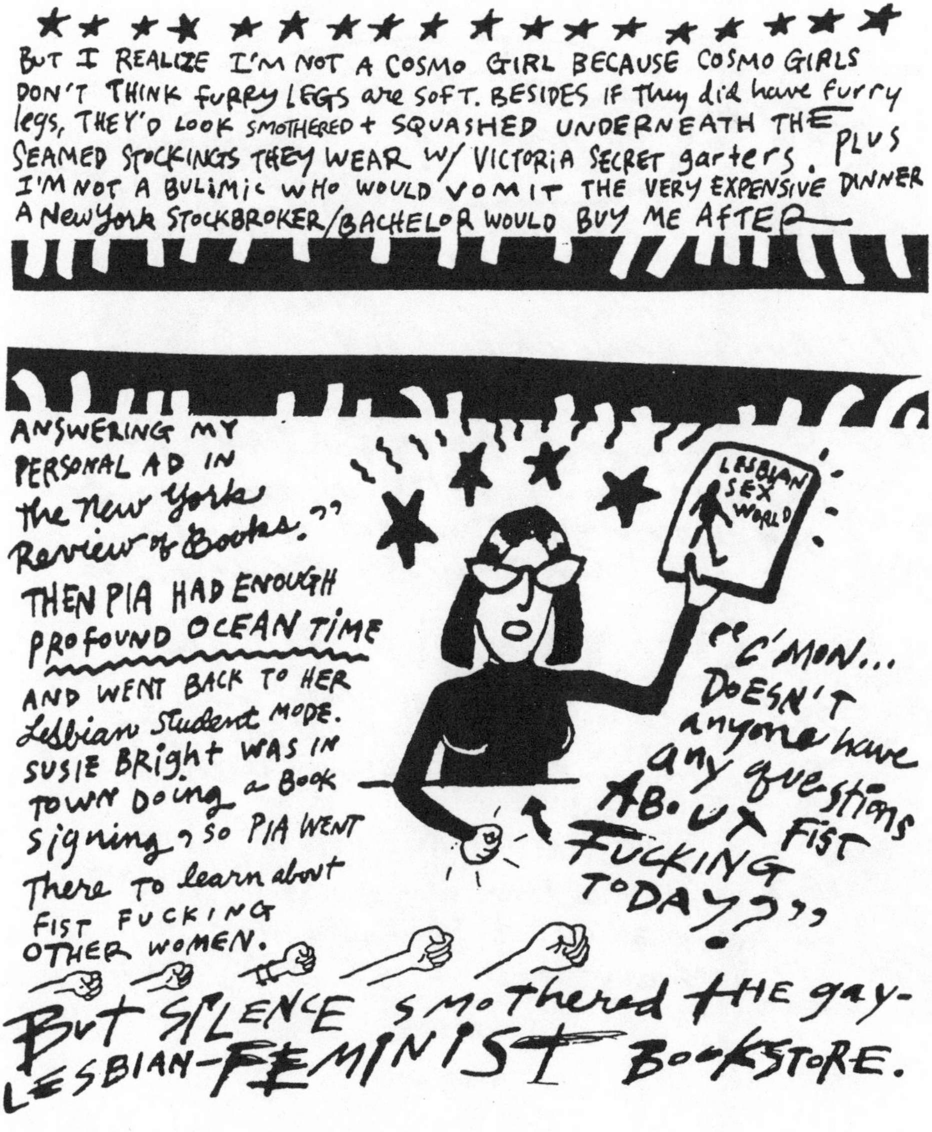
BUT I REALIZE I'M NOT A COSMO GIRL BECAUSE COSMO GIRLS DON'T THINK furry LEGS are SOFT. BESIDES IF they did have furry legs, THEY'D LOOK SMOTHERED + SQUASHED UNDERNEATH THE SEAMED STOCKINGS THEY WEAR w/ VICTORIA SECRET garters. PLUS I'M NOT A BULIMIC WHO WOULD VOMIT THE VERY EXPENSIVE DINNER A New York STOCKBROKER/BACHELOR WOULD BUY ME AFTER
ANSWERING MY PERSONAL AD IN the New York Review of Books."
THEN PIA HAD ENOUGH PROFOUND OCEAN TIME AND WENT BACK TO HER Lesbian Student MODE. SUSIE BRIGHT WAS IN TOWN DOING a BOOK signing, SO PIA WENT There to learn about FIST FUCKING OTHER WOMEN.
LESBIAN SEX WORLD
"C'MON... DOESN'T anyone have any questions ABOUT FIST FUCKING TODAY?"
BUT SILENCE smothered THE gay-LESBIAN-FEMINIST BOOKSTORE.

"Don't be shy, speak up,"

she said. One woman in the corner did:

"Well, Susie, you've changed my life. Now I can admit I like to be roughed-up by my woman + tied up to motel beds for days. Now I can be open about this w/my parents. And boy, I thought they had a hard time when I told them I was gay..."

Then Pia got the idea that she would like a little rough sex herself. No more slow/caring lovemaking for her!

She decided to start out slow with her lover at home so he wouldn't freak out & think she was a heavy-duty closet S+M chick.

SHE WENT HOME AND GAVE HIM A BLOWJOB AND BEGGED HIM TO PULL HER HAIR. HE HAD THIS HORRIFIED/DISGUSTED/IRRITATED LOOK & SAID HE COULDN'T POSSIBLY DO ANYTHING LIKE THAT. BUT HE WANTED THE BLOWJOB ANYWAY. SHE BEGGED AGAIN FOR HAIR/HEAD PULLING. HE LOOKED AWAY. THE ROUGHEST HE GOT WAS WHEN HE SLIGHTLY MOVED HIS HIPS ONCE AS HE CAME, AND HIS HANDS HOVERED AROUND HER HEAD. Needless TO SAY, PIA SWEDEN WAS QUITE DISAPPOINTED.

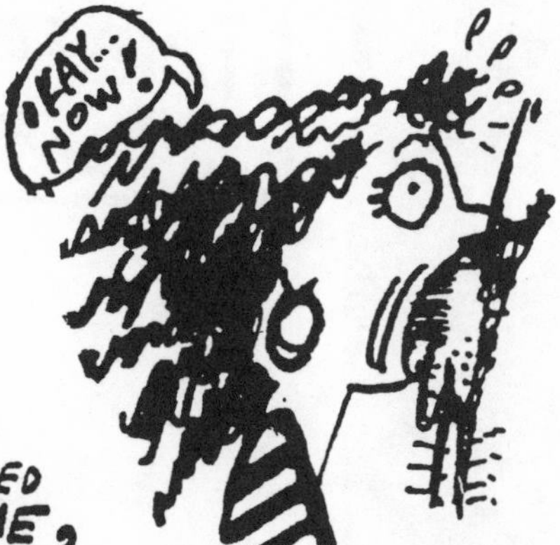
'KAY.. NOW!

THE END.

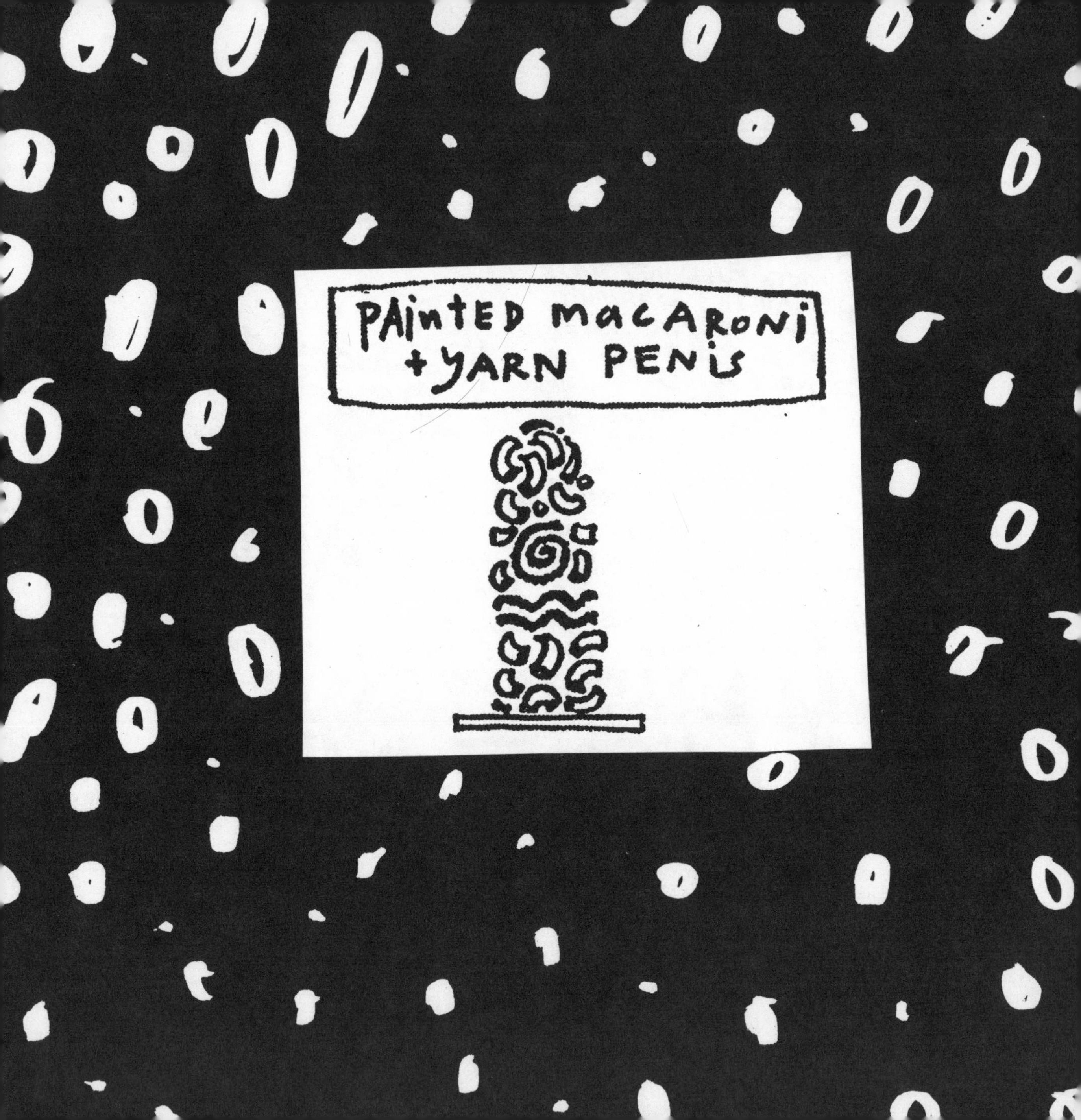
PAINTED MACARONI
+ YARN PENIS

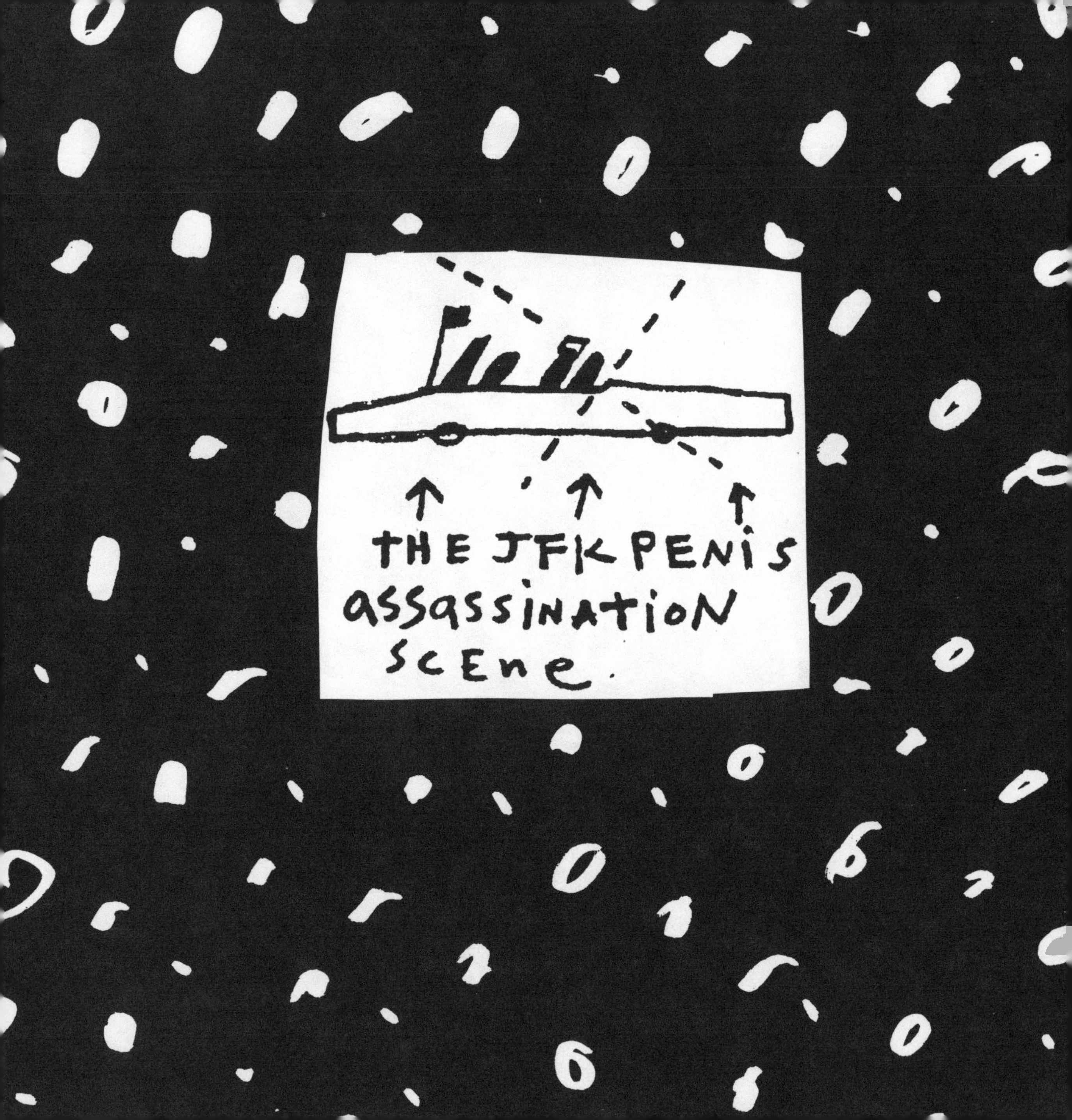
THE JFK PENIS
assassination
scene.

THE Lopez STRAP-ON CARTOON

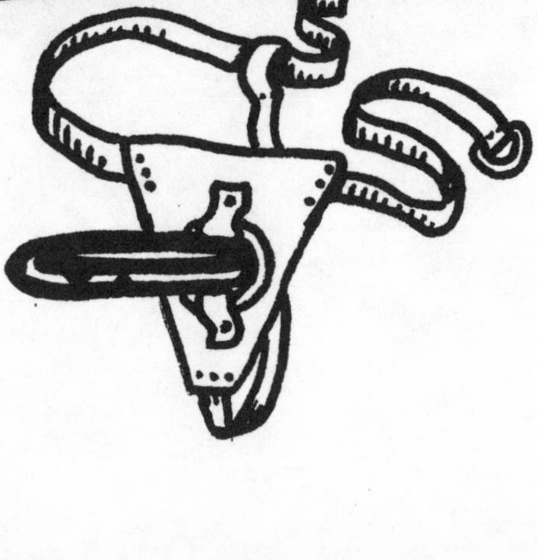

THIS IS NOT ABOUT WOMEN WHO
PICK UP 1/2·FULL BOTTLES OF
BEER w/THEIR LABIAS + DO
HEADSTANDS. / No. / THIS is
ABOUT OCCASIONAL BOUTS
OF "PENIS ENVY" w/ "BREAST
CONTENTMENT" AT THE SAME
TIME.

STRAP-ONS ARE GOOD. YOU
PUT ONE on + you ARE
IMMEDIATELY IN YOUR OWN
SAFE, ANDROGYNOUS, k. d. lang
KIND of world. / YOU WILL
NOTICE A RUSH AS YOU FEEL
LIKE WARREN BEATTY OR MR.
T, AND you WILL WANT
YOUR OWN MONSTER TRUCK
THAT you CAN Fill up WITH
ALL your OWN SPERM.

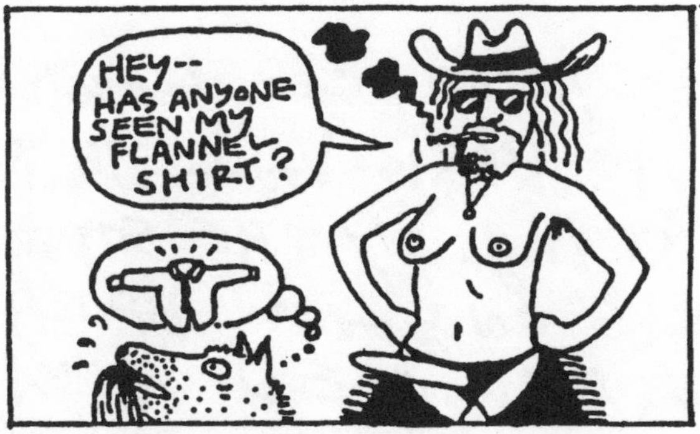
HEY-- HAS ANYONE SEEN MY FLANNEL SHIRT?

TAKING PRIDE IN YOUR APPENDAGE,
YOU HAVE FITTED THE HEAD OF
IT W/STEEL + NOW YOU'RE
MAKING HOLES ALL OVER
THE BACK OF THAT
BROWN RECLINER THAT
SHINES → AND YOU'RE ON
YOUR WAY UP TO CHEAP
FOAM SOFAS FROM IKEA
WHEN NO ONE'S LOOKING.

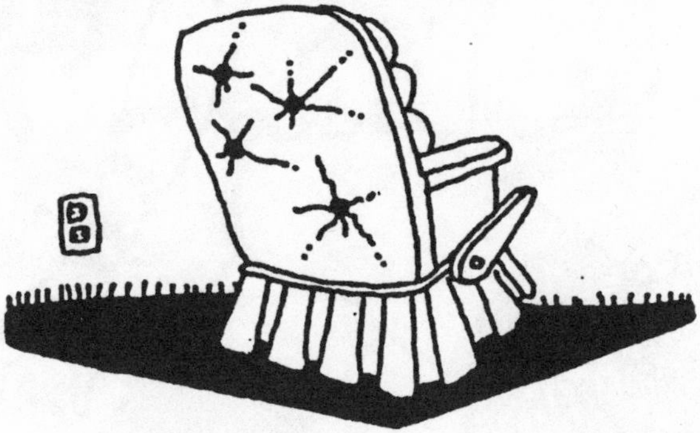

You later see yourself in A BORIS VALLEJO FANTASY PAINTING w/ THE STRETCH — MARKS ON your BREASTS AIRBRUSHED AWAY...

AND NOW YOU'RE PROPELLED
BACK ～～～ BACK TO A TIME
WHEN DWARVES LIVED IN CAVES,
PYTHONS HAD OPINIONS THAT
MATTERED + THEY COULD FLY,
AND CONAN THE BARBARIAN
WALKED THE EARTH... GIVING
AWAY FRUIT.

"HI. GIVE ME FRUIT, CONAN, MY FRIEND."

"SURE, YOU SWEET PYTHON W/OPINIONS THAT MATTER."

YOU'RE UNDEFEATABLE W/ YOUR
STEEL-TIPPED VINYL STRAP-ON
AND YOUR WELDED BRA...
YOU ARE DESIRED BY EVERY-
ONE ~~and~~ EVERYTHING ~~in~~
THIS HOBBIT-INFESTED WORLD:
MEN LUST AFTER you; WOMEN
CRAVE you; DOGS AND
ELVES DREAM ABOUT YOU;
WHILE MOLLUSKS AND TROUT
WOULD DIE FOR YOU. / YOU
ARE RULER OF THIS WORLD.

THEN, LIKE A XXX PINOCCHIO,
YOU FIND THAT IF you LIE,
YOUR PENIS ACTUALLY GETS
LONGER.

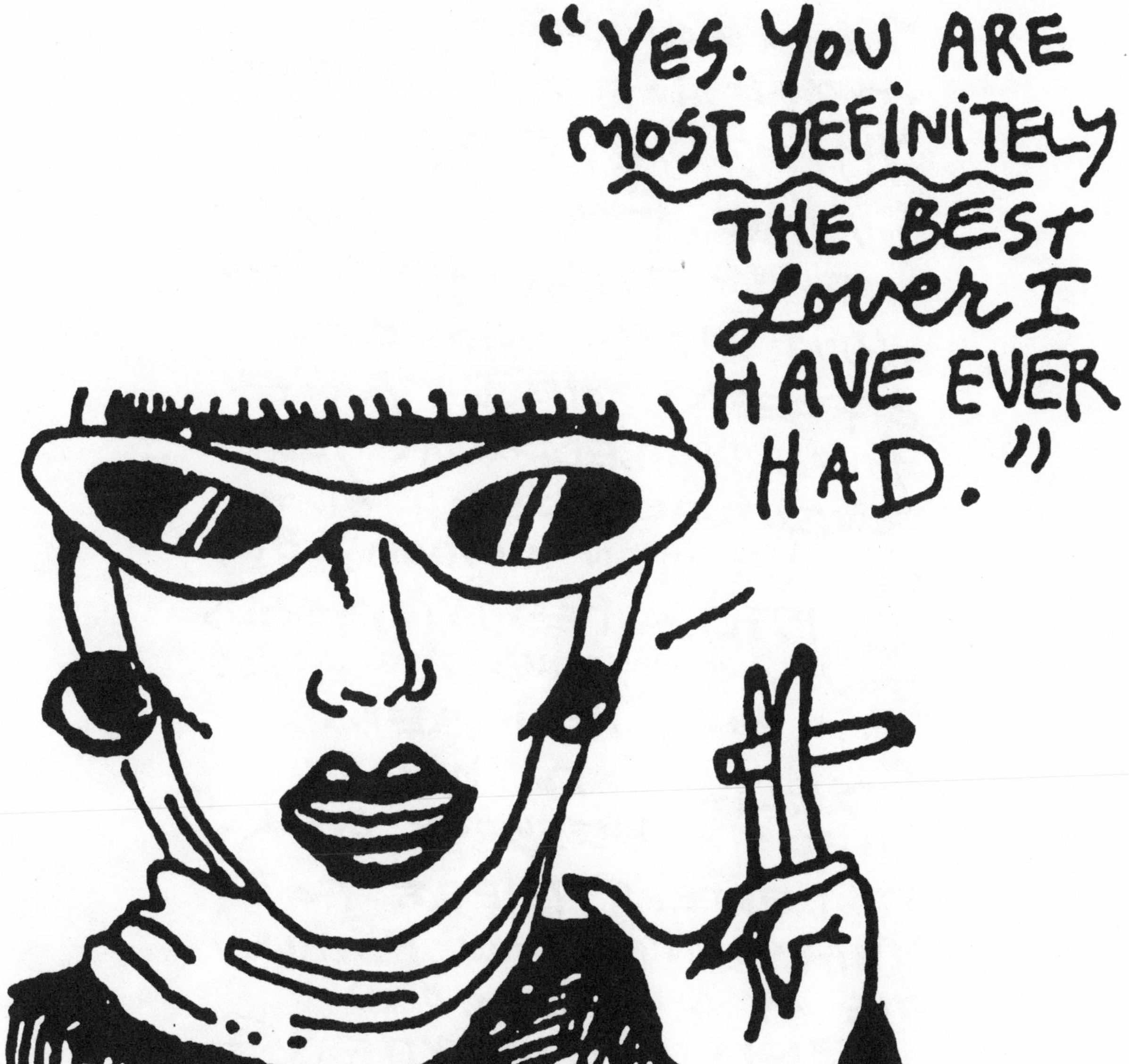
"YES. YOU ARE MOST DEFINITELY THE BEST Lover I HAVE EVER HAD."

Months later, you awake to a Kafkaesque Nightmare ~~~~ :
you have finally become nothing but ~~a~~ huge penis w/out arms who can't ~~open~~ the door of your own bedroom. You ~~eventually~~ jump out of the open window, but a 1970s feminist sees you and throws an apple at you. It imbeds itself into what used to be your back. It festers there for years until you finally die as a lonely, old penis somewhere in Maine.

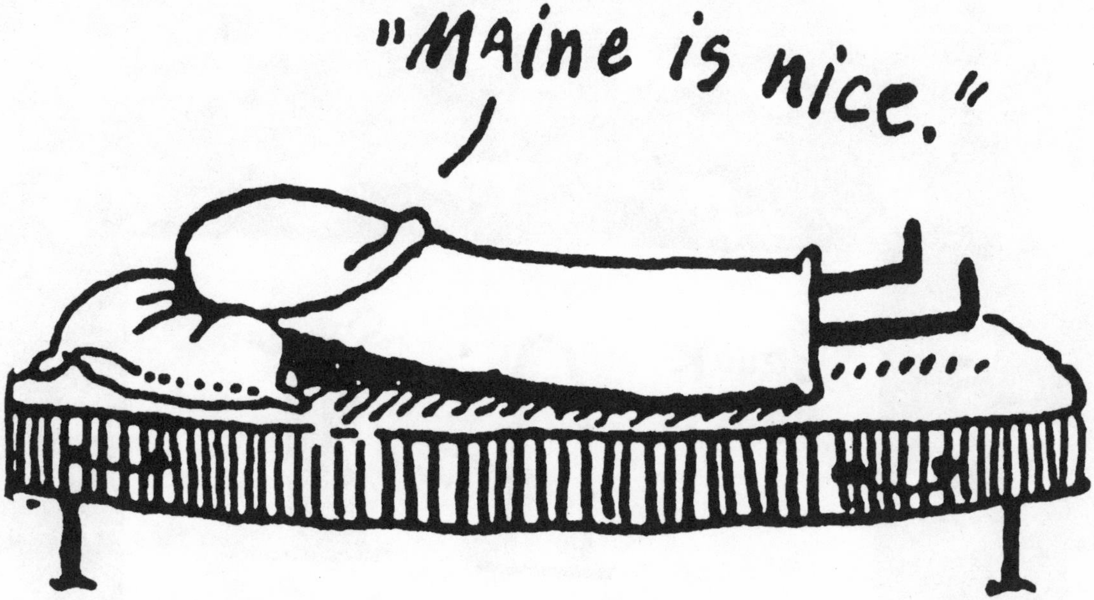
"Maine is nice."

The End.

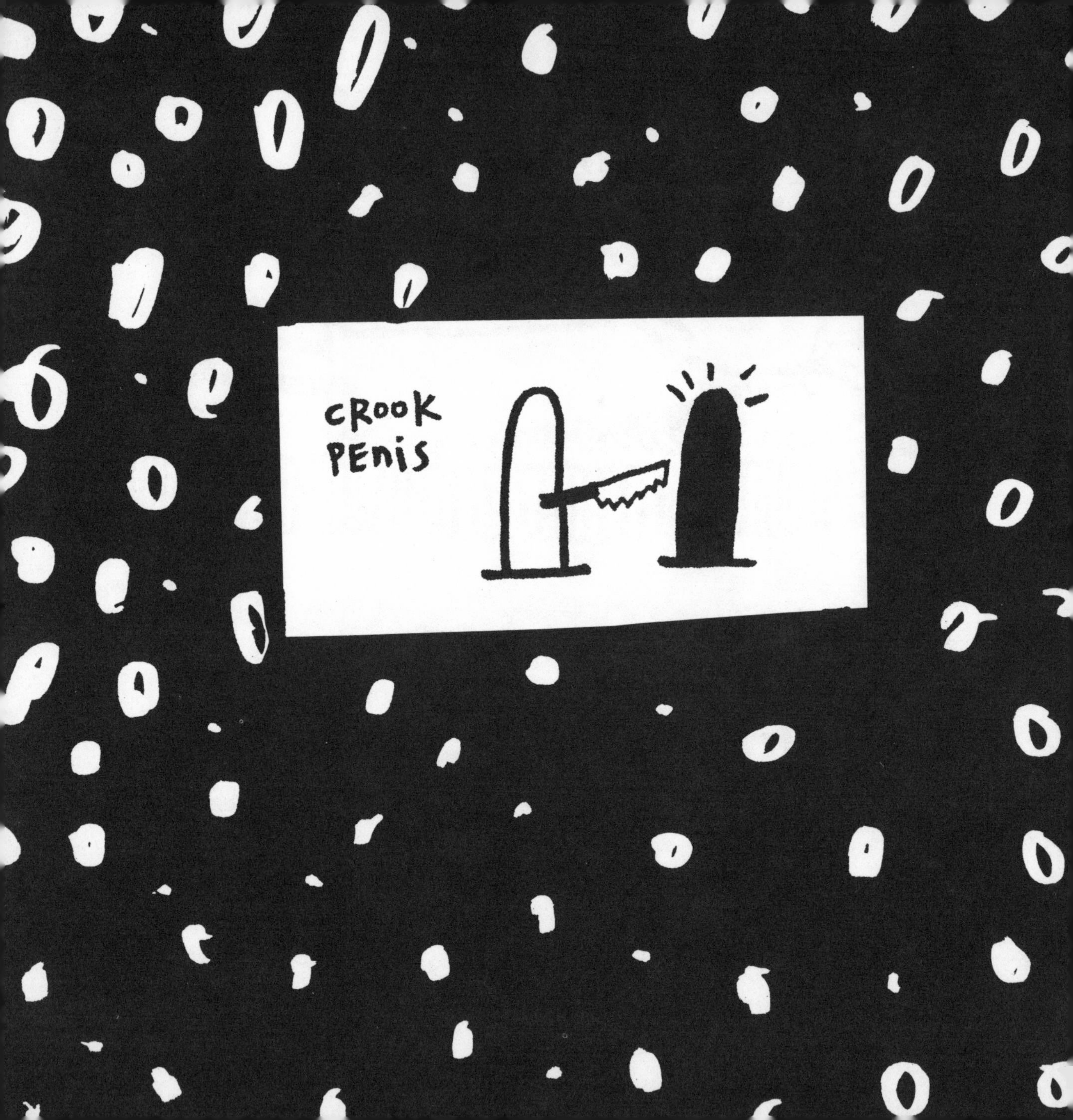
CROOK
PENIS

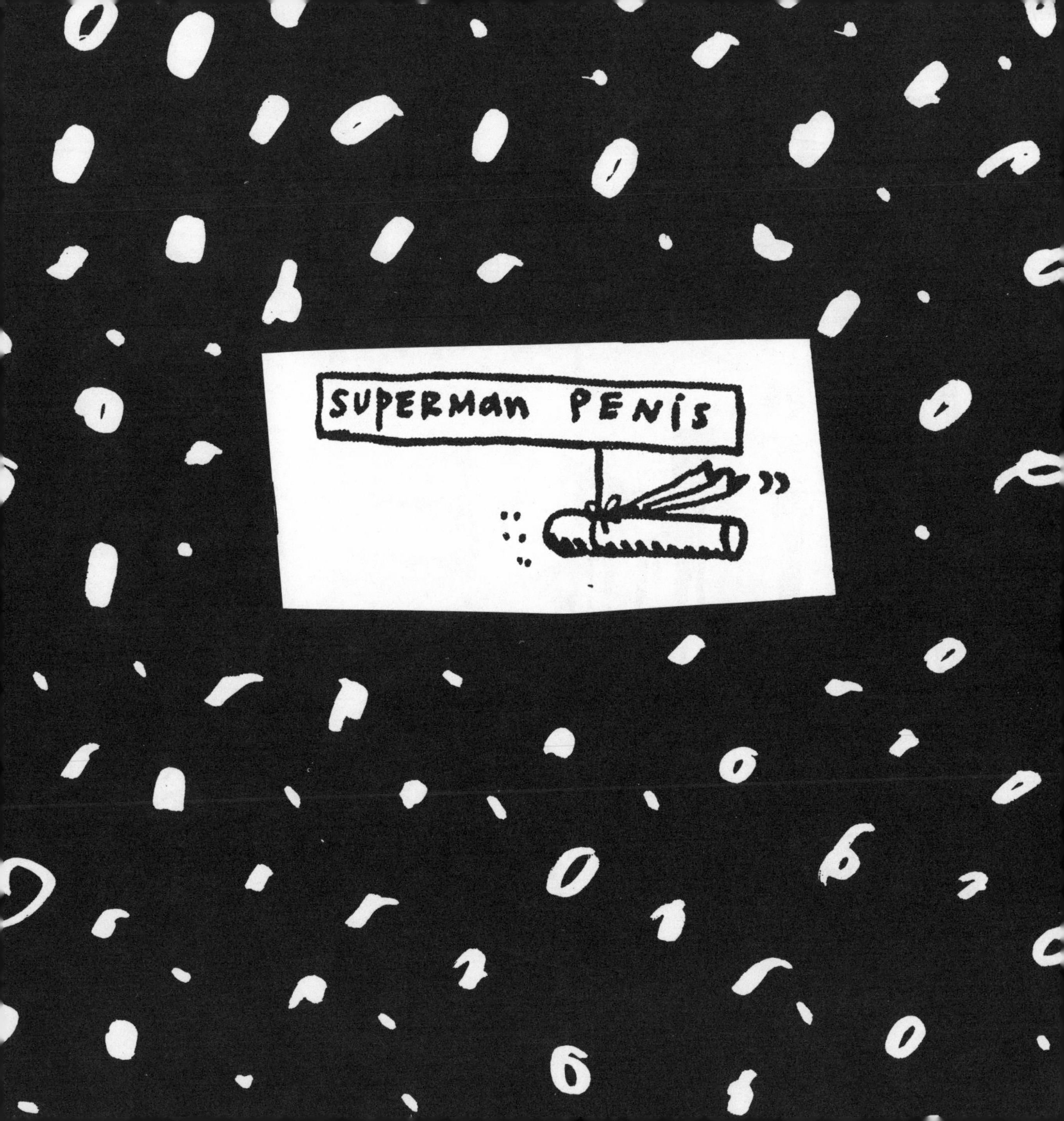
SUPERMAN PENIS

DRAINING LiKE A DEAD CHICKEN

A little tampon. 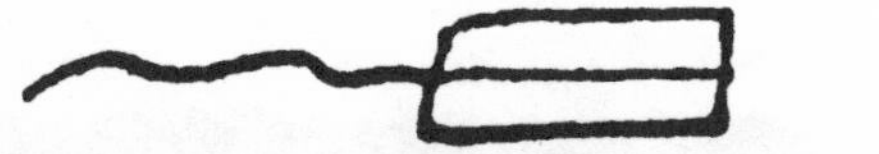

I AM ANGRY AT TAMPONS + I DON'T WEAR THEM ANYMORE. IT'S NOT only THAT I CAN'T AFFORD THEM, BUT that I WOULDN'T wear them EVEN if I could. I'm against paying close TO FIVE BUCKS FOR A BOX of what is basically COMPRESSED Toilet paper.

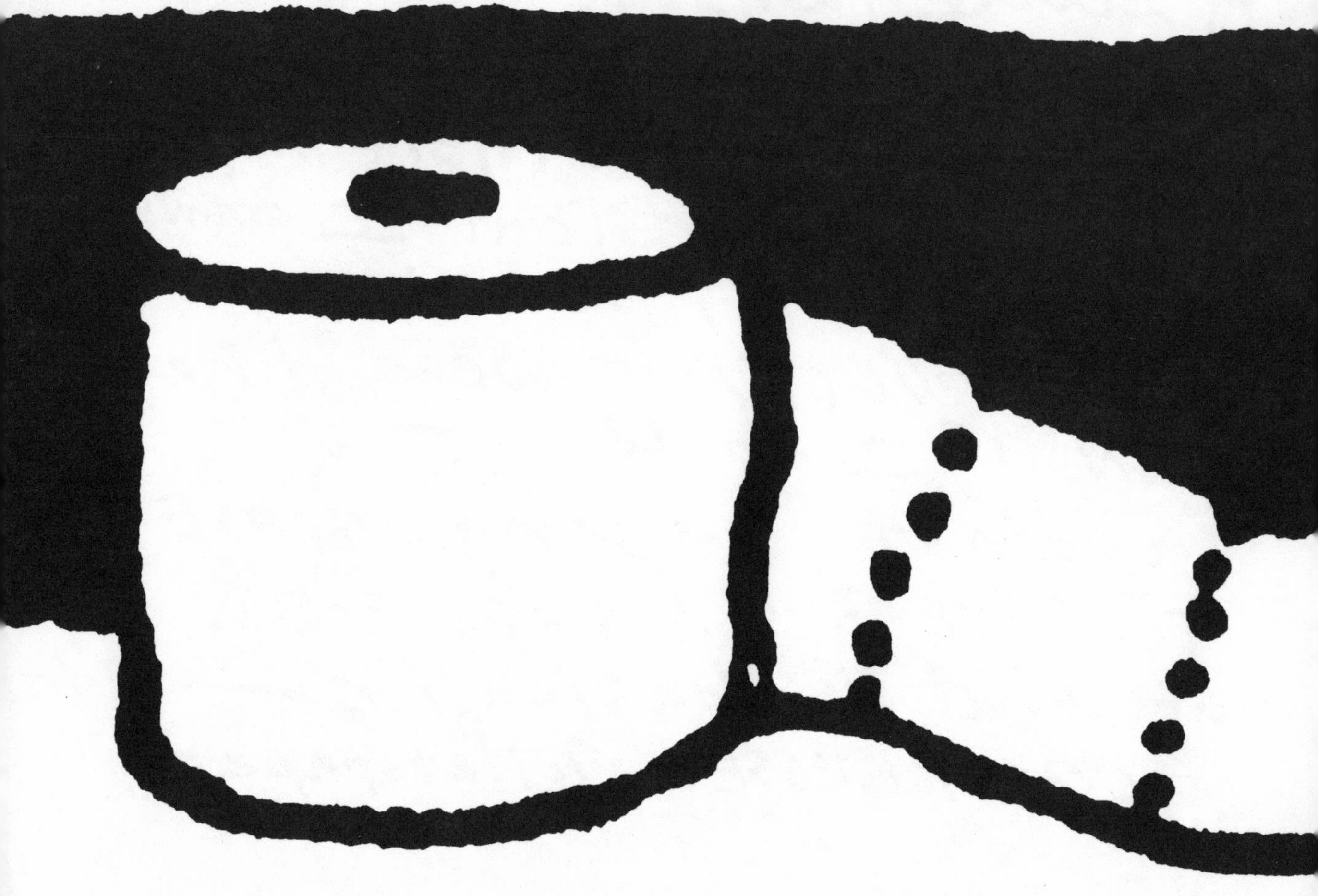

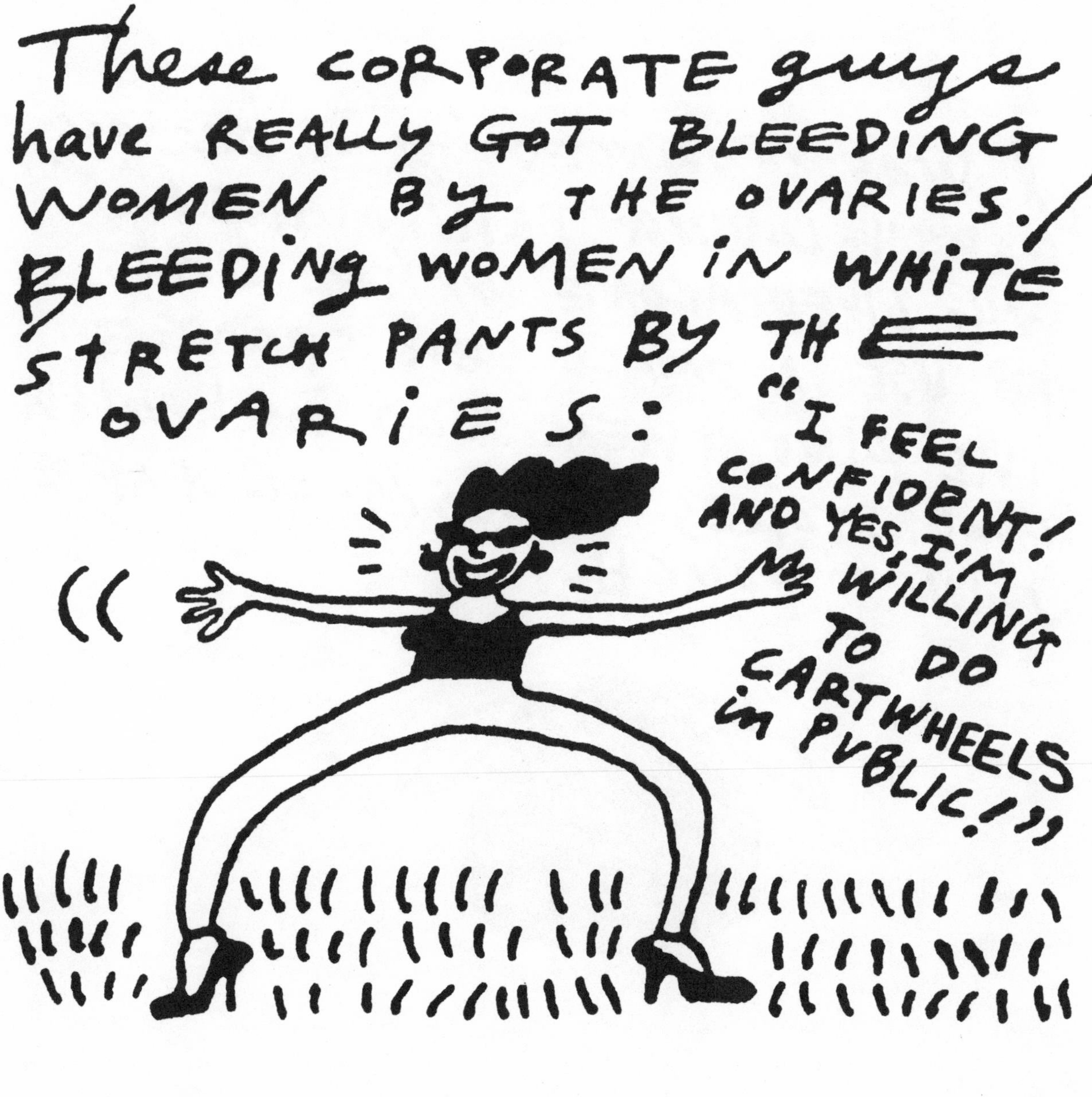
These CORPORATE guys have REALLY GOT BLEEDING WOMEN BY THE OVARIES./ BLEEDING WOMEN IN WHITE STRETCH PANTS BY THE OVARIES:
"I FEEL CONFIDENT! AND YES, I'M WILLING TO DO CARTWHEELS IN PUBLIC!"

I was convinced by a braless,
EARTH-LOVING PRINTMAKER
WHO LIVED ALONE w/her CAT,
TO USE A SMALL SEA SPONGE.
THE KIND THEY SOLD in health
FOOD STORES in a SMALL FAKE
VELVET POUCH.

Then, while I was at THE HEALTH food STORE, I ALSO Bought SOME PATCHOULI FOR MY UNBLEEDING PREMENSTRUAL WRISTS.

THEN. / THEN w/ MY HANDS
LOOKING LIKE ARTHRITIC
YAMS, I BUMPED INTO A
BOOK ABOUT WOMYN-
STUFF. IT WAS POLITELY
PRINTED IN SOY INK ON
UNBLEACHED PAPER.
IT WAS *called*:

Hygeia/A WOMAN'S HERBAL.

It was written in the 70s, AND I COULD hear JOAN BAEZ's song, "Diamonds and Rust" as I turned the FIRST PAGE...

"On The Rag" and Other menstrual Rituals -- for you, fertile SISTER

THAT's what the FIRST CHAPTER WAS CALLED. + BEING THE FERTILE SISTER THAT I WAS, I READ ON...

(I shall paraphrase)

“DO NOT BE ASHAMED OF YOUR BLOOD, OH SISTER.

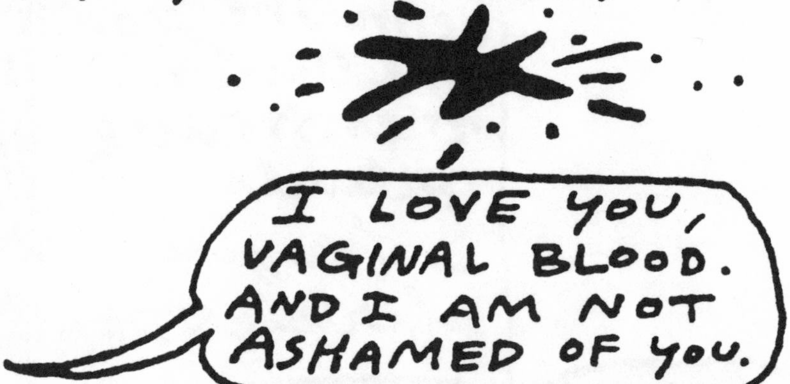
I LOVE YOU, VAGINAL BLOOD. AND I AM NOT ASHAMED OF YOU.

DO NOT <u>HIDE</u> YOUR SOILED NAPKINS IN THE **DARK** TRASH.

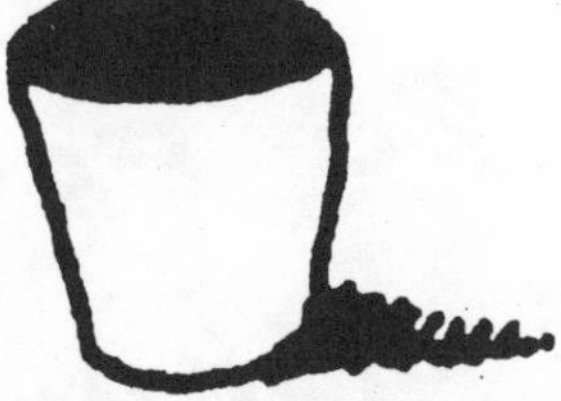

TAKE YOUR PROUD BLOOD TO THE **AIR**, THE **SUN** 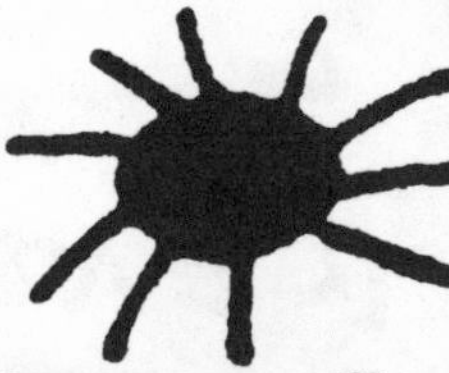, THE **EARTH** 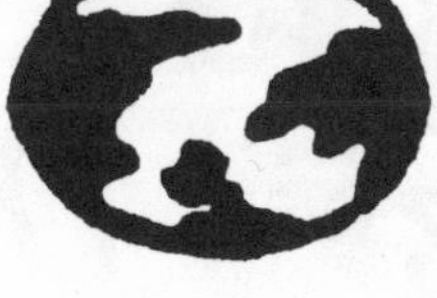.

Let Go OF THE EGG,
AND SAY (GOOD-BYE, EGG)
And THE PAIN WILL
BE EASIER / DO NOT
BE ashamed of bleeding.
PROCLAIM YOUR BLEEDING!
YOUR FERTILENESS! — LET
THE WORLD KNOW / AND
BE PROUD! GET in touch
w/ YOUR MENSTRUAL
CONSCIOUSNESS.

Squat over your HOUSEPLANTS THAT NEED minerals. AND do NOT PLUG YOURSELF UP W/WHITE PATERNAL PLUGS. BLEED

FREELY

--- AND MAKE YOUR OWN MENSTRUAL PAD. MAKE IT HUGE. / MAKE IT PROUD. A PROUD menstrual PAD, BECAUSE There Is an art to BLEEDING. (RINSE! RECYCLE! DO NOT SUPPORT A HUGE POLLUTING INDUSTRY!)

Maybe choose a purple FLANNEL To REST NEXT to your EARTHLY VAGINA.... AND applique a gold MANDALA on the front.... WHO SAID THAT EVERYTHING Must BE WHITE LIKE THOSE HERMETICALLY SEALED TAMPONS + WEDDING DRESSES?

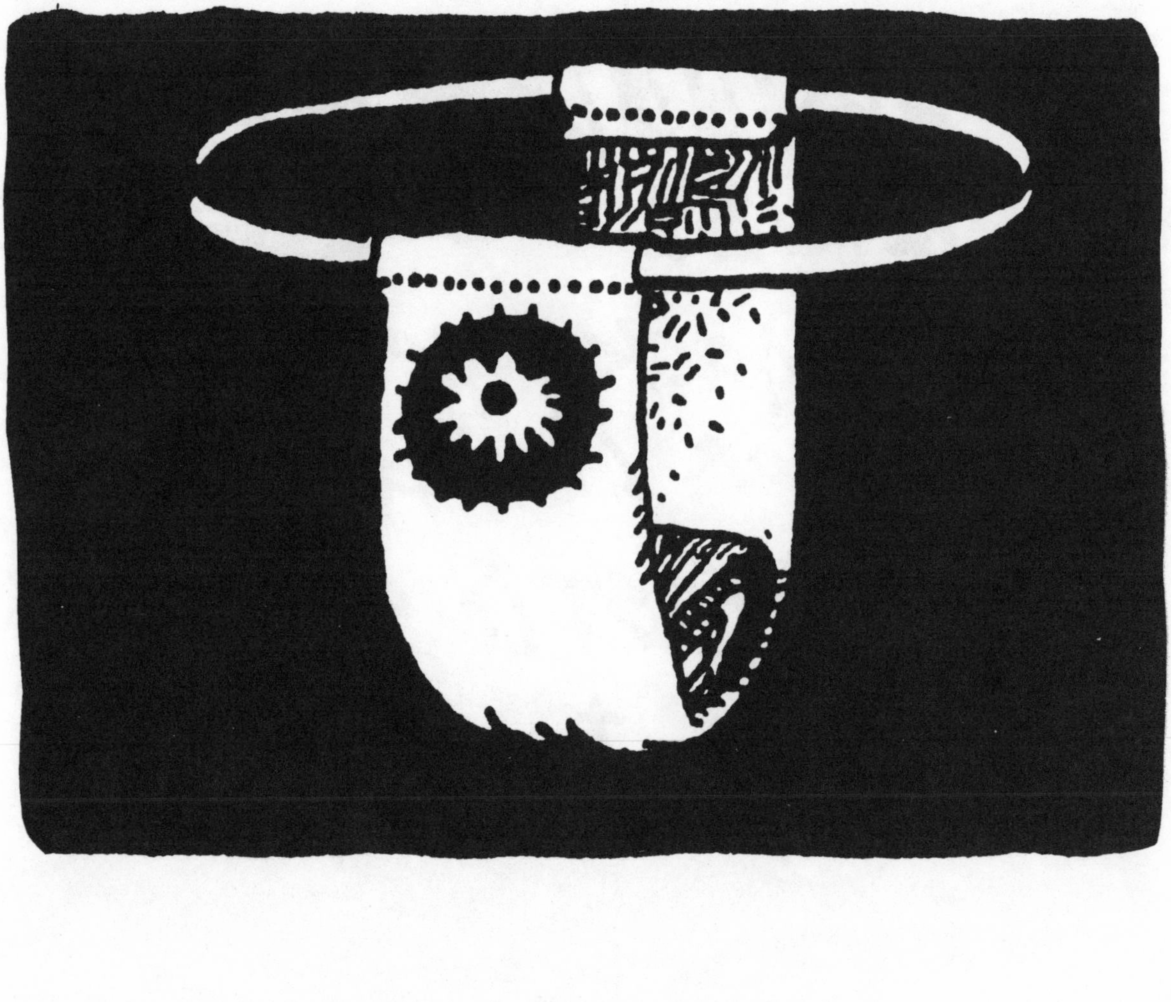

WHITE

MOCKS YOU
FOR LIVING,
EXISTING
+
SECRET ING?"

THAT WAS IT. THAT WAS ALL I NEEDED TO READ./I PUT THE BOOK DOWN + WALKED AROUND MY APARTMENT CARRYING A SPIDER PLANT BETWEEN MY LEGS, AND SINGING MADE UP SONGS ABOUT GERMAINE GREER TO CLASSICAL MUSIC WRITTEN BY EXTREMELY DEAD MEN.

My CAT FREAKED OUT
ssssss
AND threatened to
leave me forever if
I didn't quit it./
But I WAS SO EXHAUSTED
BY MY IRON DEFICIENCY,
I DIDN'T HAVE THE
STRENGTH TO TALK her
out of it./ SHE WAS
WALKING out THE DOOR
+ ALL I COULD SCREAM
BEFORE PASSING OUT ON
THE FLOOR WAS:

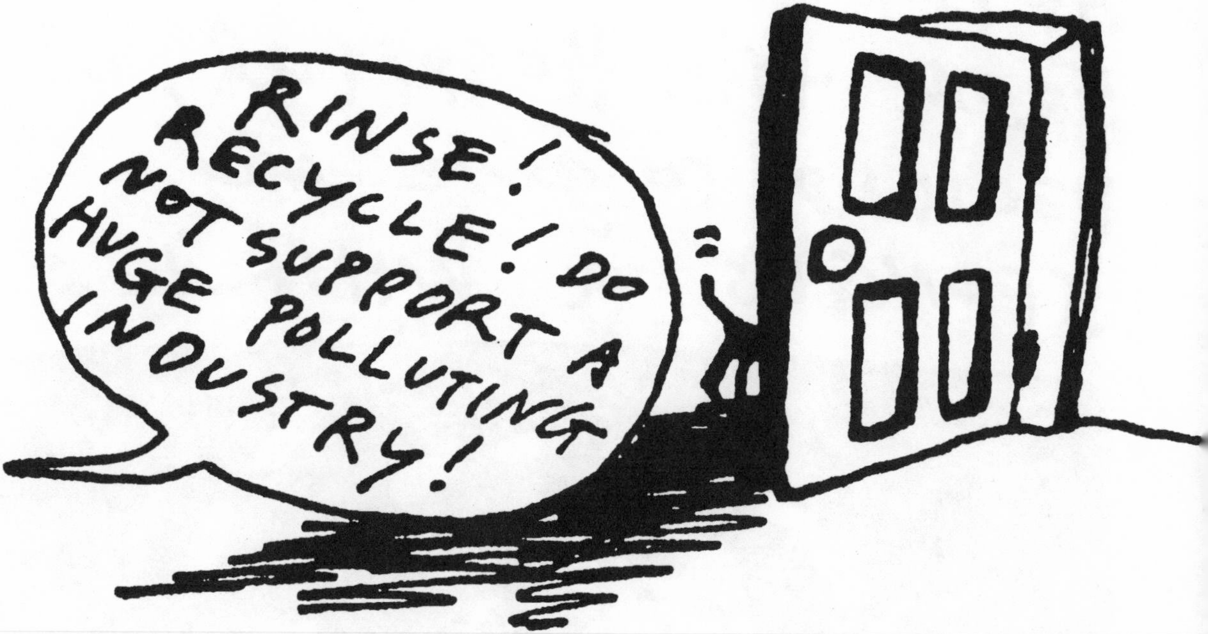
RINSE! RECYCLE! DO NOT SUPPORT A HUGE POLLUTING INDUSTRY!

AND a FEW DAYS LATER,
AFTER I WAS RELEASED
FROM the Hospital, I
DECIDED TO give MY
SPONGES a WHIRL.

I was PROUD AS I RINSED
them in PUBLIC SINKS,
Jamming my FOOT against
the BATHROOM DOOR. /
I FELT SUPERIOR. /
SUPERIOR LIKE A SUPERIOR
PERSON, IN BEING CONNECTED
TO MY Blood / my Eggs.

ME

EGG

I SAID: "FAREWELL, MY LITTLE EGGS, FAREWELL" AS I SET MY BLOOD FREE, DOWN THE DRAIN. / LIKE A SAD BIRD-MOTHER OR SOMETHING.

I WALKED BACK INTO THE DENNY'S DINING ROOMS FEELING CONNECTED, IF NOT WAITED ON, AND I WAS AT A FEMALE kind of peace...

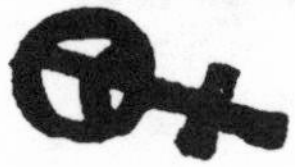

But the SPONGES DETERIORATED,
and the ROMANCE FADED
w/ RED FAMILIARITY. / PAST
DUE therapy bills STARTED
TAKING PRECEDENCE, AND I
still HAD NO MONEY w/all
the TAMPON BOYCOTT
CASH I SAVED.

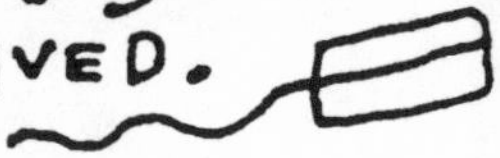

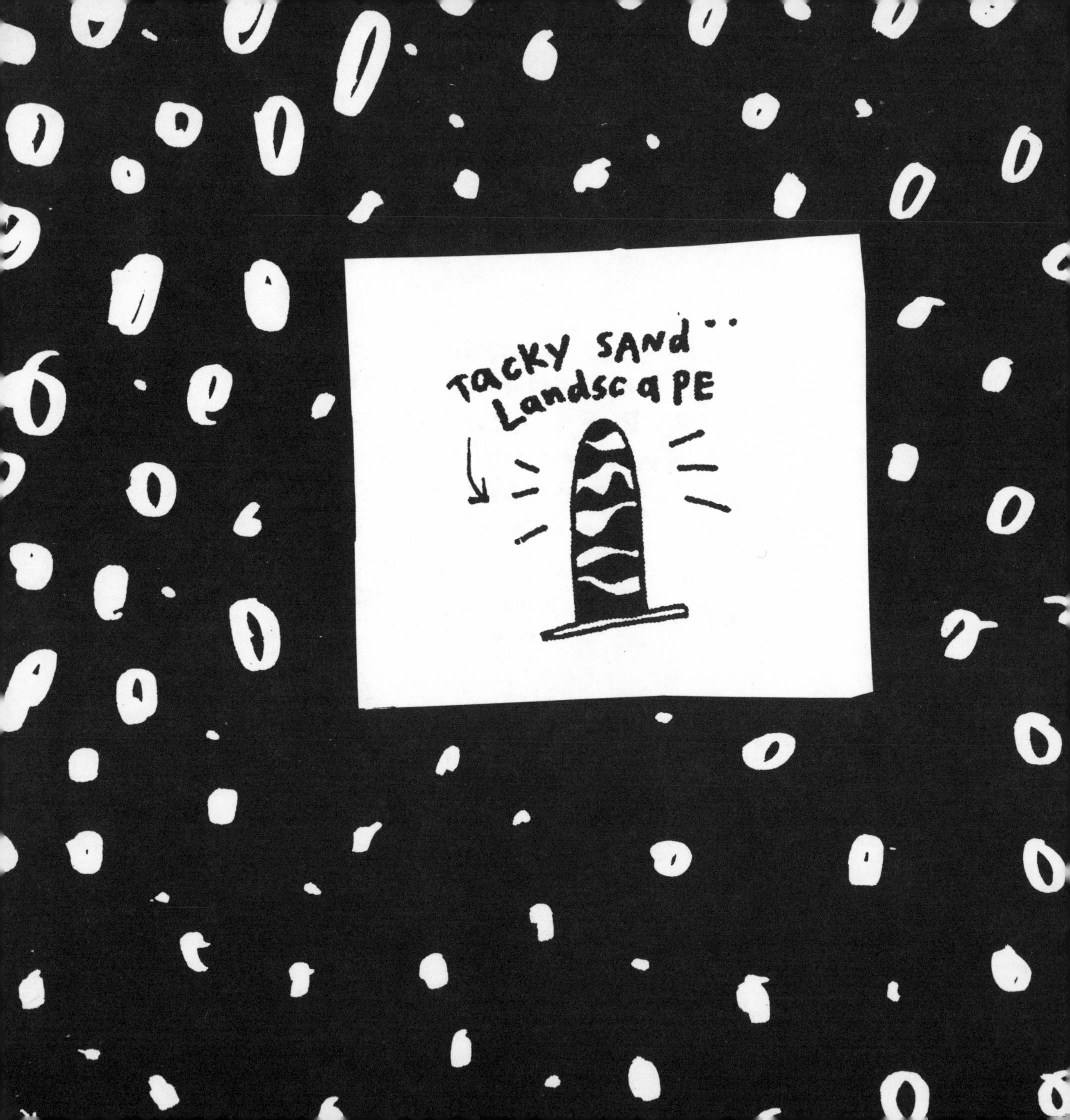
TACKY SAND..
Landscape

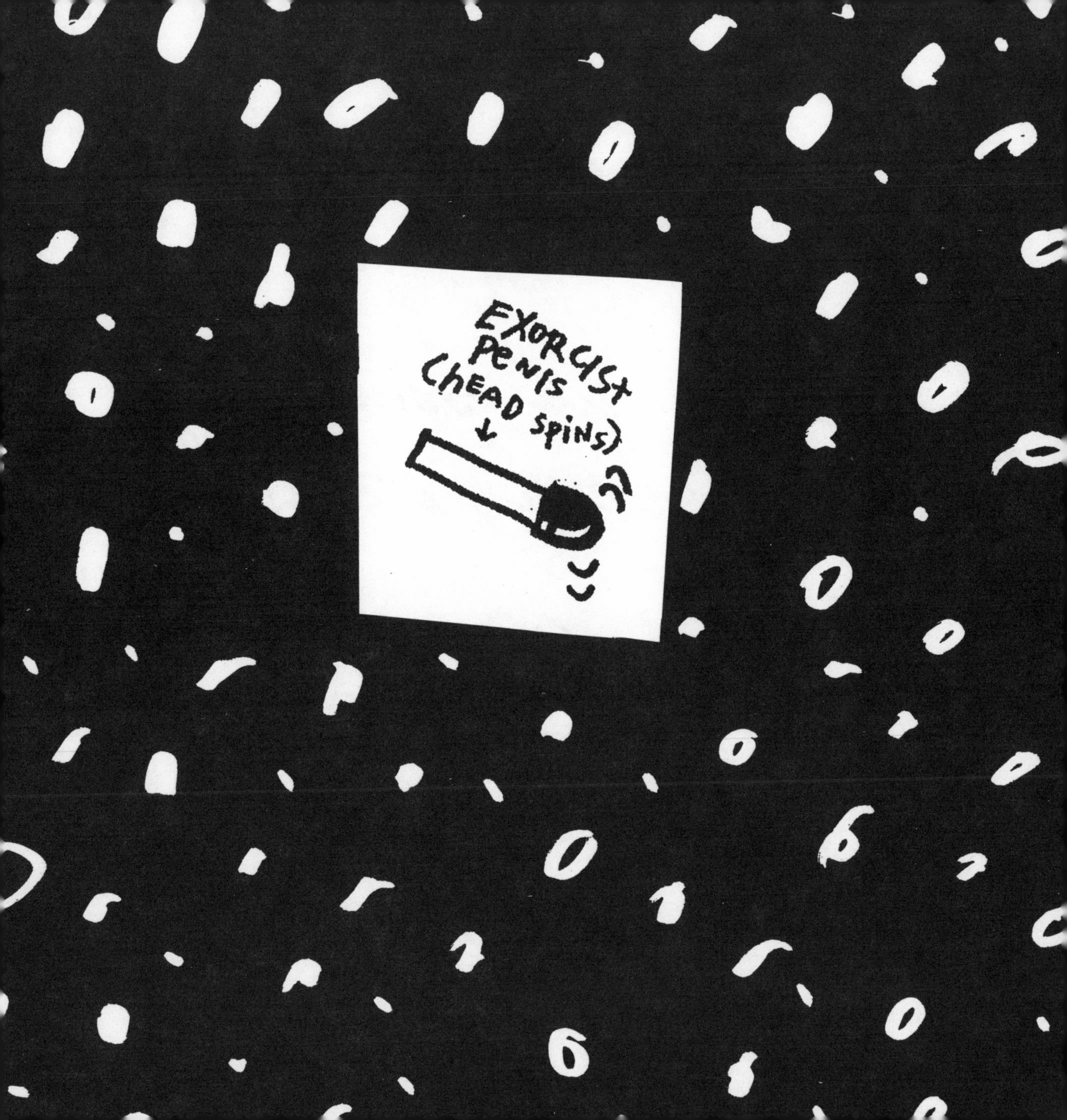
EXORCIST
PENIS
(HEAD SPINS)

℮

children as something to wear, etc...

IN SAN Francisco, DESPITE all the test tubes, turkey BASTERS + FROZEN FEtuses, people don't have children. → they hAVE (DOGS). AND cHEAP-o calENDArs ON their REFRIGERATORS w/COLOR copiES OF their dogs iN SANta outfits.

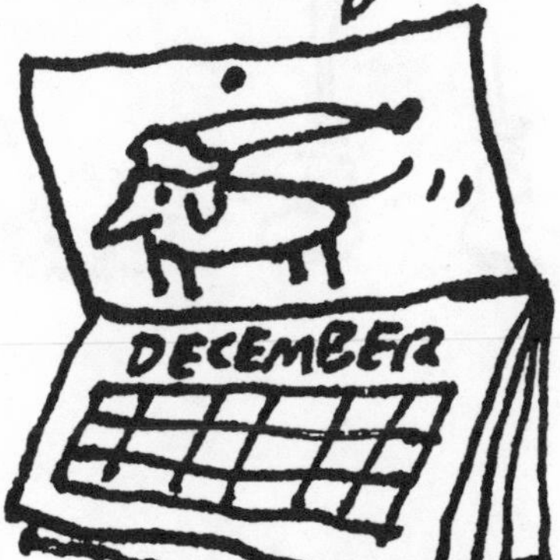
DECEMBER

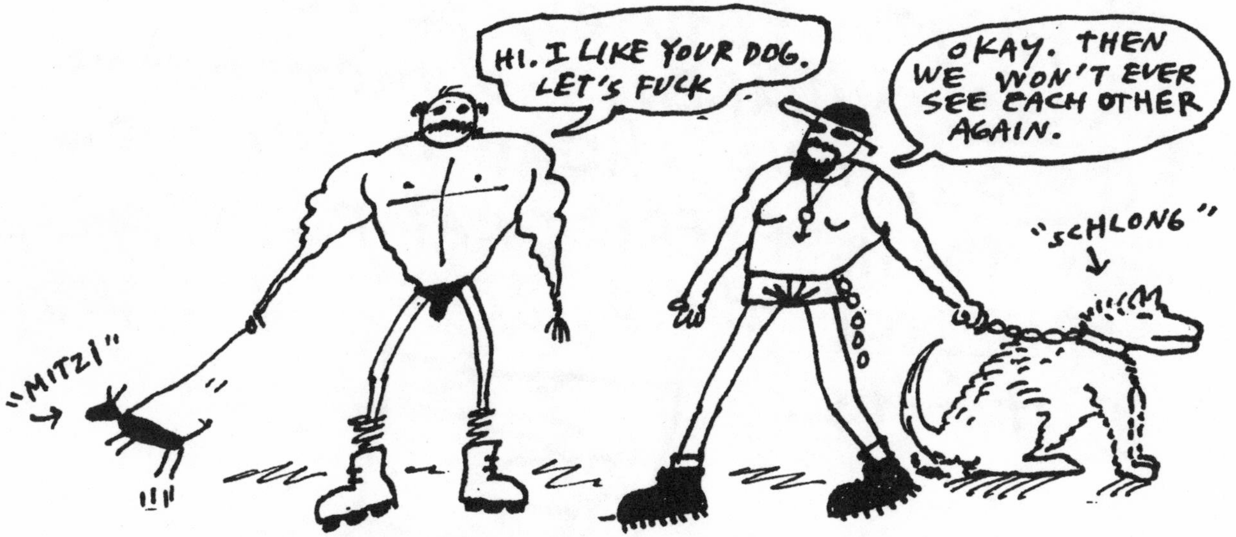
HI. I LIKE YOUR DOG. LET'S FUCK
OKAY. THEN WE WON'T EVER SEE EACH OTHER AGAIN.
"MITZI"
"SCHLONG"

And in NorthHampton where minimum wage Lesbians Have cats or...

No butt

"I'm allergic to everything. This entire planet. organic just isn't good enough anymore. I'm allergic to cats, Puerto Ricans + Italians Basically anything that isn't wheat-free or hairless or Nordic people, I'm fine w/ Nordic people though."

HOW will
she indulge her
Maternal
instinct?

WILL SHE START LOOKING AT HER VINYL COAT Lovingly?

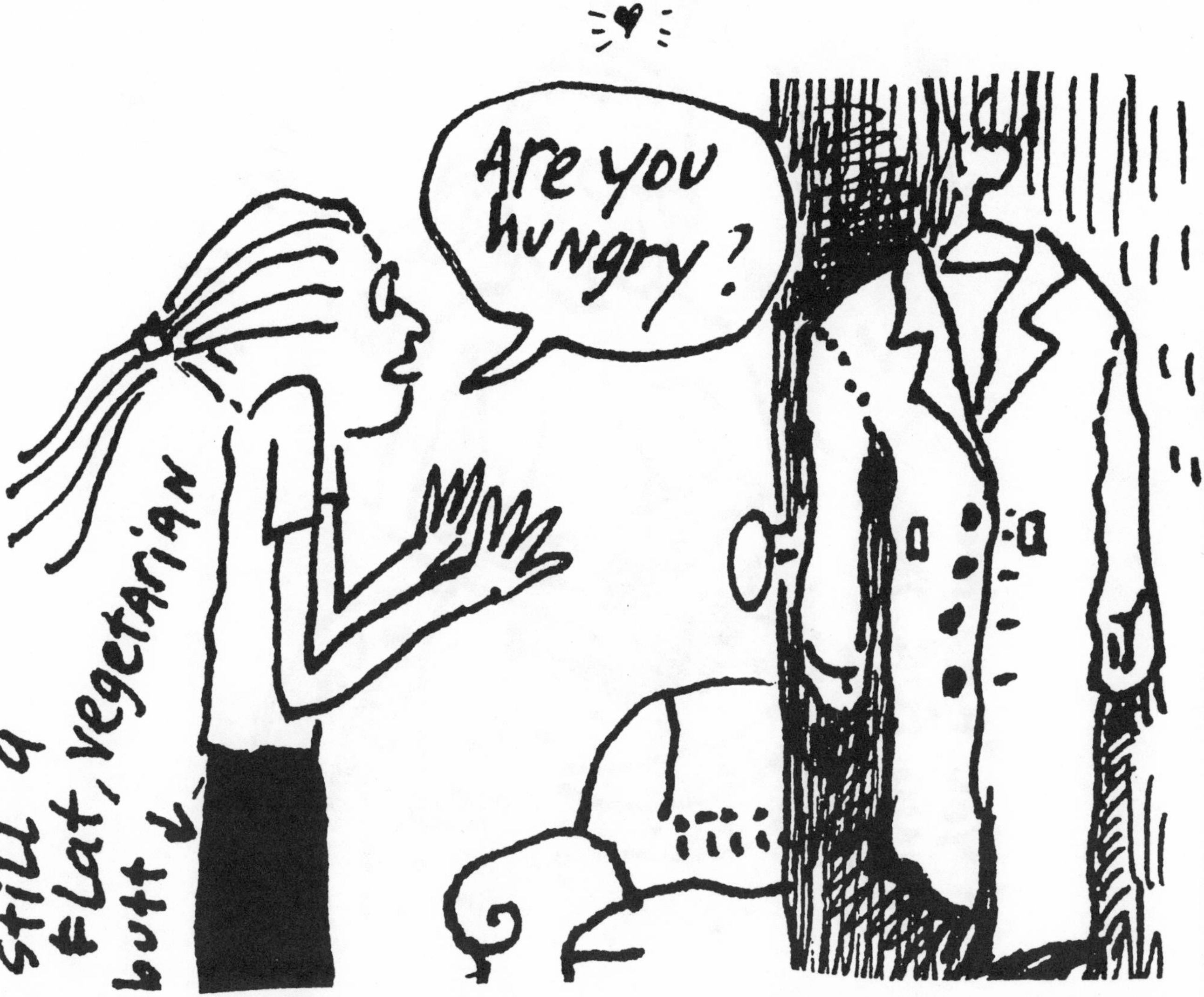
Are you hungry?
STILL A FLAT, VEGETARIAN BUTT

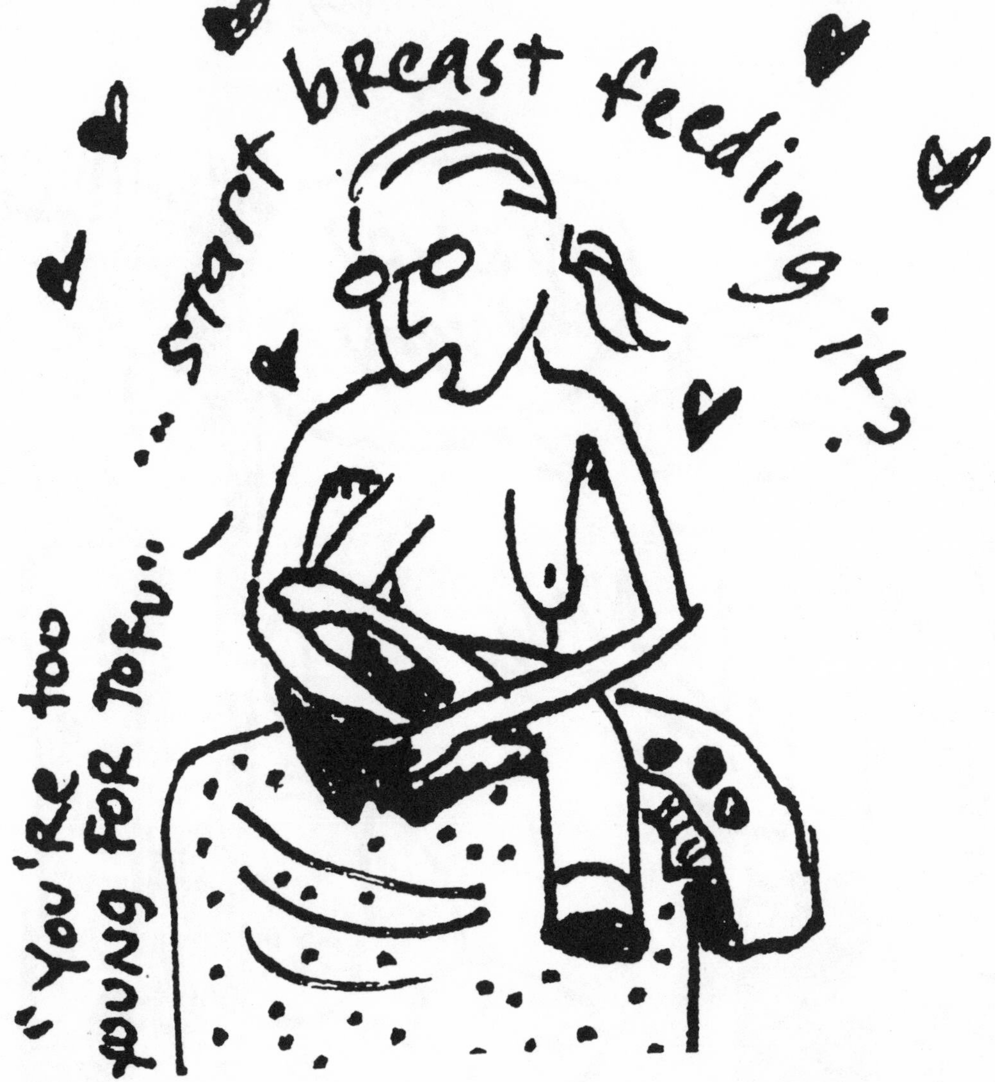
"You're too young for tofu"... start breast feeding it?

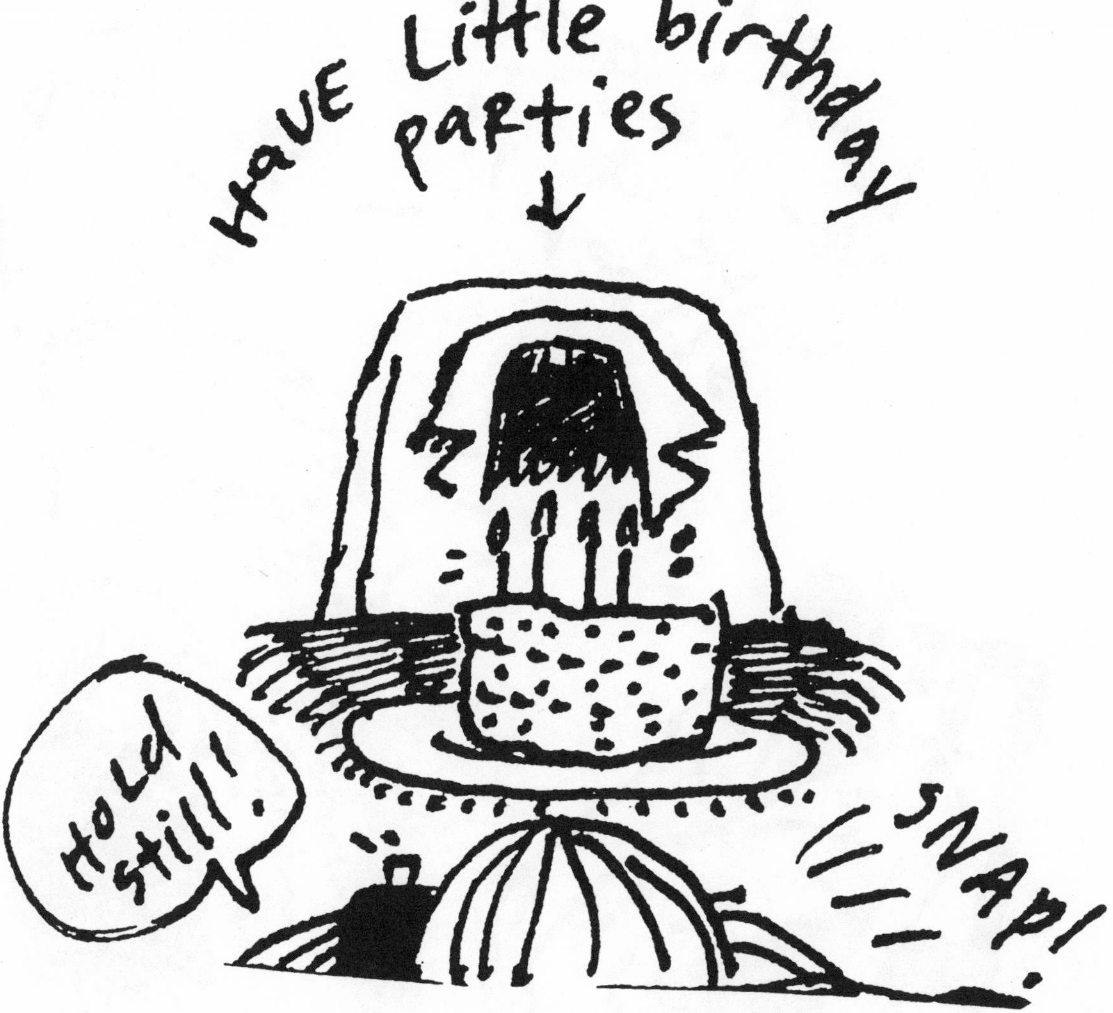
HAVE Little birthday parties
Hold still!!
SNAP!

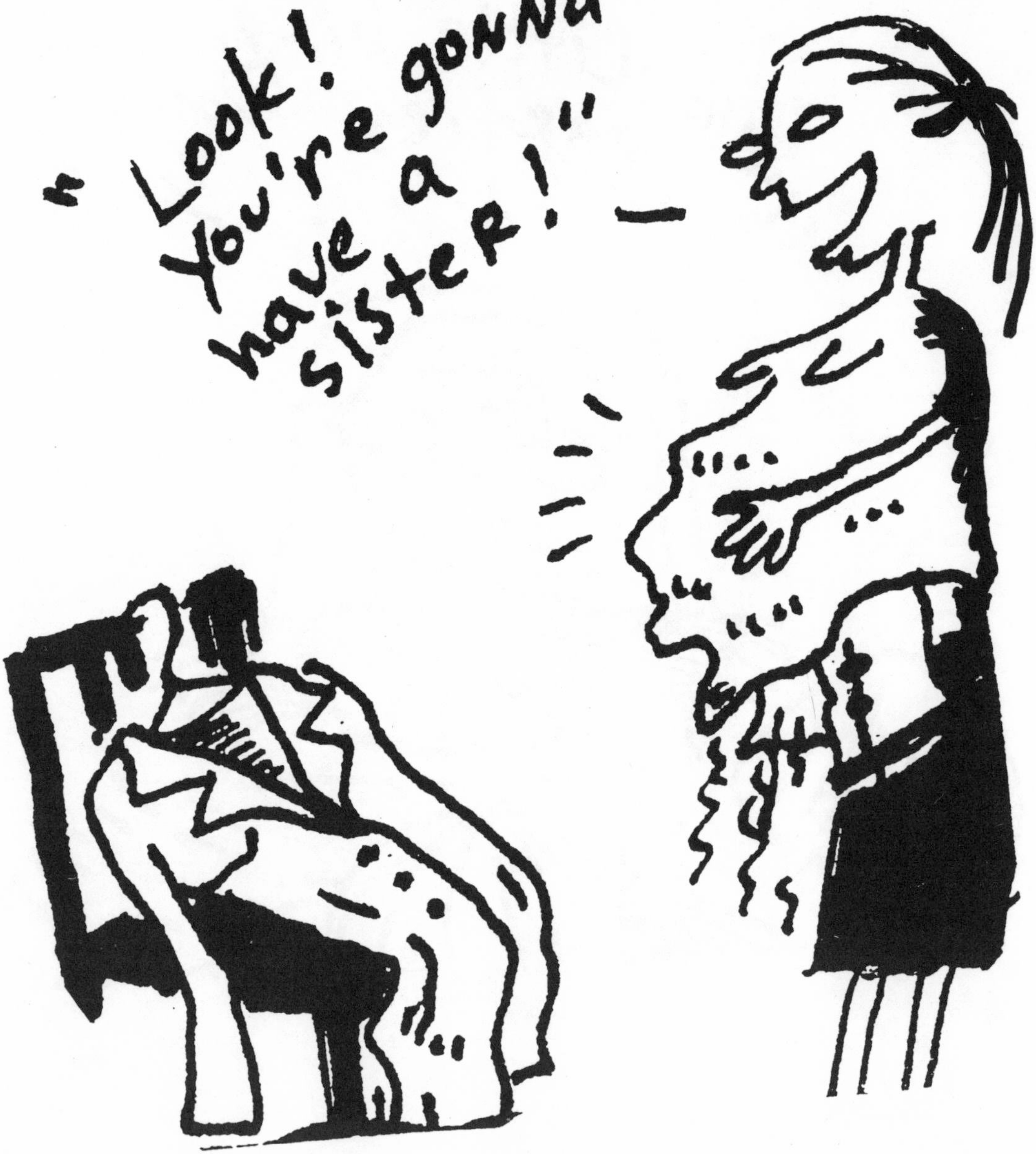
"Look! You're gonna have a sister!" —

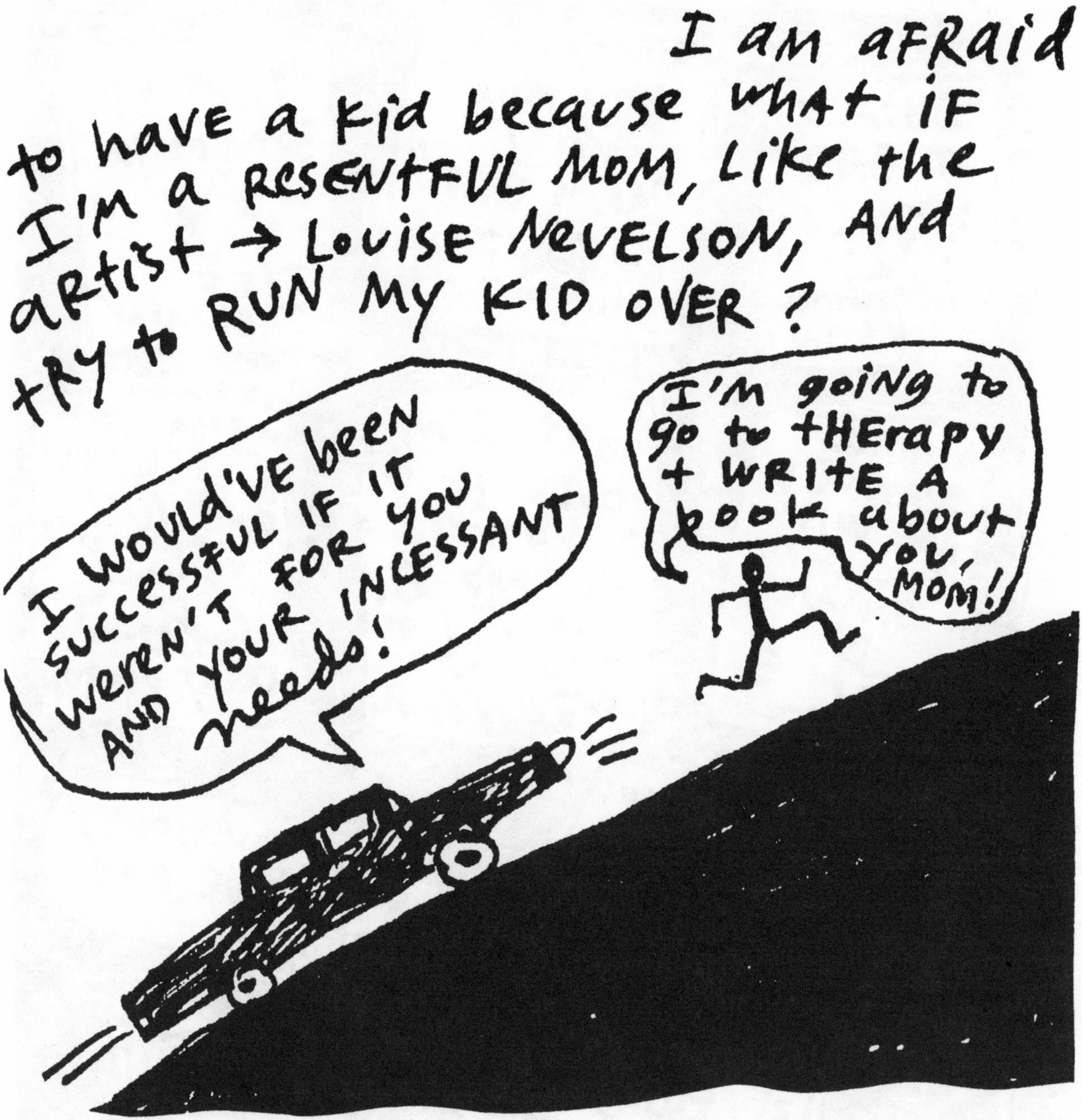
I am afraid to have a kid because what if I'm a RESENTFUL MOM, like the artist → LOUISE NEVELSON, AND try to RUN MY KID OVER?
I WOULD'VE been SUCCESSFUL IF IT weren't FOR YOU AND YOUR INCESSANT needs!
I'm going to go to tHErapy + WRITE A book about YOU, MOM!

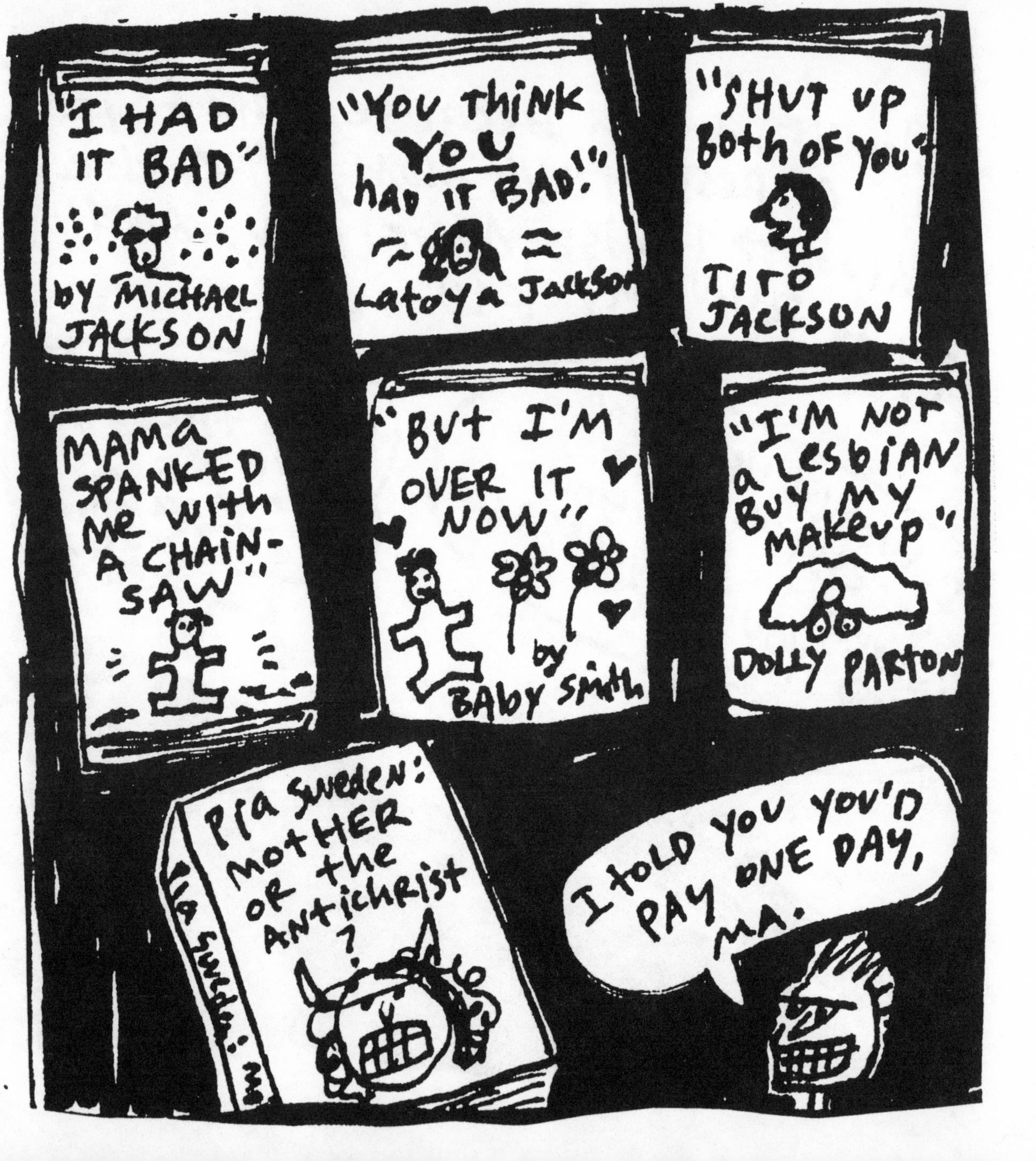
"I HAD IT BAD" by MICHAEL JACKSON
"YOU THINK YOU HAD IT BAD!" LaToya Jackson
"SHUT UP BOTH OF YOU" TITO JACKSON
MAMA SPANKED ME WITH A CHAIN-SAW"
"BUT I'M OVER IT NOW" by BABY SMITH
"I'M NOT A LESBIAN BUY MY MAKEUP" DOLLY PARTON
PIA SWEDEN: MOTHER OF THE ANTICHRIST?
PIA SWEDEN!
I TOLD YOU YOU'D PAY ONE DAY, MA.

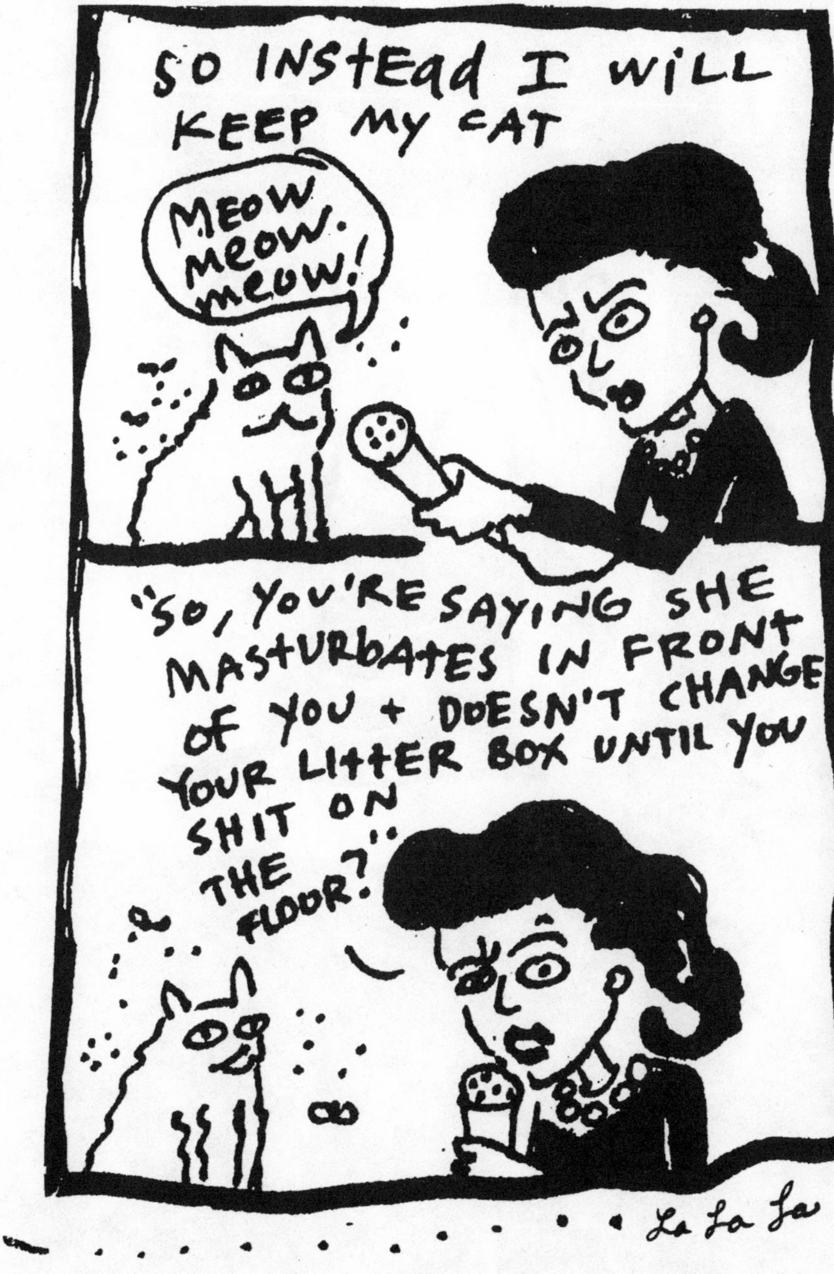
SO INSTEAD I WILL KEEP MY CAT
MEOW. MEOW. MEOW!
"SO, YOU'RE SAYING SHE MASTURBATES IN FRONT OF YOU + DOESN'T CHANGE YOUR LITTER BOX UNTIL YOU SHIT ON THE FLOOR?"
La La La

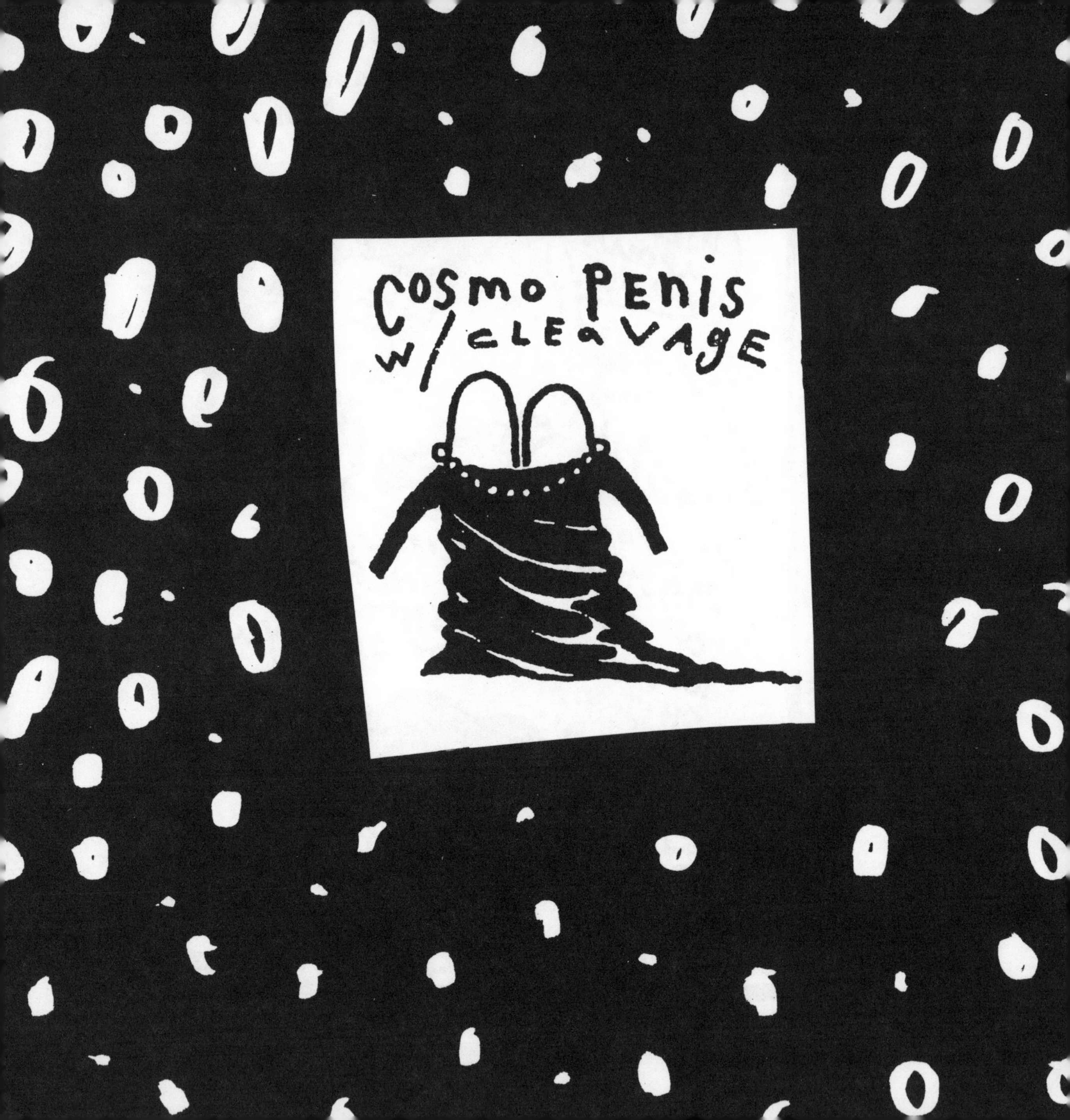
COSMO PENIS
w/ CLEAVAGE

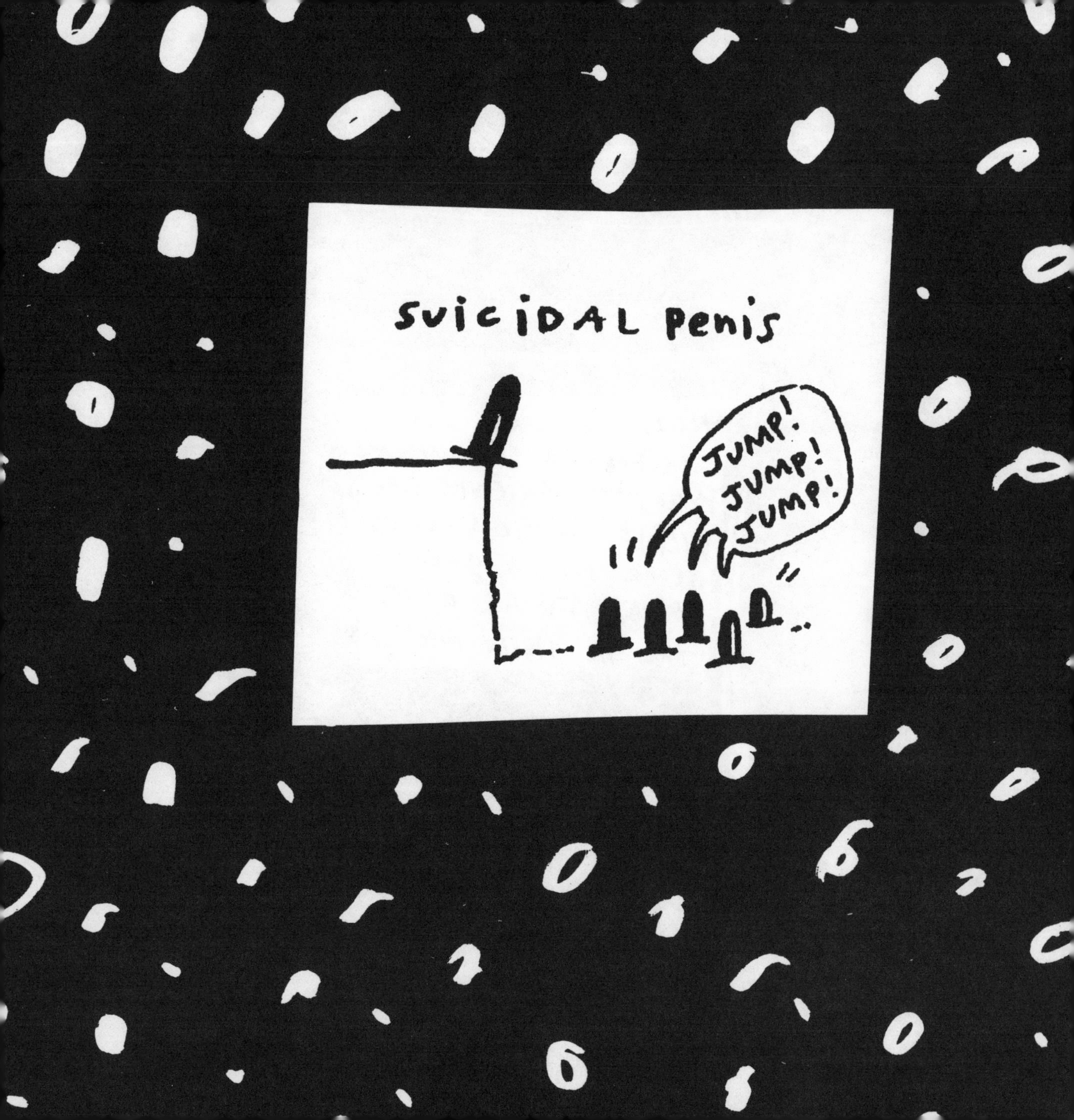
SUICIDAL penis
JUMP! JUMP! JUMP!

PORN MOVIE REVIEW of "Gemini" → A gay boy PORN

no FAMILY should be without

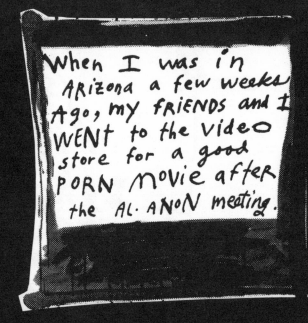

When I was in Arizona a few weeks ago, my FRIENDS and I WENT to the video store for a good PORN Movie after the AL.ANON meeting.

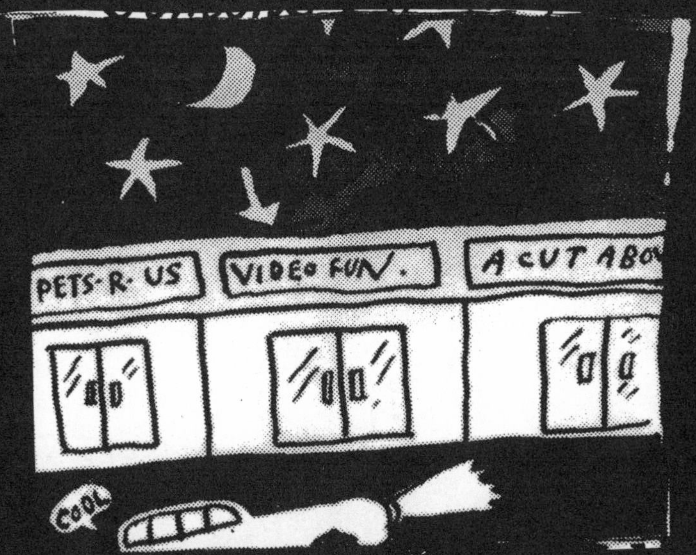
PETS-R-US
VIDEO FUN.
A CUT ABO
COOL

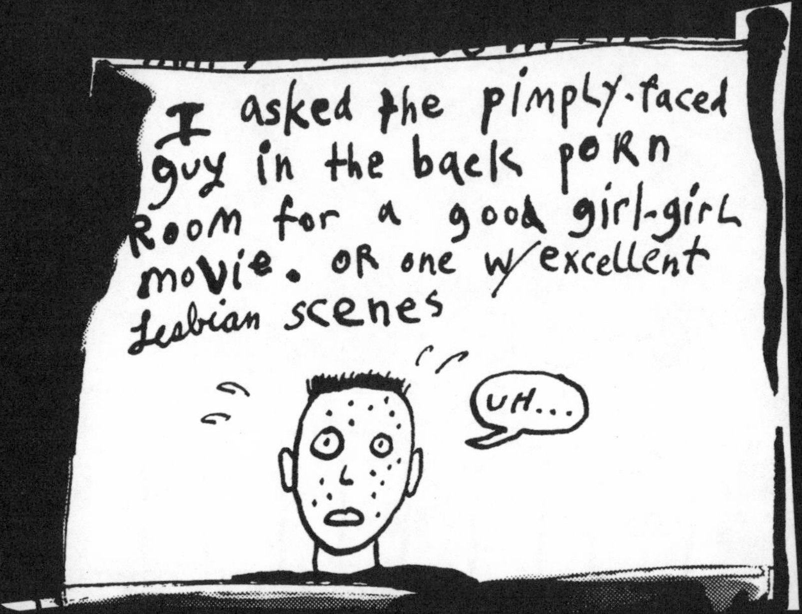
I asked the pimply-faced guy in the back porn room for a good girl-girl movie. or one w/excellent lesbian scenes
UH...

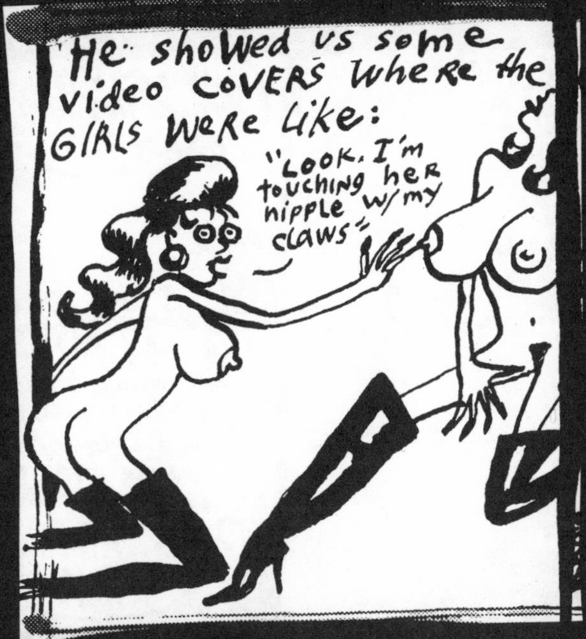
He showed us some video covers where the girls were like:
"Look, I'm touching her nipple w/my claws"

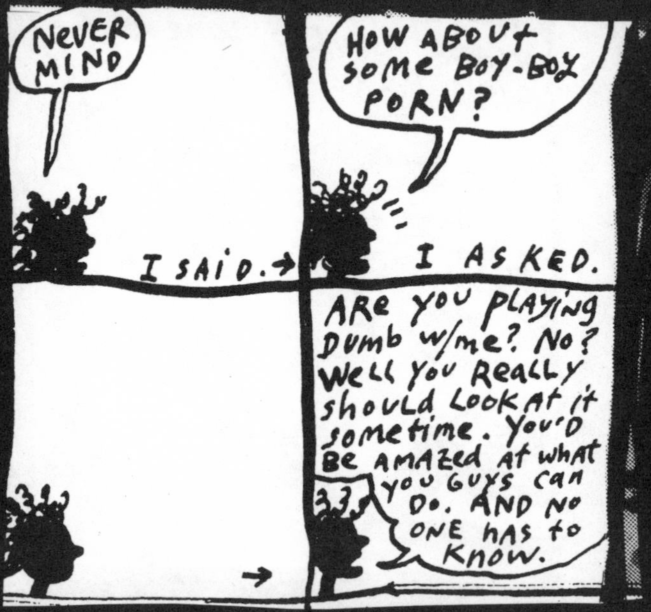
NEVER MIND
I SAID.
HOW ABOUT SOME BOY-BOY PORN?
I ASKED.
ARE YOU PLAYING DUMB W/ME? NO? WELL YOU REALLY SHOULD LOOK AT IT SOMETIME. YOU'D BE AMAZED AT WHAT YOU GUYS CAN DO. AND NO ONE HAS TO KNOW.

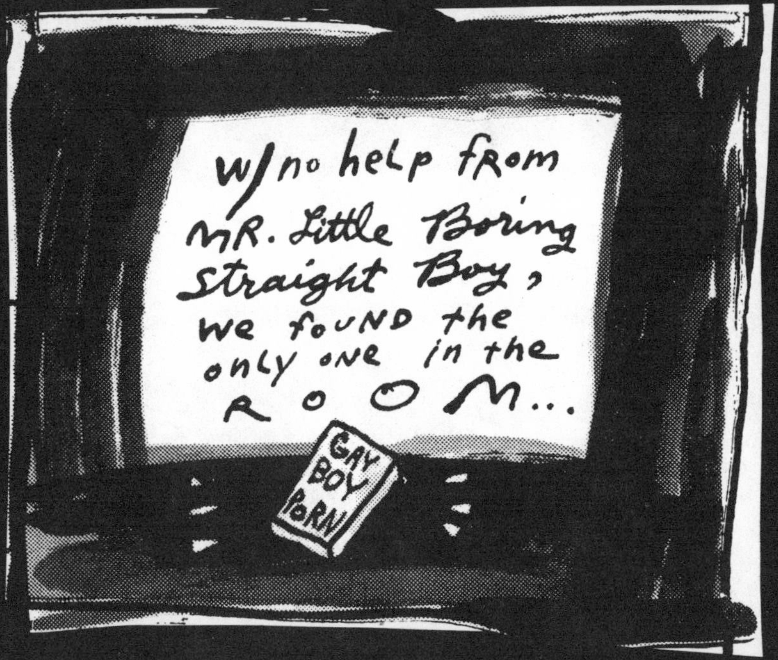
w/no help from
MR. Little Boring
Straight Boy,
we found the
only one in the
R O O M...
GAY
BOY
PORN

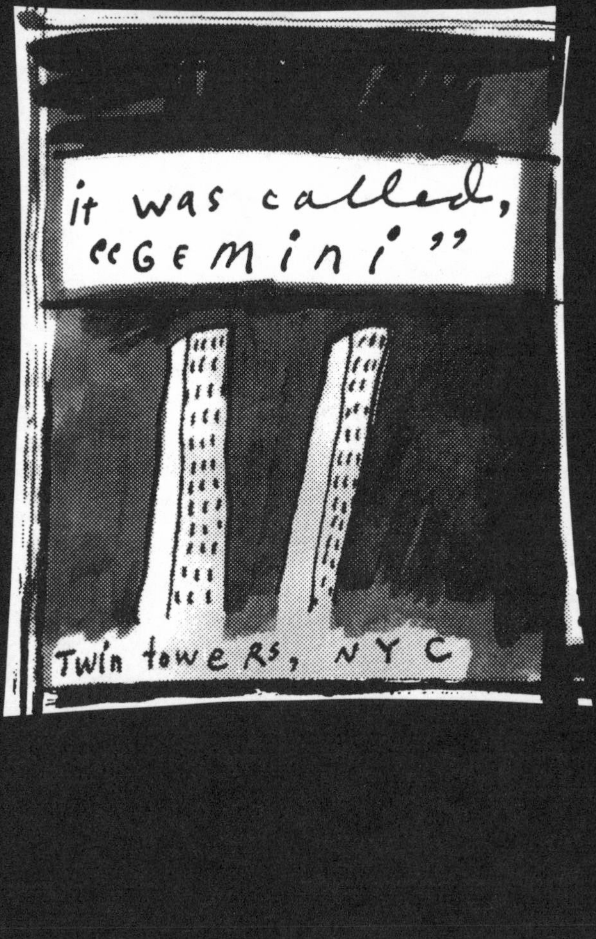
it was called,
"GEMini"
TWin toweRs, NYC

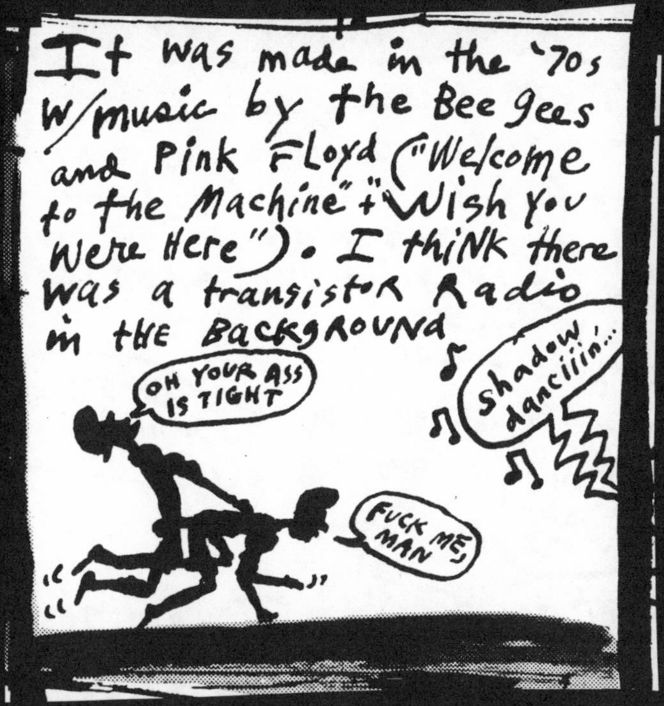
It was made in the '70s w/music by the Bee Gees and Pink Floyd ("Welcome to the Machine" + "Wish You Were Here"). I think there was a transistor Radio in the BACKGROUND
Shadow dancIiin'...
OH YOUR ASS IS TIGHT
FUCK ME, MAN

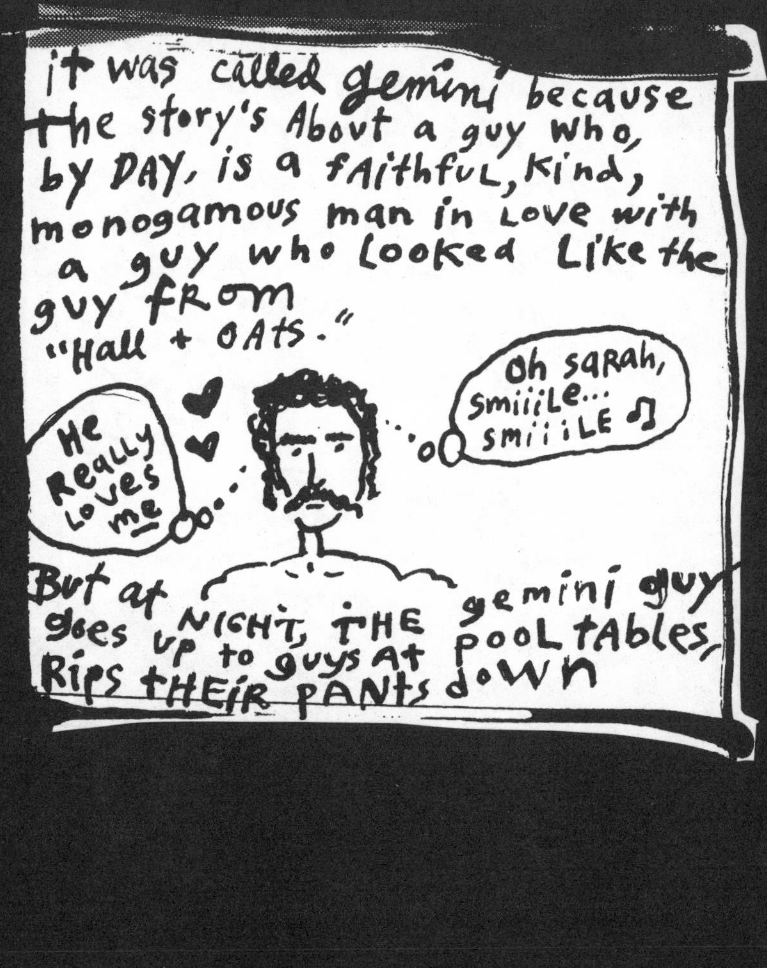
it was called gemini because the story's About a guy who, by DAY, is a fAithfuL, kind, monogamous man in Love with a guy who Looked Like the guy FROM "Hall + OATS."
He Really Loves me
Oh sarah, smiiiLe... smiiiLE ♫
But at NIGHT, THE gemini guy goes up to guys At pool tAbles, Rips tHEIR PANTs down

AND fucks
them.

I'm sure we all
know someoNE
exactly like this,
but We won't mention
Names, WiLL WE?

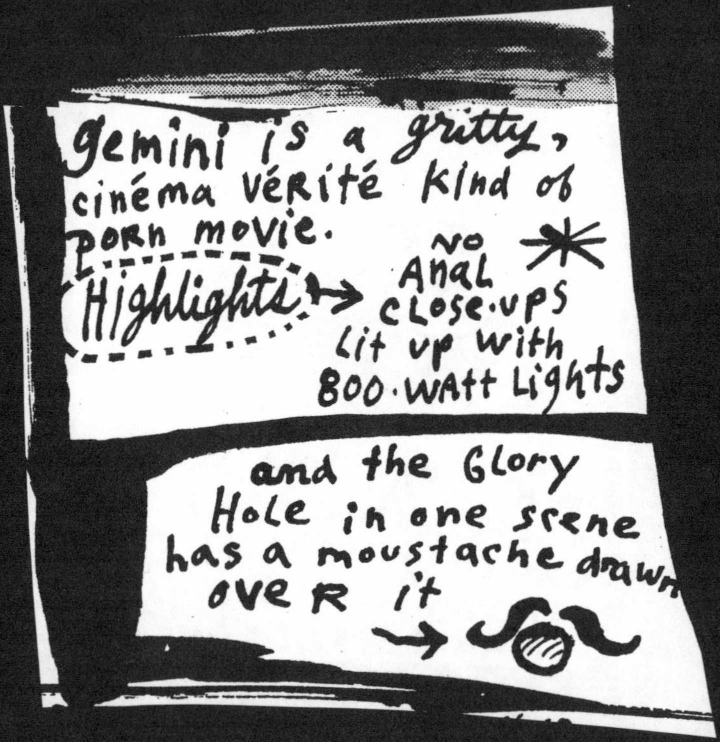
gemini is a gritty, cinéma VéRité kind of porn movie.
Highlights → NO ANAL CLOSE-UPS LIT UP WITH 800-WATT LIGHTS
and the Glory Hole in one scene has a moustache drawn over it →

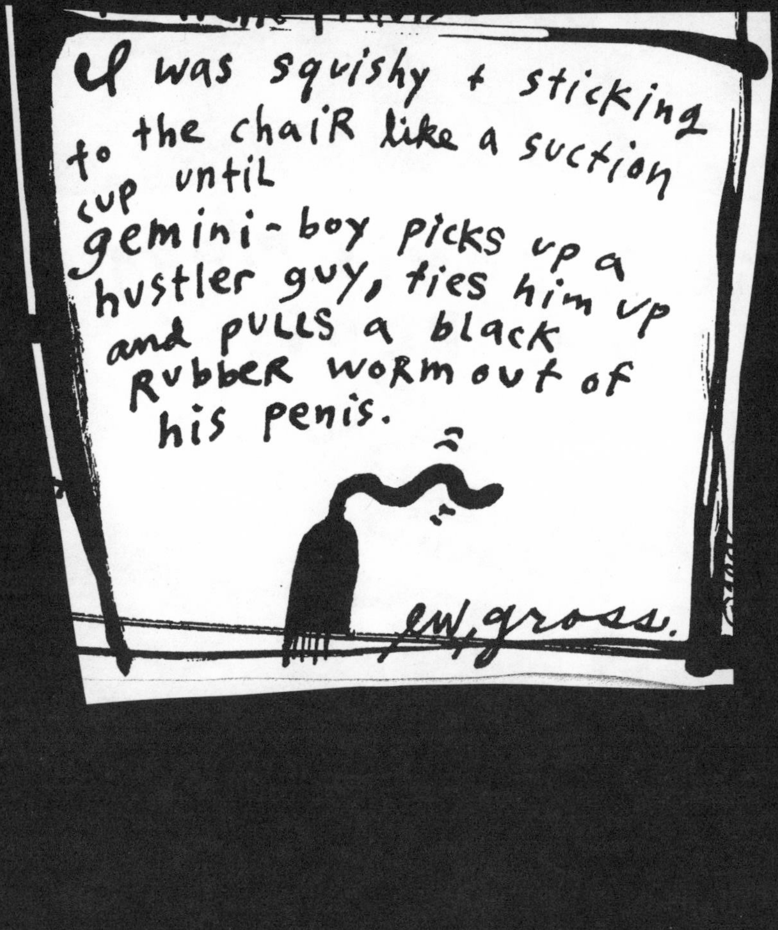
I was squishy + sticking
to the chaiR like a suction
cup until
gemini-boy picks up a
hustler guy, ties him up
and pulls a black
RubbeR worm out of
his penis.
ew.gross.

GIDDEE YUP.

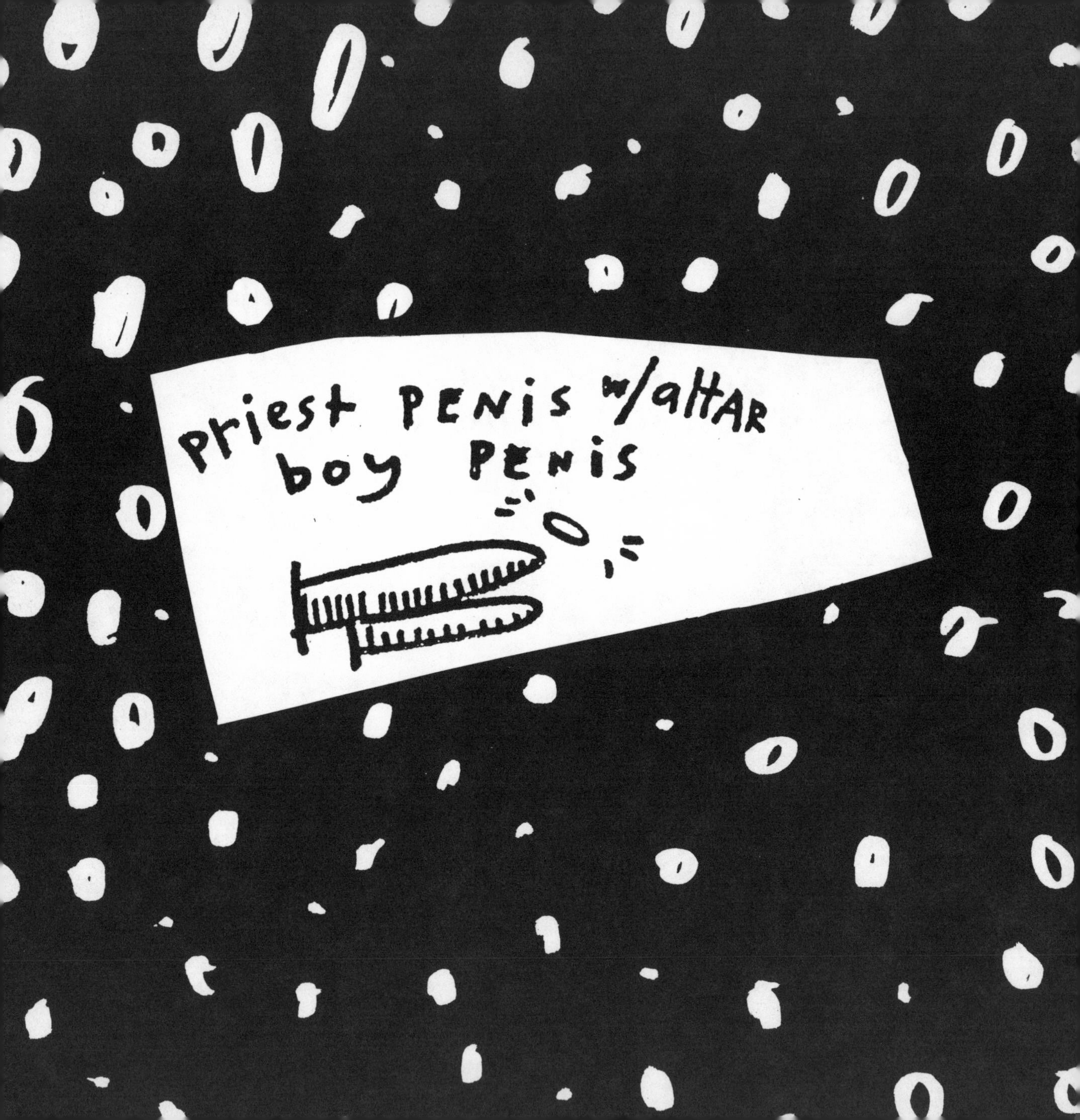
priest PENIS w/altAR
boy PENIS

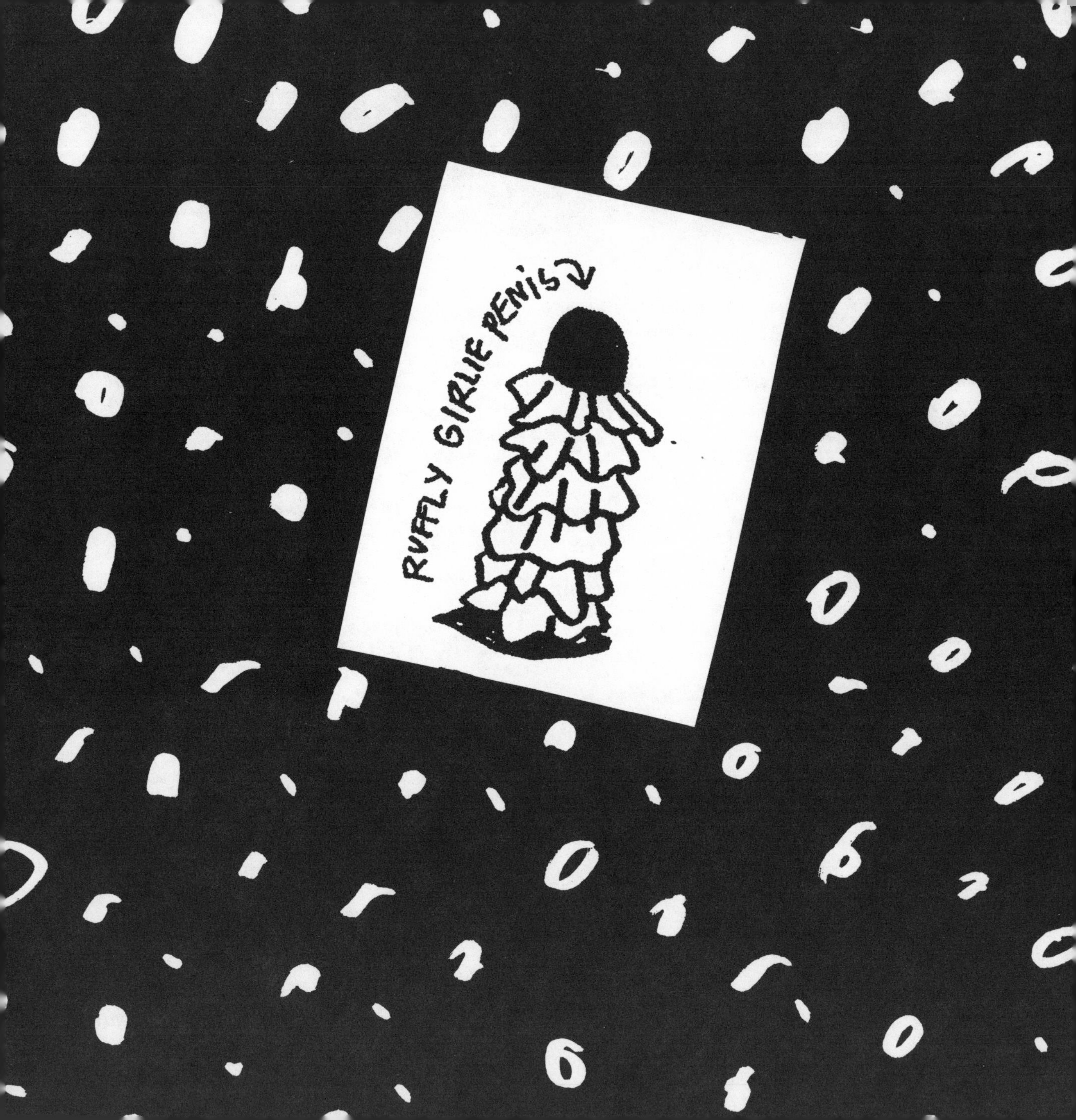
RUFFLY GIRLIE PENIS

"waiting for self-esteem + financial independence"

HERE I AM... MINING MY OWN MISERY FOR CARTOONS. I WIPE the whiskey FROM MY LIPS LIKE CHARLES BUKOWSKI + THINK CRUDE thoughts. MY MISERY is PLOPPED LIKE MASHED POTATOES ONTO AN INSTITUTIONAL PLATE IN A PRISON OF SELF DOUBT.

I'M SLOUCHED IN THE CORNER OF MY ROOM, ON THIS DAY, THE 50th ANNIVERSARY of THE LIBERATION FROM AUSCHWITZ, Listening to MUSIC MADE by PEOPLE who DIED CHOKING ON THEIR OWN VOMIT. No vegetarian New Age Yanni for me ⟶ SKEWER the COW + DEEP throat SAUSAGE LINKS, Lovergirl.

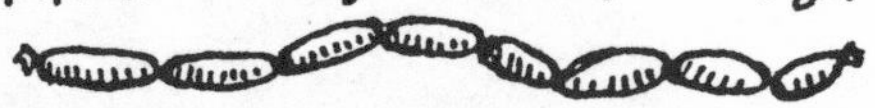

I'm CHAIN-SMOKING CLOVE cigarettes because REGULAR SMOKES MAKE MY HOUSE STINK LIKE A CHEAP GUY./ and it's THE best way to ROMANTICIZE the fact THAT I look + feel Like shit.

The phone NEVER Rings + when it does, I DON'T even bother to sound Busy, + successful./ I only GO OUT to pick up my REJECTION Letters FROM THE MAILBOX + THAT'S why I take showers. I can't even open my front DOOR w/out showering first, no MATTER what, and I GUESS that's GOOD. The holes in my lungs whistle like KAZOOS. I'm 27 + look like Kate Millett after the Looney Bin, but I spit and I don't care./ JIMMY CRACK CORN.

I Really SHOULD Be Happy ☺: FOR ONCE in MY LIFE I SUSPECT I'VE GOT A POSITIVE NET WORTH, but NO ONE'S SENDING the CHECKS. They'll all PROBABLY ARRIVE ON SOME WAY FUTURE Monday when I'M Ready to Retire in some aged Artists' commune where we EARN OUR KEEP by MOWING golf greens FOR OLD FAMILY DOCTORS and SUBURBAN ACCOUNTANTS. Then I'll be Able to Afford SWEATSHIRTS with SHOULDER PADS + RHINESTONES.

BUT UNTIL THAT wealthy/ wealthy DAY, I Might have to GET a DEMEANING PART-TIME job/ WORK FOR SOME bitter, UNTALENTED, SCAMPERING, UNDERACHIEVING BUTT-HEAD in a cheap POLYESTER OXFORD SHIRT, OR a SWEATSHIRT w/SHOULDER PADS + RHINESTONE DESIGNS.

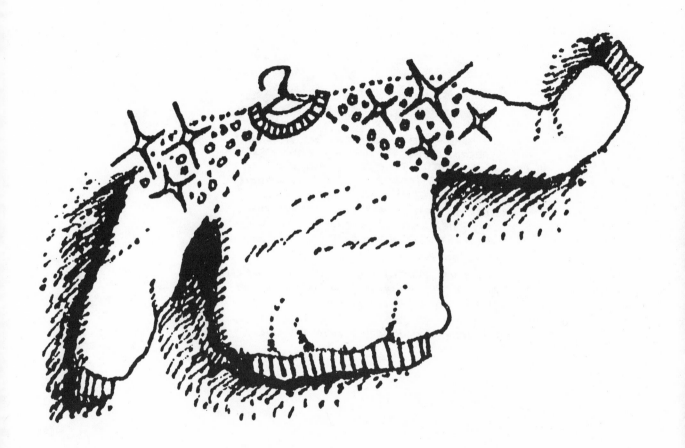

OH GOD → I'D RATHER BE ROAD KILL,
A DECOMPOSING POSSUM w/ MAGGOTS
OR SOMETHING. / I SCREAM ALONE
IN MY APARTMENT and MY NEIGHBOR
UPSTAIRS DOESN'T HEAR ME: SHE
HASN'T STOPPED VACUUMING FOR THREE
DAYS. HER DOG IS BARKING + HER NEW
MOTION-SENSITIVE PORCH LIGHT KEEPS
GOING ON + OFF.

MY ONCE FLUFFY EGO NOW LOOKS LIKE
AN OLD SHRIVELED RAISIN w/ PIECES OF
PUBIC HAIR STUCK TO IT.

I PRACTICE GOING OUT IN PUBLIC AND
ACCIDENTALLY RUNNING INTO SOMEONE
I KNOW.

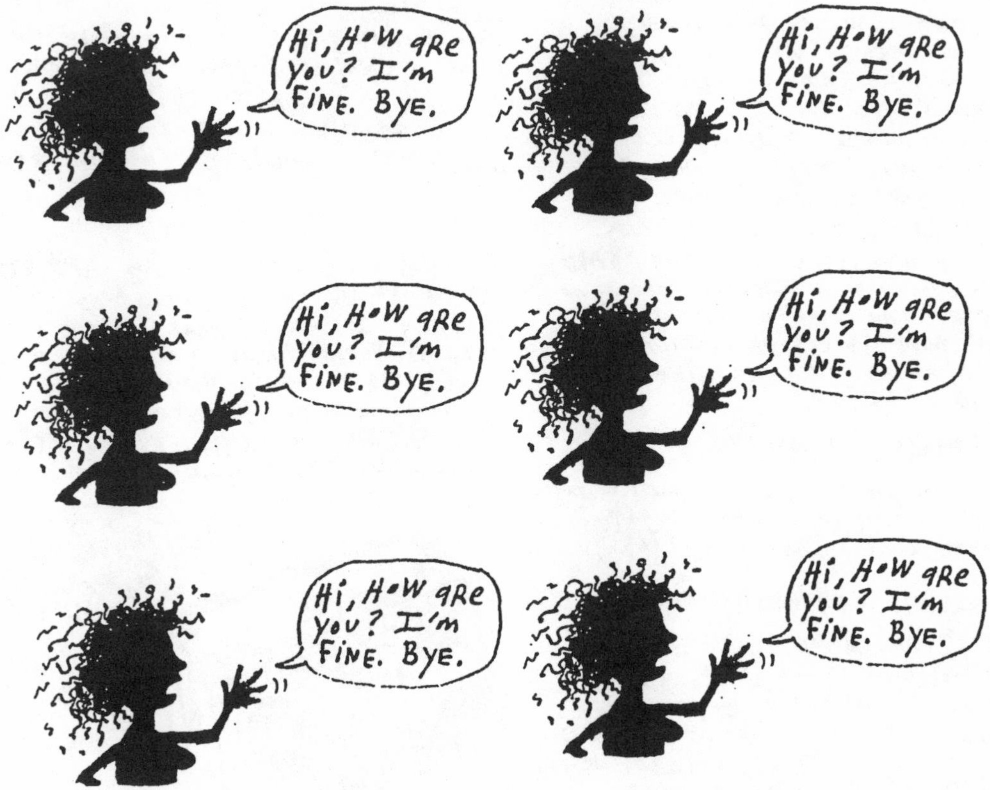
Hi, How are you? I'm Fine. Bye.
Hi, How are you? I'm Fine. Bye.
Hi, How are you? I'm Fine. Bye.
Hi, How are you? I'm Fine. Bye.
Hi, How are you? I'm Fine. Bye.
Hi, How are you? I'm Fine. Bye.

THE PHONE RINGS + I WADE through the knee-deep piles of rejection letters. It seems like I get rejection letters from people I didn't even write to. / I answer the phone + some creepy, velour-voiced guy says: "Erika Lopez? 2 friends of yours called up our (blah blah blah) company + bought you a 15 minute fantasy phone call. They said it was a surprise so I can't tell you who they are until we're finished. Uh, they must think it's your birthday... so, uh... what do you look like? What are you wearing?"

"What friends?" I asked.

"I can't tell you. I guess you're not into this, so I'll give them their Visa money back. Bye." (click)

Obscene callers are getting creative.

Maybe I should be an obscene caller instead of an artist. I could talk to drooling guys with phlegm in their throats and know that I've probably seen them before at 16th and Mission / sexy. I could return cans + bottles to pay for the ads.

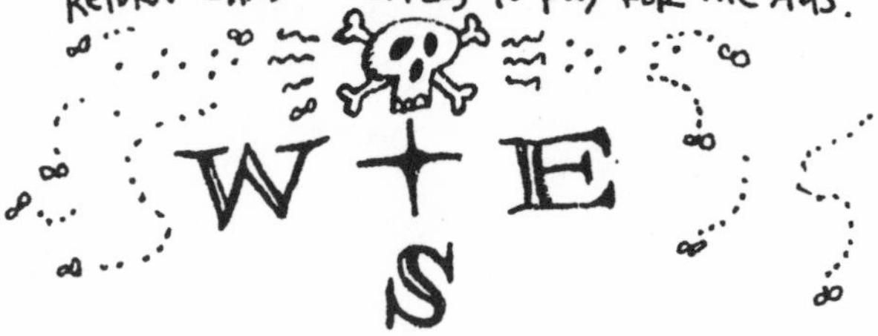

W
E
S

Were these my best options for the future? Everything pointed like a compass North → to → roadkill. I'd have a chance at being reincarnated into a *king*! or an American white guy in the '80s.

I could be a rich + cocky artist, stockbroker or gay man! → My lover + I would make more money than 7 Puerto Rican families + we could write books about being discriminated against for being gay. Terry Gross would interview us + we'd be righteously angry, damn it.

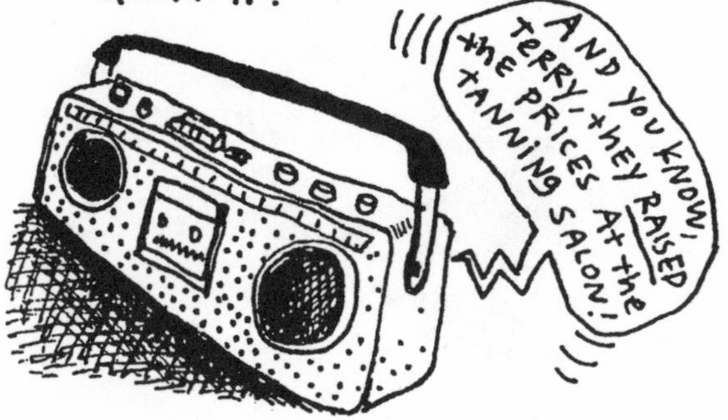

AND YOU KNOW, TERRY, they RAISED the PRICES At the TANNING SALON!

OR I COULD SIGN MYSELF INTO A MENTAL HOSPITAL SO I COULD GET LOTS OF SHOCK TREATMENT LIKE KATE MILLETT. THEN I COULD BE A CONTENT RECEPTIONIST AT AN AD AGENCY + SAY, "HI, CAN I HELP YOU, YOU INSIGNIFICANT PIECE OF SHIT?" I'D BE HAPPY + IN LOVE W/SOME GUY WHO MAKES OBSCENE CALLS AS A FAVOR TO WOMEN EVERYWHERE.

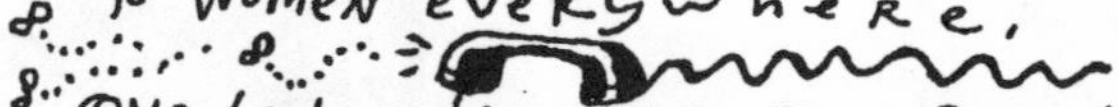

ONE LAST OPTION THAT I'VE FAVORED SO FAR, IS TO HISS IN THE FACE OF PROFOUND REJECTION + GO AHEAD AND WRITE THE GREAT AMERICAN LESBIAN ROAD NOVEL. I CAN DELUDE MYSELF INTO COUNTING ON THE FACT THAT COLUMBIA PICTURES + OLIVER STONE WILL OPTION THE NOVEL + MAKE A BLOCKBUSTER LESBIAN ROAD MOVIE: "FLAMING IGUANAS." THERE'LL BE HUGE POSTERS AT BUS STOPS EVERYWHERE. YOU WON'T BE ABLE TO ESCAPE THIS TRAVELING LESBIAN THING.

EVERYONE WILL WANT TO BE A LESBIAN. COPS, CHILDREN, ANIMALS, WELFARE RECIPIENTS AND MEN WHO GO TO TANNING SALONS.

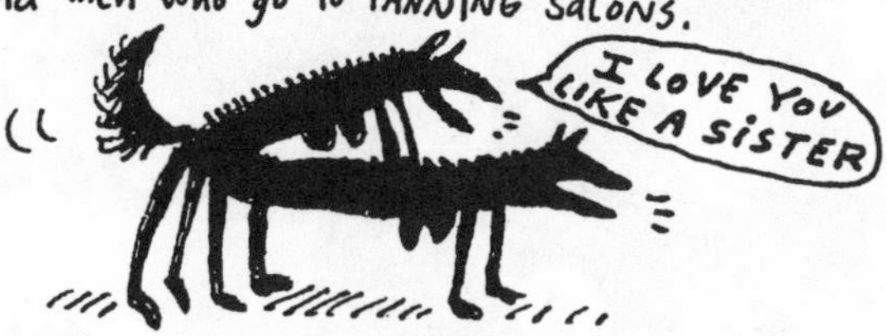
I LOVE YOU LIKE A SISTER

SURE! → AMERICA WOULD CREAM OVER A MOVIE WHERE WOMEN CAN DO COOL THINGS W/OUT HAVING TO RUN AWAY FROM WIFE BEATERS AND RAPISTS. YES! AND I WANT TO GAIN ENTRANCE INTO A WORLD OF ADVANCES + ROYALTIES!

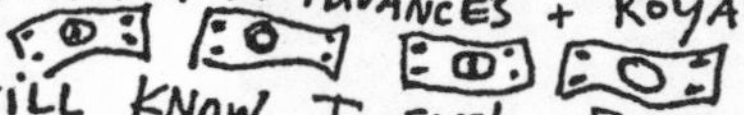

I STILL KNOW I SUCK. BUT I WILL WAIT A LITTLE LONGER WHILE KEEPING AN EYE OUT FOR OVERSIZED CARDBOARD BOXES + A SPACE UNDER THE BRIDGE. BAD CRAP GETS PUBLISHED ALL THE TIME. / HEY. HEY YOU LOOK AT ME. AND KATHY ACKER'S STILL TRYING TO RIP THE WAX OFF YOUR LEGS THE WAY SHE DID THE FIRST TIME.

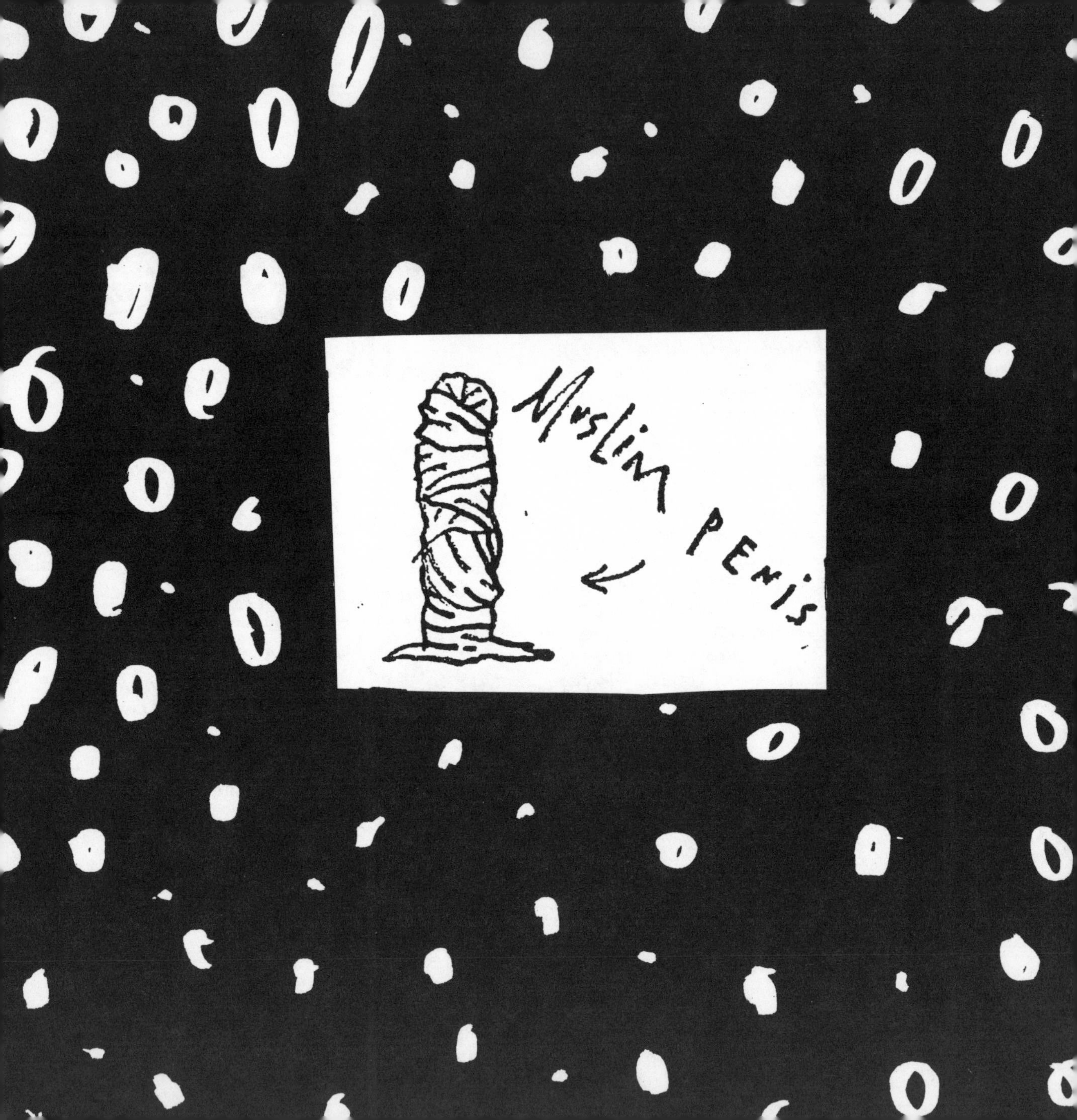
Muslim penis

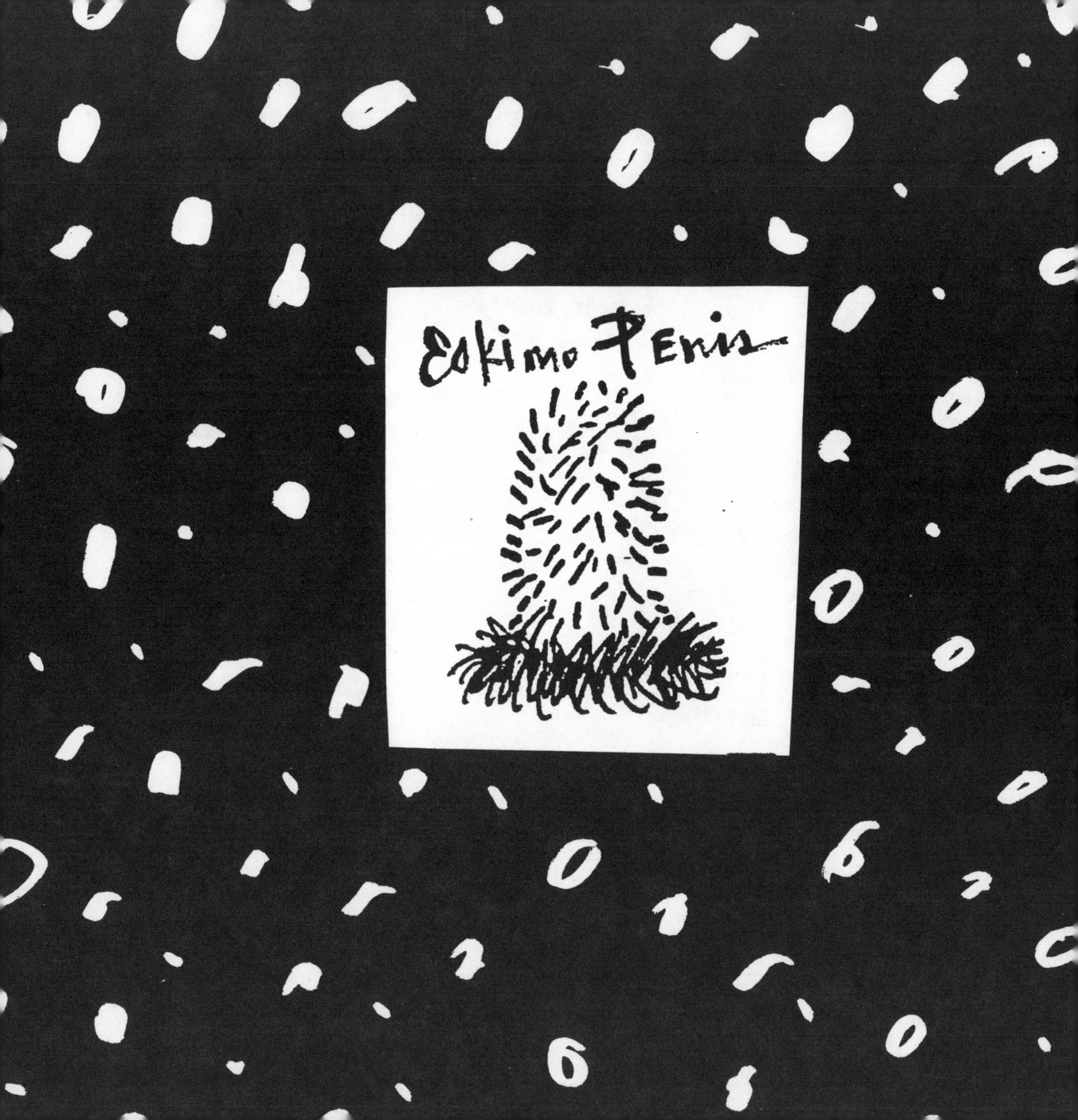
Eskimo Penis

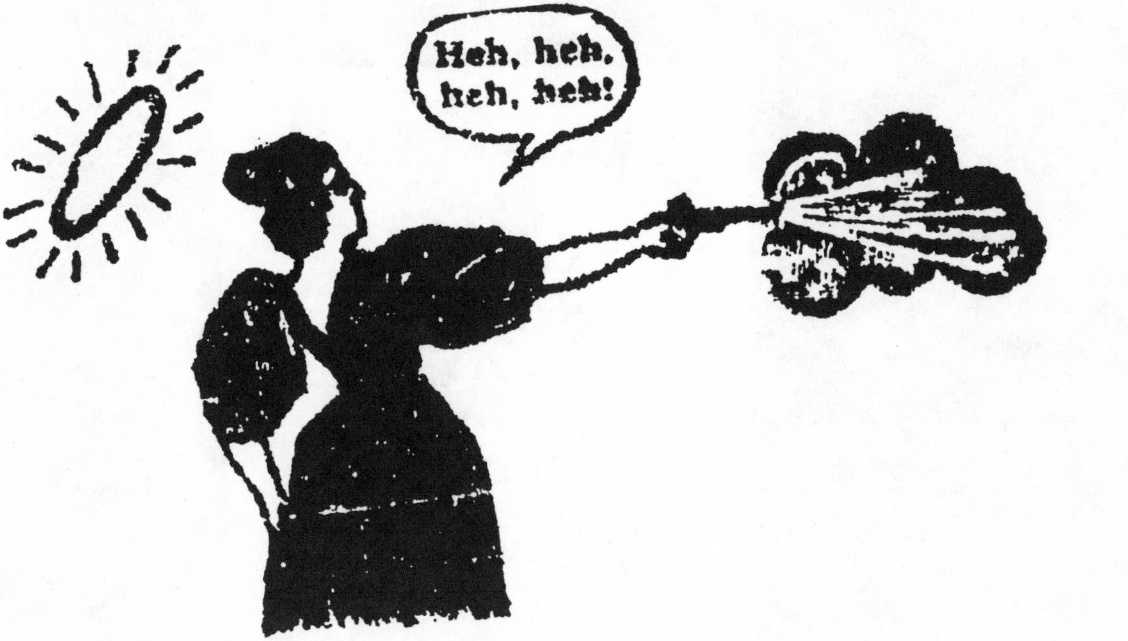
Heh, heh,
heh, heh!

The Queen of Everything

She has a "queen of everything" magnet on her 'fridge, a glass of wine in one hand and a 400 dollar Pomeranian in the other. Last weekend I met Kay Wolff, who wrote THE LAST RUN, a book about her life as a Colombian drug smuggler who fucked her bosses' South American wives to keep them busy and cracked open the legs of North American girls like a dozen eggs / Back before the salmonella scare. Then she adopted a couple of street kids from Colombia, came back to the States and ended up going to PTA meetings with uptight straight people. "My daughter's high school soccer coach patted me on the back and said, 'we know how hard it is for a single mother,' and I said, 'I'm not a single mother, I'm a LEZZBian.'"

Kay Wolff is one of those forever San Francisco lesbians who doesn't much care for that word, and was around before the word "dyke" became as cute as the word "nigger." Since I wasn't really around before panties got scary, I'd have to assume Lesbian San Francisco used to be just like that porn movie "Aerobisex Girls" I reviewed a while ago, where all the girls drive to aerobics class in Gremlins or Dodge Colt hatchbacks, and end up wrestling each other in vegetable oil / except without the red and white striped leotards and leg warmers.

I cannot even imagine a San Francisco of lesbians who are able to fuck each other without demanding by the second date where you were last Thursday and why you didn't call.   Back then they shared girls like a box of tampons in a high school bathroom, and I can't help but sigh because I've definitely missed something.   My idea of a raucous good time is researching bankruptcy laws because i'll never be able to pay off my student loans / Chapter 7 has become pillow talk and hanging up on creditors is like wrestling in vegetable oil, circa 1996.

Wahoo/yeeha.

So why do I even consider children?   That's how this whole conversation started with Kay Wolff, by the way.   She said, "what the hell are all these girls doing turkey baster and artificial insemination babies for, anyway? There are tons of unwanted children out there if you want a kid.   We're overpopulated as it is.   And do you have a quarter of a million dollars? Because that's what it costs by the time they go to college.   Think about the prom dresses, soccer uniforms.   I'm not kidding!   And it's not like you can take a year off when you're tired, and go on welfare.   Welfare?   Hah!   Pretty soon, what welfare?   I had to work 50 hours a week at two jobs and move across from the high school so I wouldn't have to run my kids around."

She said she doesn't know if she'd do it all again, even though she loves her kids more than anything.   And she had tons of help because she had status orphans.   Her little family became like some kind of fetish because her kids were brown.   Everyone wanted to baby-sit and some lovers found the LEZZbian mother/kid thing really sexy.   But by the time it amounted to much, her kids were pounding on the door asking for pancakes.   She said that's a total buzz kill when you've finally got the energy to fuck.

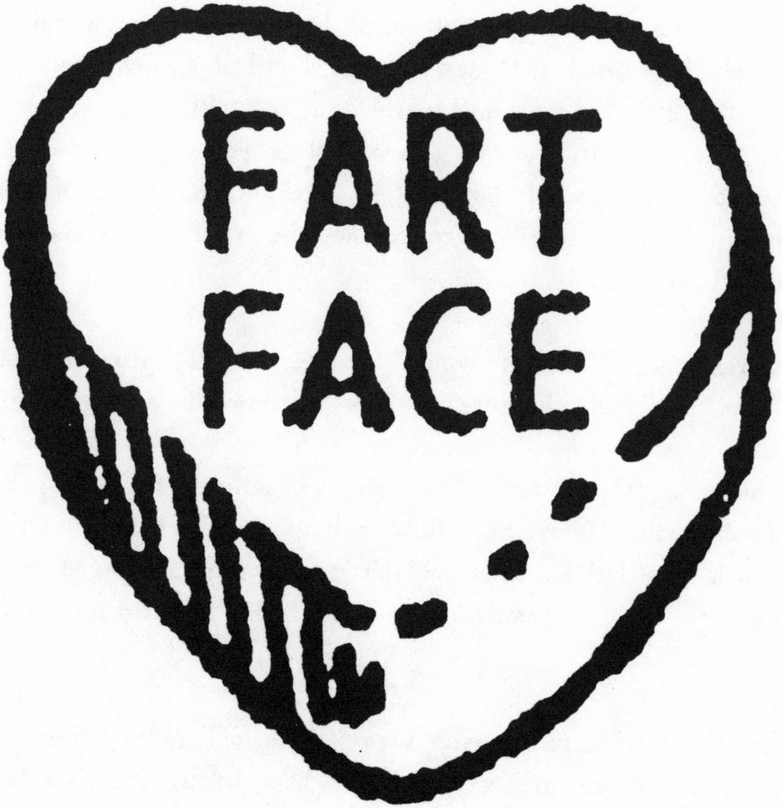
FART
FACE

Still, it's hard for me to let go of this mass biological clock hallucination that seems to be going on right now. So many people I know without even a *place* to put a pot to piss in, are thinking it must be time to have a baby. A lot of my straight friends back east got married and knocked up as soon as they saw what a pain in the ass the working world can be. Being a mother is a job you don't have to apply for, and if you've got a partner who sticks around, they're supposed to take care of you w/out bitching so you have time to walk around smelling sunflowers like you're in a baby food commercial, nurturing *The Future of America.*

I ran, ran, as fast as my d-cups would let me. Away from the showers, birth announcements and baby talk because it was starting to look good and noble.

But now it's happening here, too. It seems so natural, the leaky breasts and public breast feeding that feels like 100% cotton and Berkeley. Oh how we'll laugh as we push our lesbian sons on the swing sets and have weekly telephone fights with members of our family back home who heartily disagree with what we did.

The same little girls who ferociously wave those old faded "down with the patriarchy" signs in the air are some of the best lifestyle pillow queens. I wonder if our moms who raged for equality through the streets are slapping their foreheads like we just didn't get it.

"It's so overrated, you wouldn't believe it." Kay Wolff shook her head. "Go to Disneyworld, stand in any long line and you'll see what it's like having a kid."

And I remembered what a pain in the ass I thought it was to change the cat litter or water my plants. I could see myself eventually having this conversation with my baby, the love of my life, apple of my eye: "Look, missy: you are <u>not</u> the queen of everything. You may be only two, but you need to start pulling some of your own weight around here. You know, answering the phone once in a while, scrubbling your own Kool-Aid out of the carpets. Hey, and if you grow up feeling whiny in therapy and want to write a book about what a horrible mother I was, fine. I'll talk about the time you ate dog shit and masturbated in front of Ralph Nader."

Wahoo/yeeha.

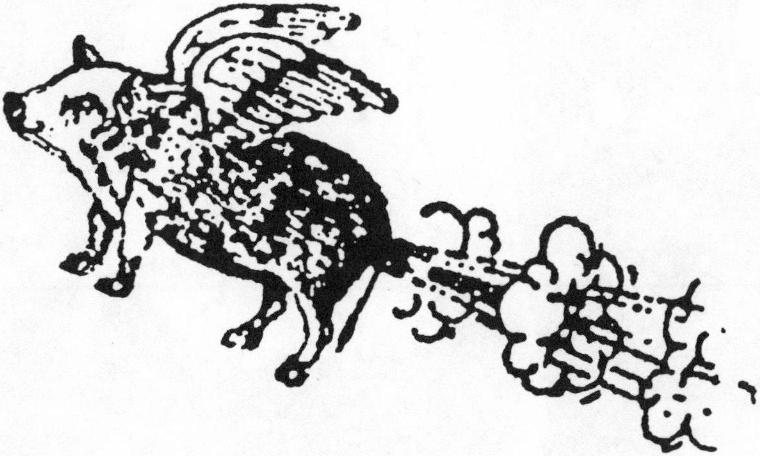

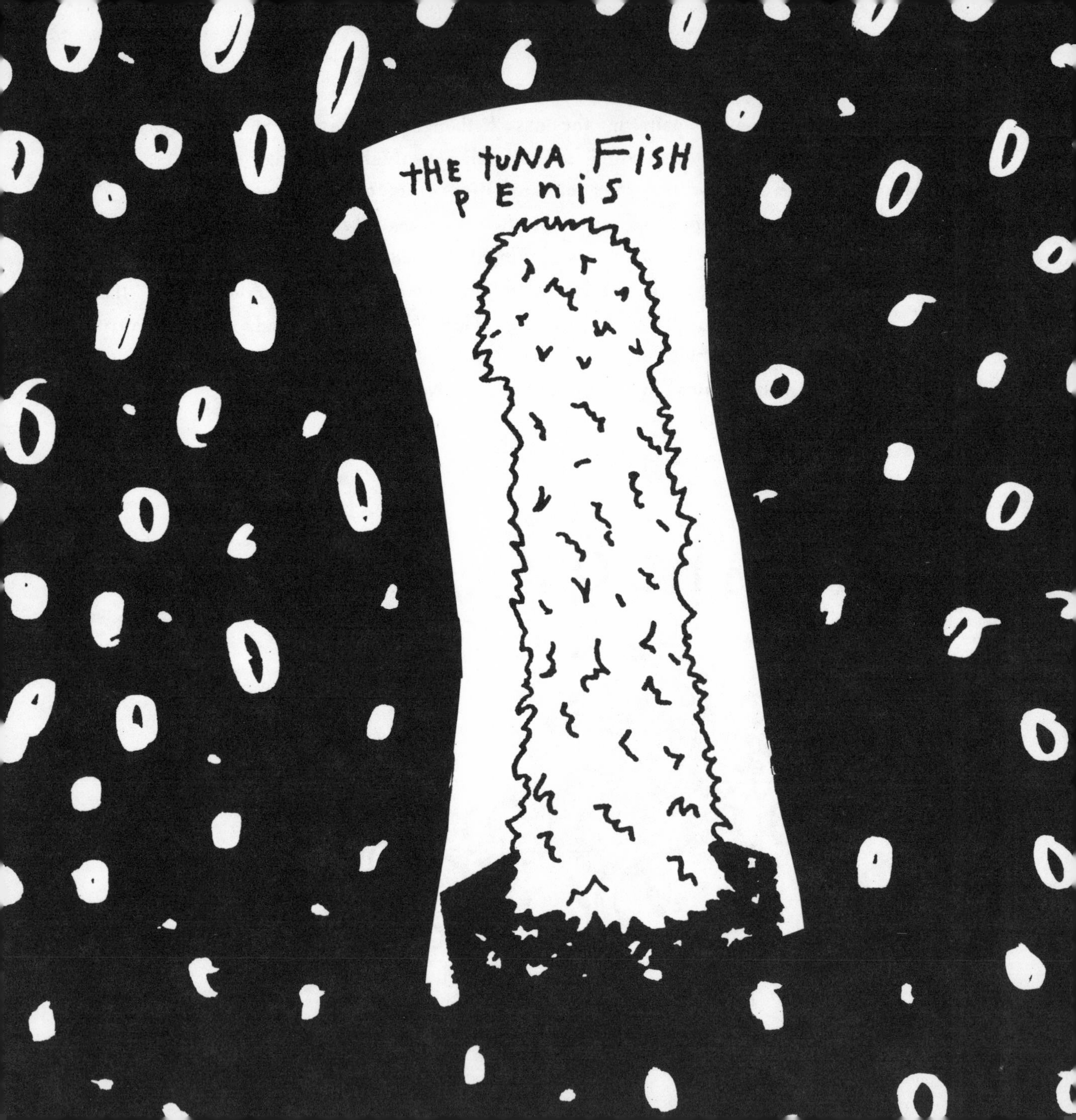
THE TUNA FISH
PENIS

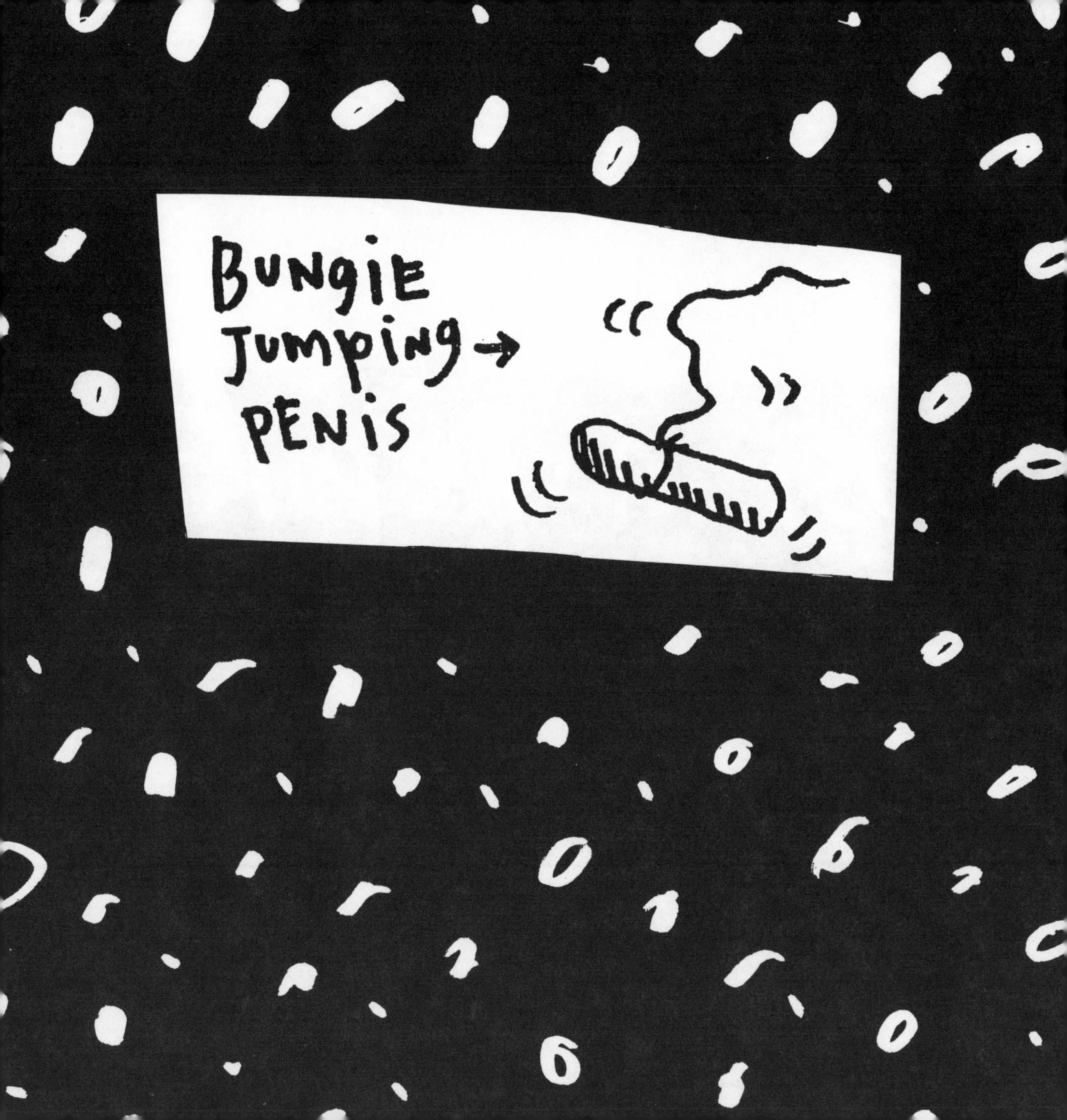
BUNGIE
JUMPING →
PENIS

Just a Report

I WENT ON A BIKE RIDE TO SEE SOME
FRIENDS IN ARIZONA. I WANTED TO SEE
WHAT TRUE love LOOKED LiKE + WHY
EVERYONE ELSE WAS SO HAPPY all tHE TiME.

'95'

I HAD a COUPLE oF ALCOHOLICS ANONYMOUS
FRIENDS UP NORTH SOMEWhere, so I RODE
15 hours FRom San Francisco. I'D LOSt
my oh-so-excellent motorcycle jacket
on POTRERO, so I hAd to borrow ELissa's
Levi jacket. I wore a ½ helmet out
there + I got deaf. SNot was flying
behind me in the wind + I thought my
nipples were gONNa tuRN black and
fall off. AS I followED the only
tRuck on the highway, going 90 miles an
hour because I couldn't cut through the
dark w/ovt him, I got less and
less sexy.

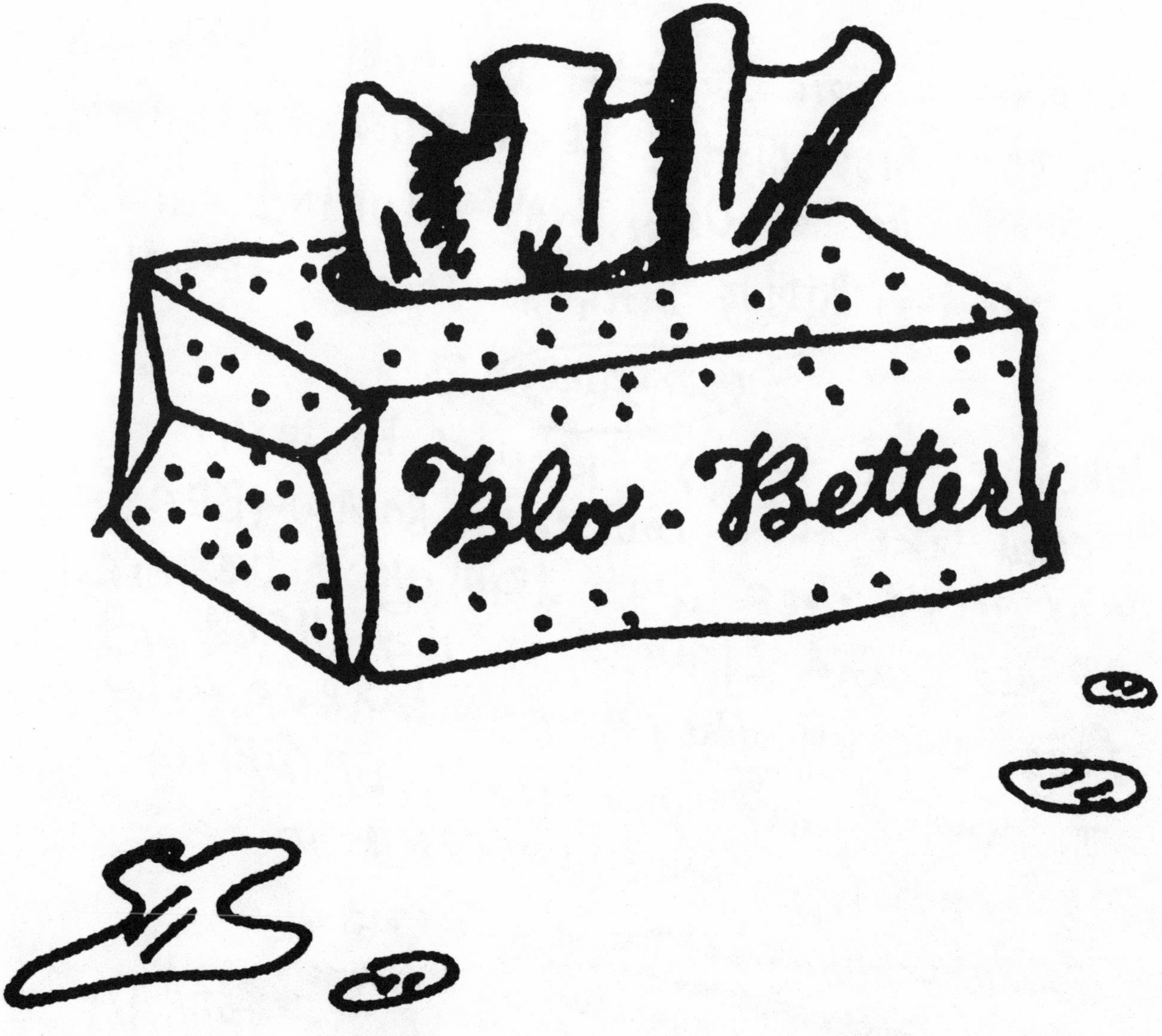
Blo Better

I made a note to clip my ankles behind my ears, ride bitch + be a Pillow Queen from now on. Ha ha. Only way kidding. After 20 minutes, riding bitch is so-o-o-o-o boring.

(anyway)

When I got to my friends' house, it seemed like they couldn't remember why they'd ever quit drinking in the first place, and figured if they held out long enough they'd remember why. I thought once you quit drinking, everything was supposed to be Little-Orphan-annie-Fine-

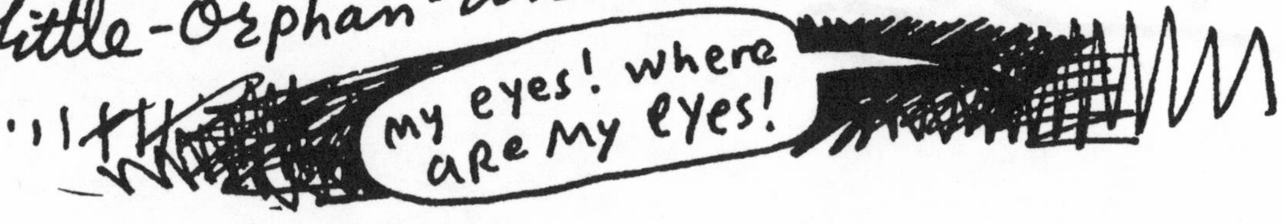

my eyes! where are my eyes!

Then I went DOWN to TUCSON where my GRandmother lives in a white REpublican retirement community. At dinner they tell ME to Smooth down my hair because it's UNRULY, but I say I'M half (½) puerto Rican and CAN't smooth anything DOWN INCLUDING my sexuality. she keeps introducing me to the waiter guy + I've had to come out to her 50 times already.

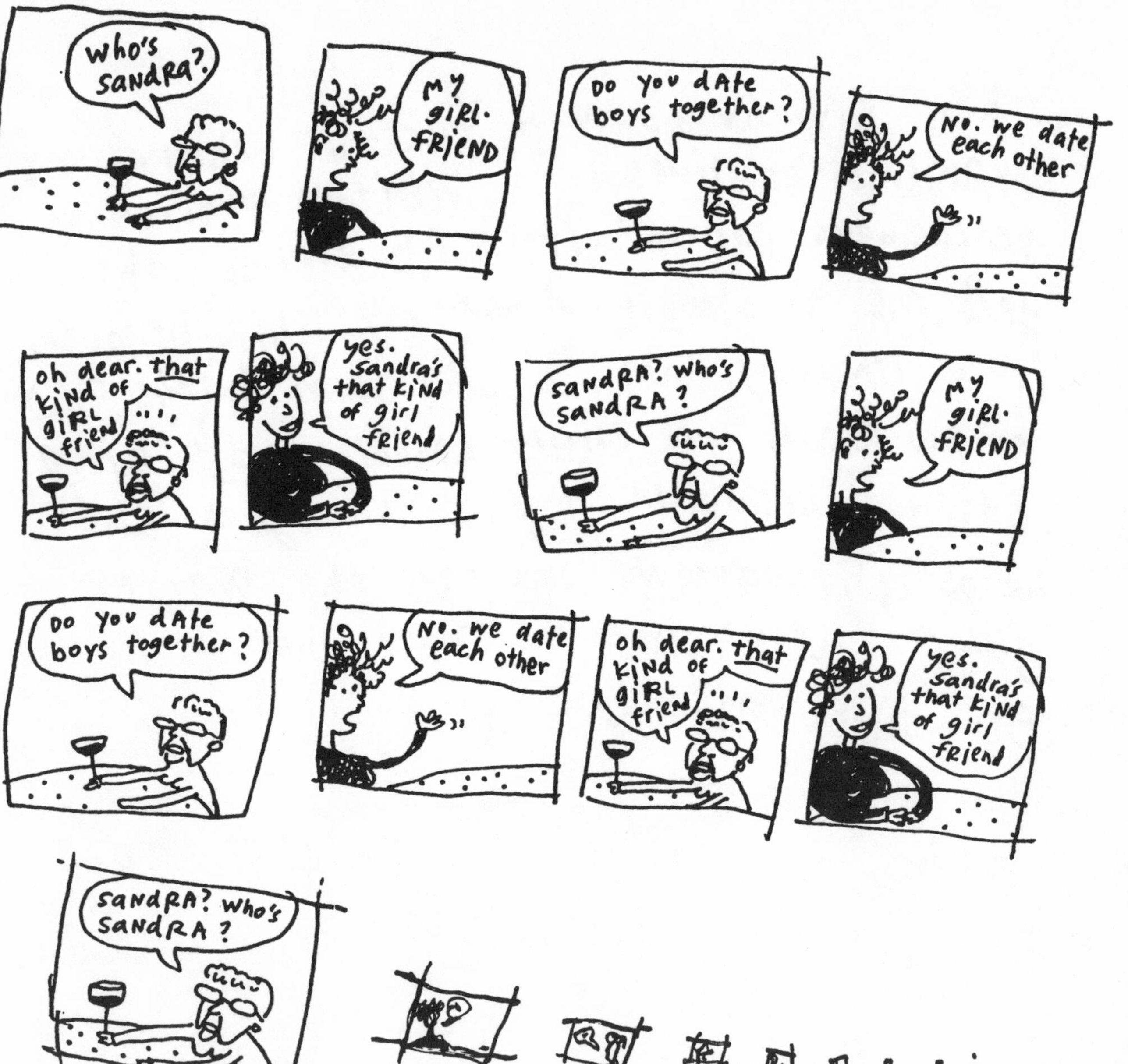
who's sandra?
my girl-friend
do you date boys together?
No. we date each other
oh dear. that kind of girl friend ...,
yes. sandra's that kind of girl friend
sandra? who's sandra?
my girl-friend
do you date boys together?
No. we date each other
oh dear. that kind of girl friend ...,
yes. sandra's that kind of girl friend
sandra? who's sandra?

Her cranky husband
with the huge ear
lobes tells me people
don't like people who

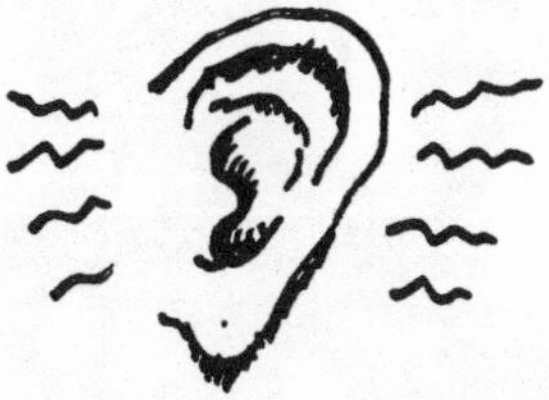

laugh loudly. He says it scares
them. He's such a wimp. He thinks asking someone to remove that rake
from your ass is bullish + demanding.
He's glad he gets what he's given +
doesn't complain when their $4,000
a month rent jumps 5% each year, as
their pensions stay the same. He says
it's only fair because the corporation
needs the money.

I thought old people hit a zen place
when they'd just say, "okay, let's cut
through all the crap, I don't have a
lot of time," but not necessarily.

And everyone's not as happy as they
look. I'm here to tell you in case you forgot.
----(YOU'RE FINE.)

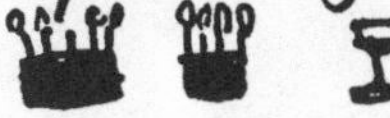

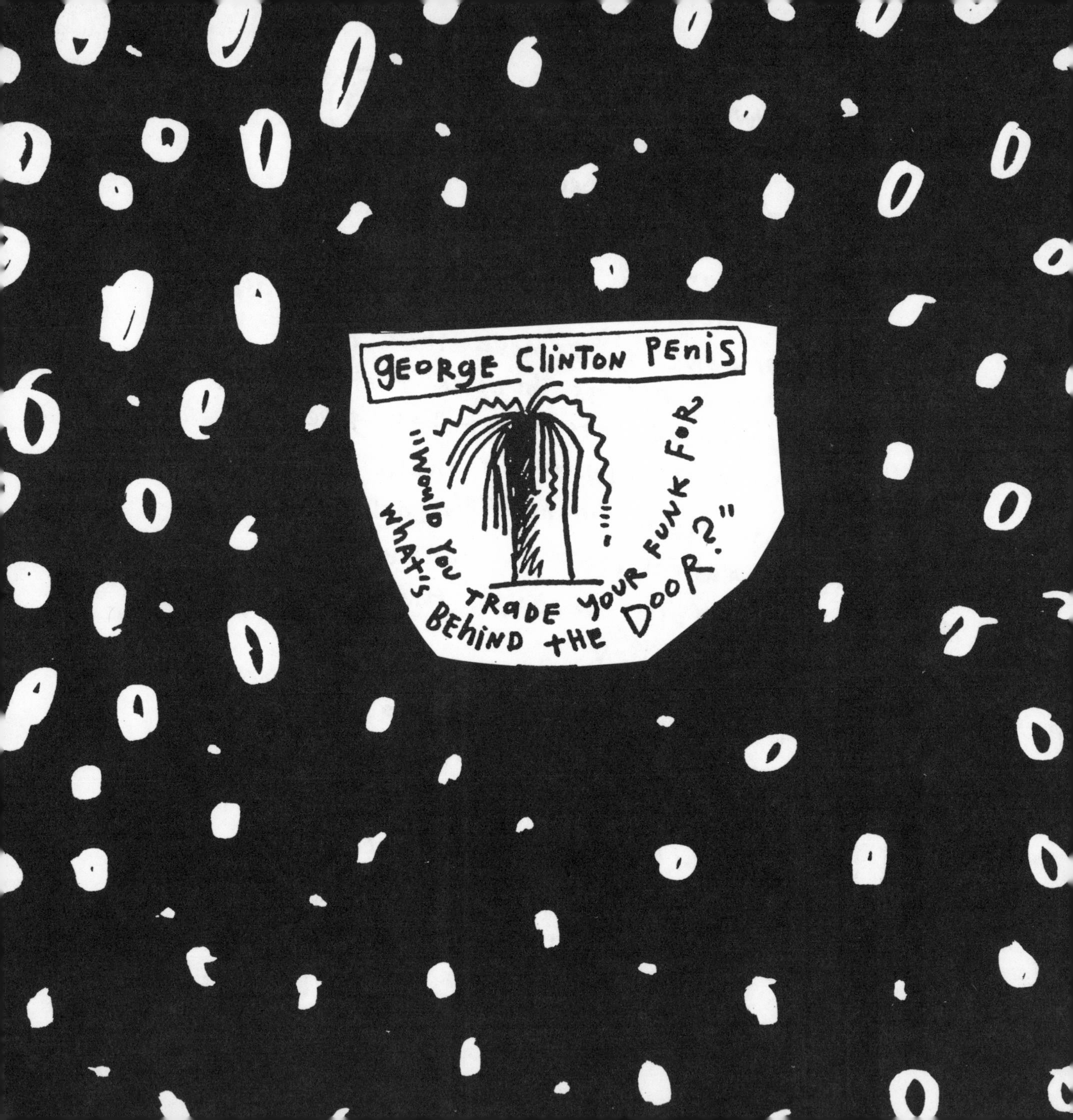

GEORGE CLINTON PENIS
"WOULD YOU TRADE YOUR FUNK FOR WHAT'S BEHIND THE DOOR?"

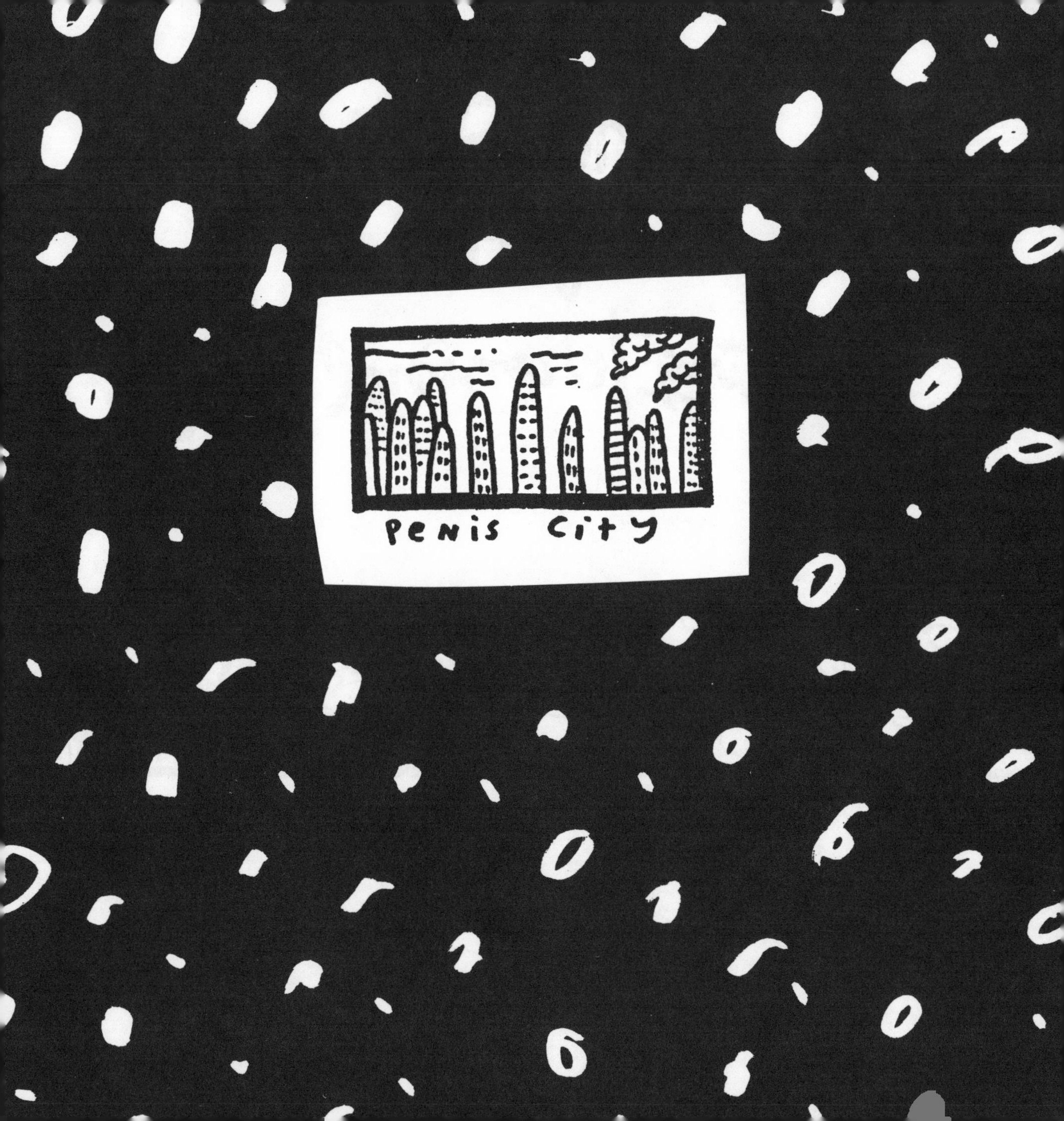
penis city

The Gift of the Reading Terminal Magi*

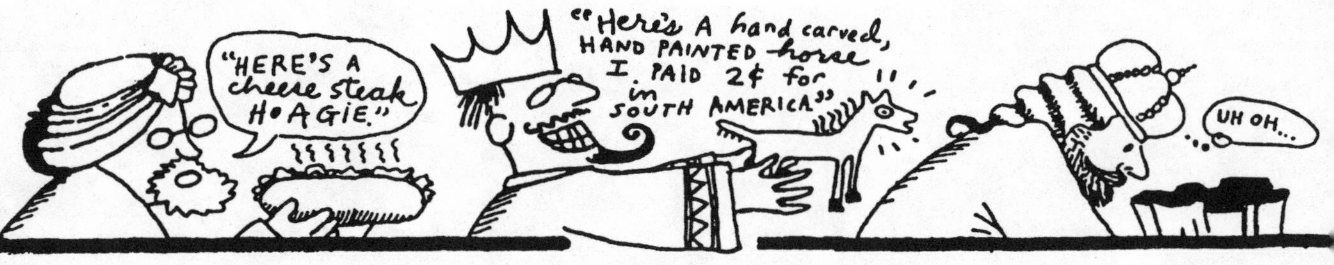
"HERE'S A cheese steak HOAGIE."
"Here's A hand carved, HAND PAINTED horse I PAID 2¢ for in SOUTH AMERICA"
UH OH...

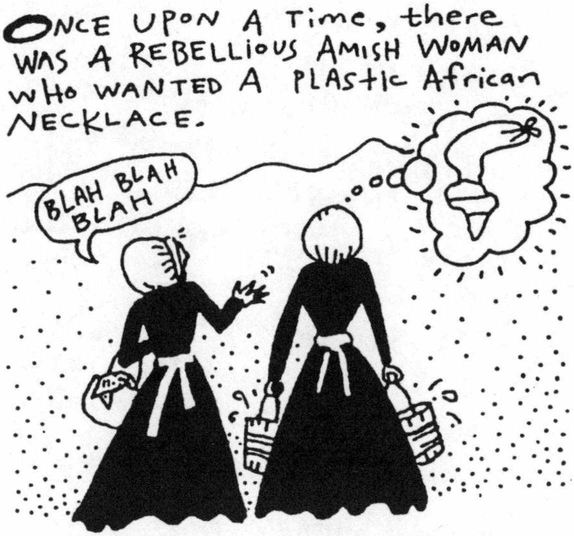
ONCE UPON A TIME, there WAS A REBELLIOUS AMISH WOMAN WHO WANTED A PLASTIC African NECKLACE.
BLAH BLAH BLAH

She untied her apron, bunched it up and threw it down on top of a PRE-SLICED LOAF of ONION BREAD IN Plastic. SHE PULLED her WHITE BONNET Tighter over her blonde hair, AND VENTURED PAST the AMISH forcefield and into the REST OF THE TERMINAL'S CONCRETE HEAths. getting lost. SHE WAS BLUDGEONED w/ TERMINAL IMAGES of Modern Day Society / ice cream flavoured COFFEE / and

veggie burgers MADE BY AN OLD WOMAN WHO TALKED w/ her mouth full, so stuff sprayed on your own VEGGIE Burger.

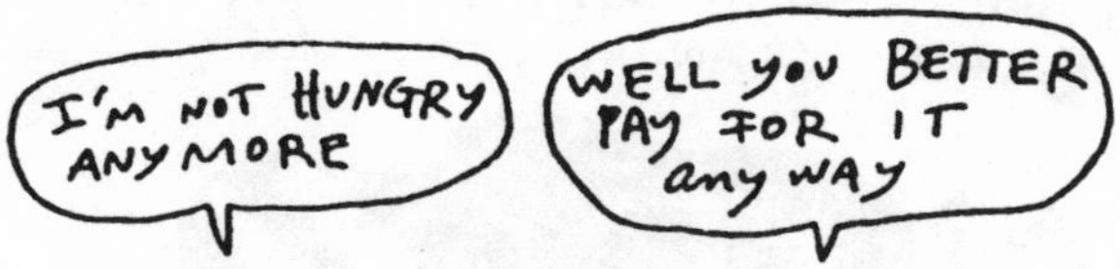
I'M NOT HUNGRY ANYMORE
WELL YOU BETTER PAY FOR IT any WAY

She TURNED, TURNED, AND TURNED
AROUND AGAIN LIKE AN AMISH
Wonder Woman whose
HUSBAND had Nothing to do w/ the
BCCI SCANDAL.

HER eyes lighted upon THE STAND of a NOUVEAU African Man In His Thirties. She SAW The INSANE DREADLOCKS AND SCHIZOPHRENIC BEARD. Medusa's lover, SHE thought AS she delicately lifted her SKIRT w/ BOTH hands and RACED OVER To Him.

She wiped the PERSPIRATION FROM her BROW w/the Back of her tiny hand, AND SAID:

"I WANT a PLASTIC-Twine NECKLACE."

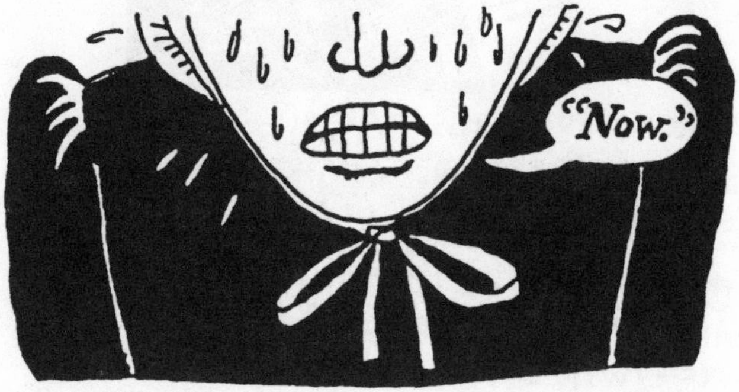
"Now."

the man pursed his lips
w/ his fingers and looked
at her w/ a furrow in
his brow: "ARE YOU,
UH... SURE ABOUT THIS???"

SHE PUT HER HANDS ON THE
EDGE OF HIS African CART, AND
leaned CLOSER to him:
"YES," SHE WHISPERED, "I'VE
NEVER BEEN MORE SURE OF ANY-
thing IN MY LIFE."

HE SHRUGGED IN HIS DASHiKi,
SAID "Okay" AND WAVED HIS
HAND OVER THE Black felt
DISPLAY BOARD. THE Amish
WOMAN QUICKLY STUDIED All tHE
PLASTIC-TWINE African NECKLACES,
AND SAID "HA!" AS SHE Lifted
Up a SMall plastic NECK pouch
in the shape of africa.

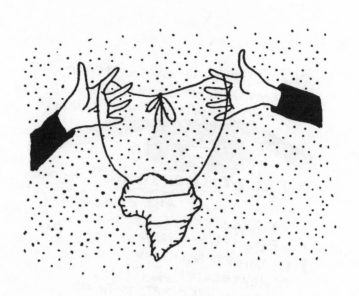

She slipped it over her neck in slow motion and patted it to her tightly bound bosom:

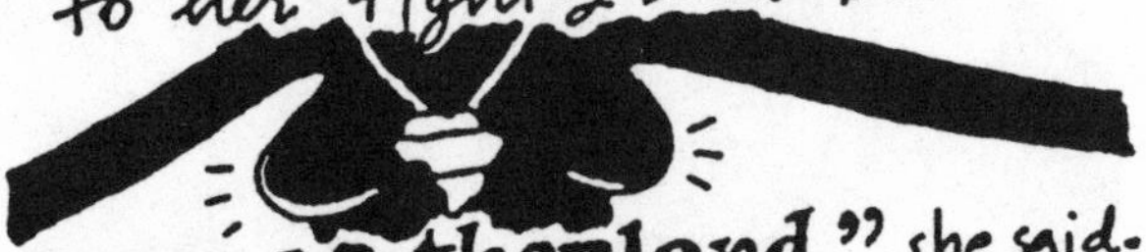

"The Motherland" she said. Looking up at the Merchant w/a huge satisfied smile, she asked, "What is your name?" He smiled back and said, "HEATHCLIFF X."

"Heathcliff X, I think I love you."

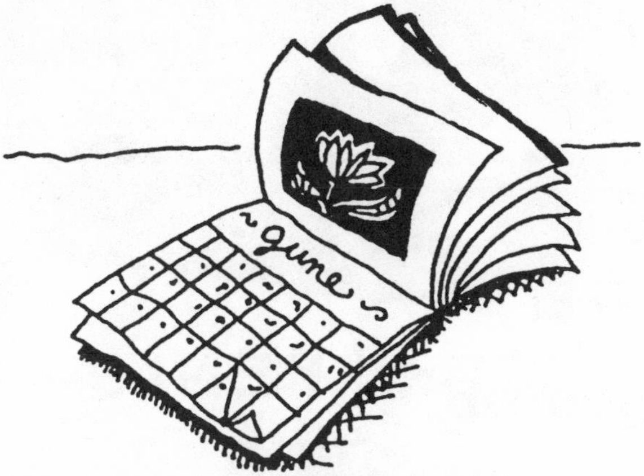
June

THAT WAS 6 MONTHS AGO. THE LAST ANYONE HEARD, THEY SHARED A HYBRID KWANZAA/CHRISTMAS-THING. They hadn't seen each other for a couple of weeks, AND HE SHOWED UP HAVING SHAVED HIS HEAD AND SPORTING AN ABE Lincoln/AMISH BEARD: HE WANTED to fit in her WORLD. SHE WAS SURPRISED BECAUSE SHE WENT OUT AND GOT A PLANET-SIZED afro perm, AND GOT skin cancer from spending too MUCH TIME in the tanning salon. HE SNAPPED his **NEW** AMISH SUSPENDERS AND THEY LAUGHED + LAUGHED LIKE IT WAS THE END of a **TV** SHOW.

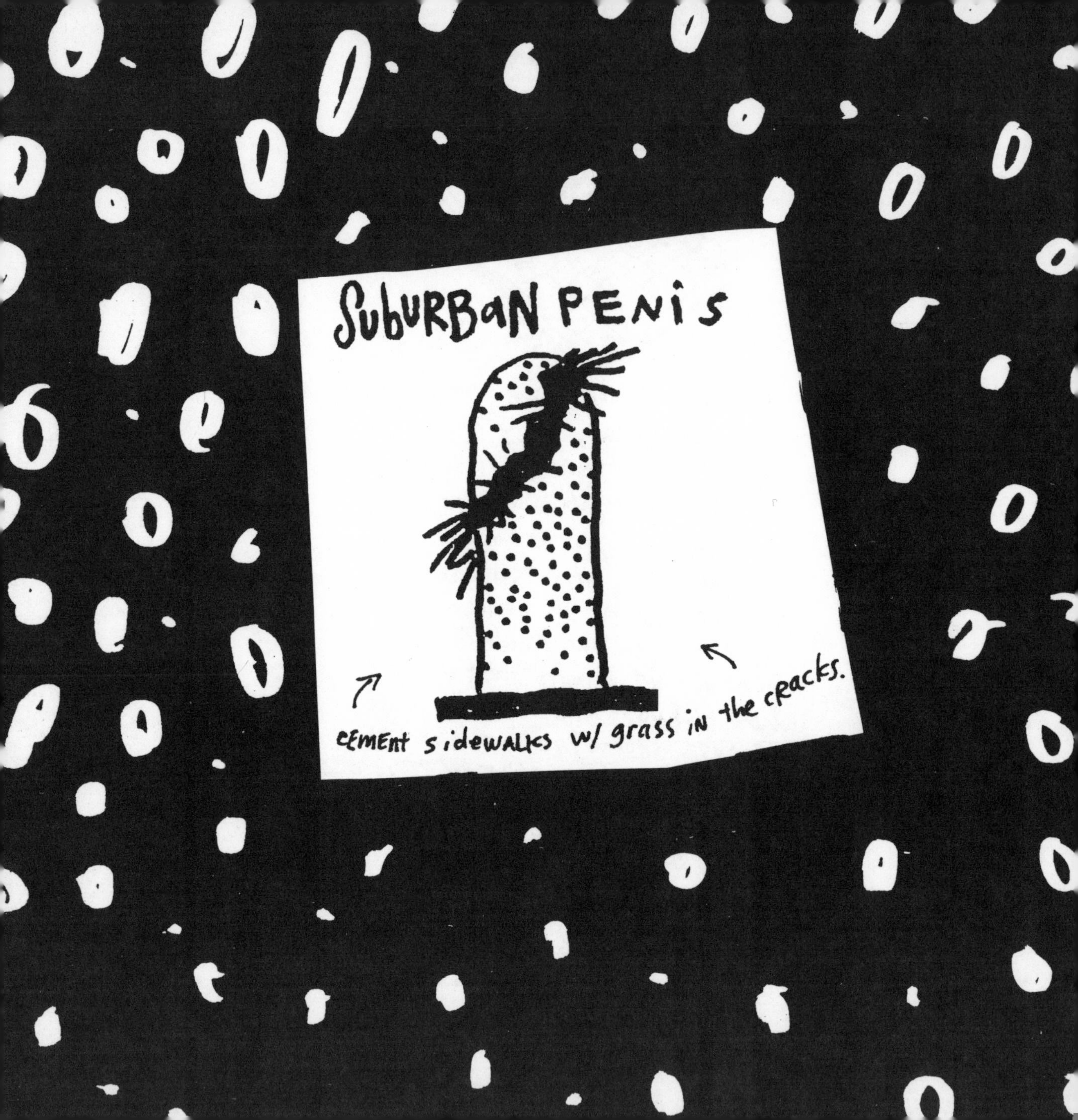
SUBURBAN PENIS
cement sidewalks w/ grass in the cracks.

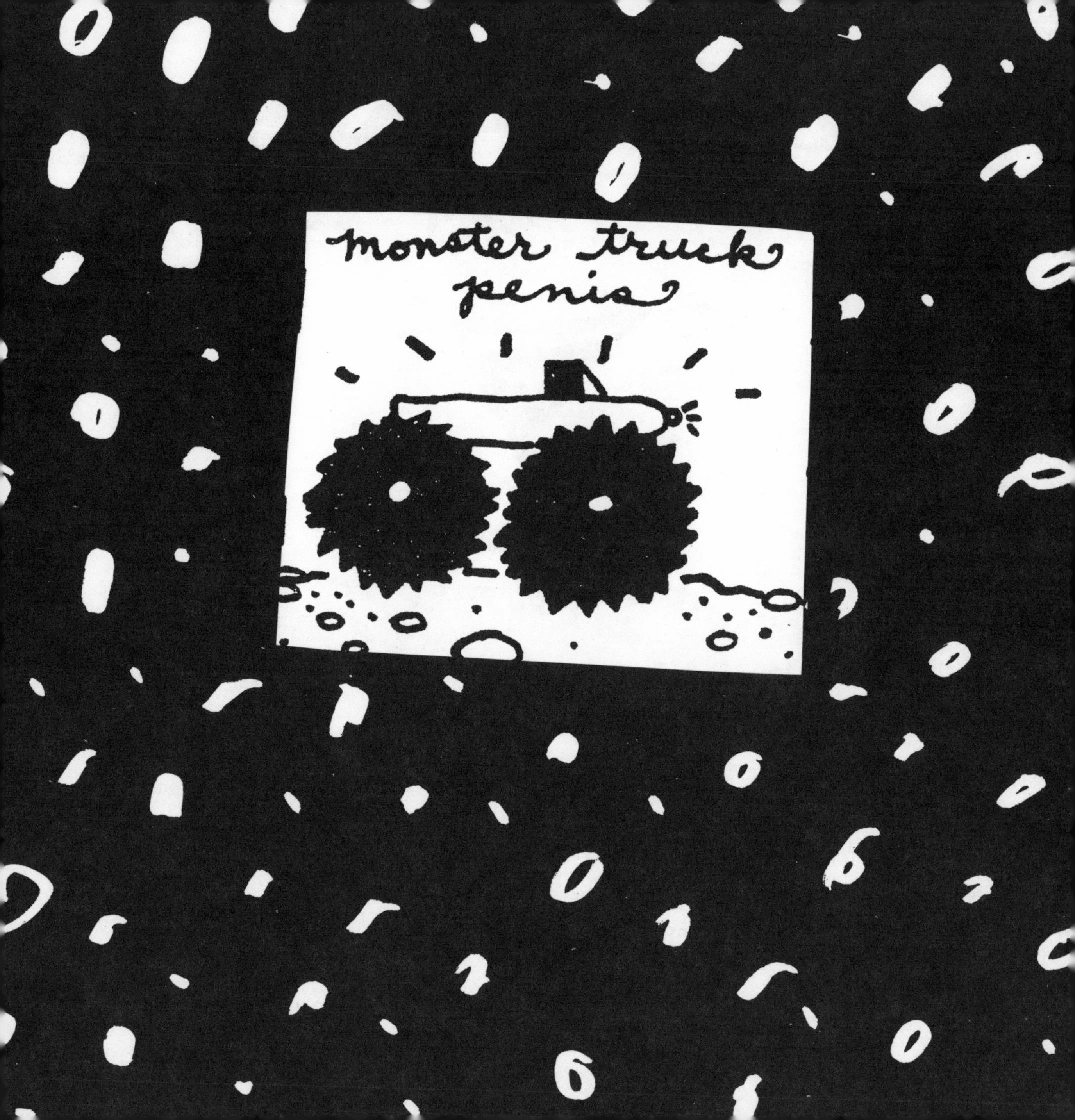
monster truck
penis

Pia Sweden Falls in Love with Hooter

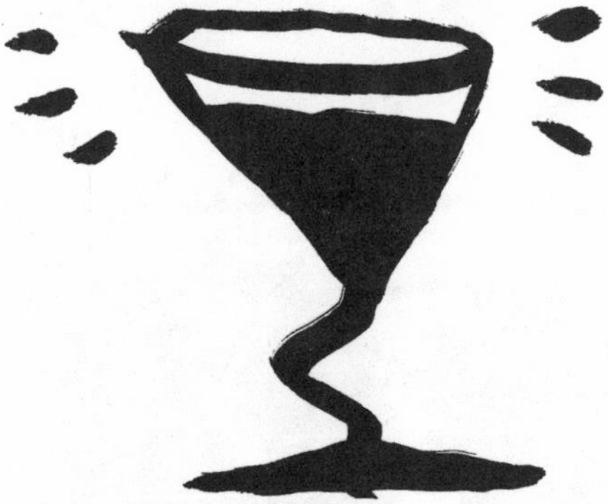

★ chapter one ★

I called her Hooter because her flagpole nipples made it nearly impossible for anyone to call her by her Christian name.

The smell of alcohol in her sweat, cigarette smoke in her curly hair, glassy eyes and the slurred pillow talk didn't really do much for me. It was the way she steered and shifted her pickup truck while never letting go of my hand. Sweet. Very sweet. That was all it took for me to promise everlasting monogamy and throw away the latex gloves so we could squirt like water fountains.

I never even paid attention to the word co-dependent because I thought I was above it. Ha ha ha. Ha ha ha.

✳ chapter Two ✳

Almost overnight I turned into a bitchy, distrustful trailer park wife. I tried to be understanding:

"Okay, you're right," I said. "Maybe I am new at this lesbian stuff, but you're telling me it's normal in the Lesbian Way for you to go out and get drunk with a former lover and give her a candle-lit bath?"

"Yeah, see that's what lesbian platonic friends do for each other," Hooter explained. "It's like a family thing."

I shrugged my shoulders and started chewing on my forearm. "Uhm, I never gave anyone in my family a bath."

"Well how about a dog or a gerbil? You had to give them baths, right?"

"Yeah."

"Well, then---there you have it!"

"Oh, okay," I said. But in spite of all those rational explanations, there was a little dark cloud of distrust and banal co-dependence growing over our dried-up field of alcoholic love.

★ ★ ★Chapter Three ★★★

I started chainsmoking with pink foam curlers in my hair and lime green polyester pants that were too tight, and remembered back to a time when I used to dance, sing and wear loose cotton clothing that didn't spotlight my cellulite as if it were in a museum.

I also used to watch that amazing pig movie over and over again, which by the way, deserved every oscar that exists, and the duck deserves best supporting actor. Fuck *Leaving Las Vegas*. Why pay to sit for that kind of depression when it's so easy to just go and slice your wrists behind some dumpster in the ghetto and watch the cuts get infected as you bleed to death?

So, one day I was at a filling-up-and-spilling-over party with non-alcoholic beer and folk singers. And this woman walked past the three bean salad wearing sunglasses that made her mouth look famous, scratched her dog behind the ear and said, "Yep, I've been clean and sober for ten years."

Sober for ten years: I thought it was the most erotic thing that could ever be said.

Then I figured Hooter and I'd have to do something about our parched field of alcoholic love, so with thirteen years of I'm Okay You're Okay therapy behind me, I fell back on what I knew best: I read self-help books by the armload.

My friend Kris once told me if you've been seeing someone six months and need to go to therapy, it's not a real good sign, so I waited until it was seven months. Then I called a therapist so Hooter and I could stay together for the children's sake. Which children, I didn't know. Any child that wanted us to stay together for their sake was fine with me in this world of country music divorce and unrealistic love songs.

Besides, what else are supposed to do with someone who takes away your fear of dying and will watch Matlock reruns with you?

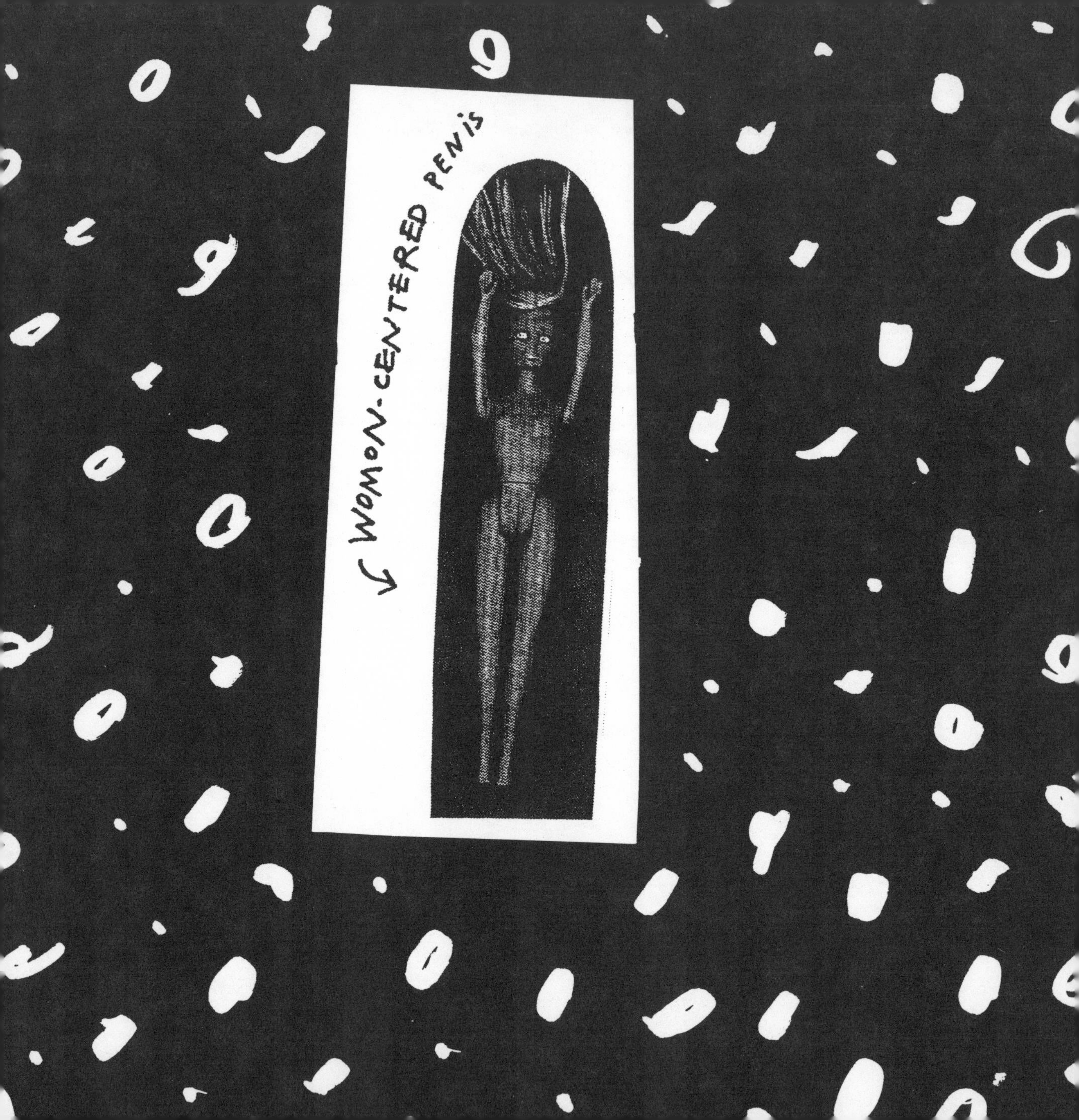
WOMON-CENTERED PENIS

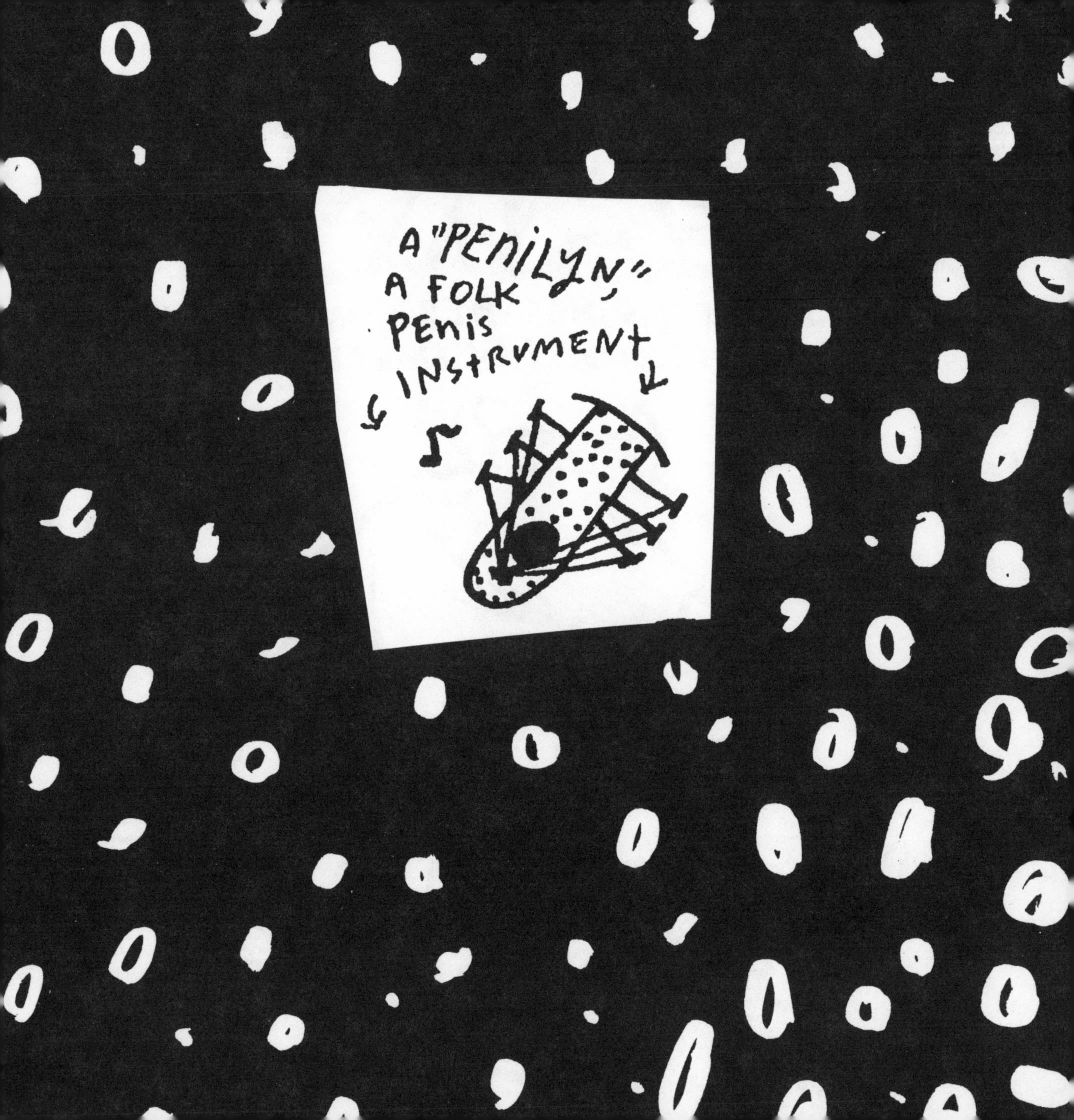
A "PENILYN"
A FOLK
PENIS
INSTRUMENT

STEAKS and RIBS

PIA SWEDEN FINDS HER INNER MATADOR IN THIS SECOND TINY NOVEL

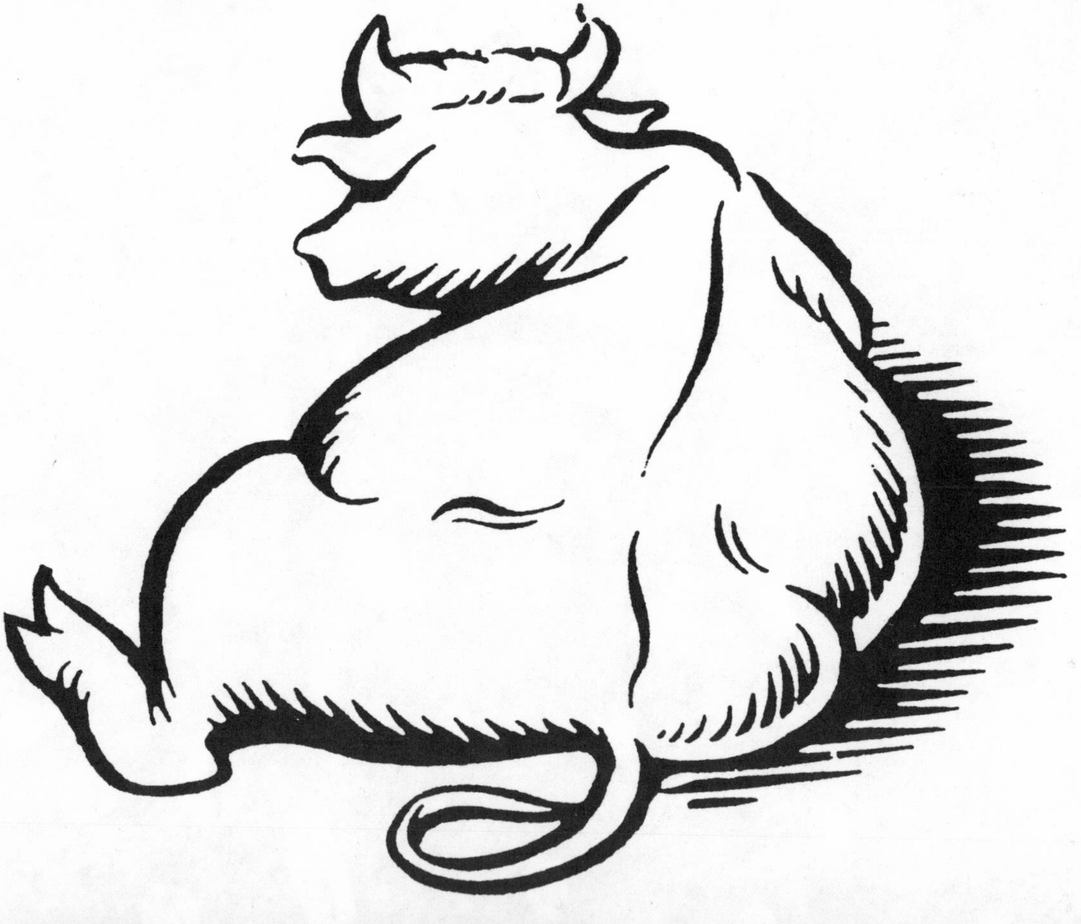

Chapter One.

The Other Woman. Her job is to rub shoulders, be understanding to the point of concussion and ask for nothing. tossed peanuts become emerald moments of time and it goes without saying that she'll refer to the wife with a sisterly love so she can stay where she is and take what she can get.

Some of the most passionate forbidden sex she'll ever have will whisper fool thoughts in her head, but an hour later when she's watching Judge Wapner alone and the sheets are dry, she'll remember it's never been about the sex anyway. It never is.

Yeah, couples therapy didn't work for Hooter and Pia, so they took a little break from their alcoholic love story that was like an endless tape loop of distrust, anger, hope and denial, spliced with occasional good sex and touches of honesty. Hooter immediately took up with Another Woman who'd been circling overhead with a bald head for quite some time. Pia's body wasn't even cold yet.

Later, Hooter did the country song thing, got on her knees and tried to convince Pia "it didn't mean a thing," but Pia finally had enough of playing whiny trailer park wife bitching about all the drinking. The role was getting so boring she could barely keep her eyes open. In truth, Pia was too much of a diva to play Wild Kingdom and fight over the carcass of a lover. Hooter seemed defiled somehow. Maybe it was the Latin American side of Pia that wanted a woman who didn't sacrifice her honor or her underwear so easily. Someone a little more expensive.

Well, whatever, Pia's heart ached horribly just the same and she had to admit she didn't really believe in this butterfly-let-it-go, free-love hippie, lesbian thing no matter how hard she tried to be modern and detached. And how many other "it didn't mean a thing" moments had there been? It was an accident she even knew about this one. Hooter had a special way of bending the truth around like a paper clip and fastening you to what you wanted to believe.

But no matter: Pia was getting in touch with her inner matador and dreamt of killing the hovering bald woman in front of a cheering audience.

MAY WE SUGGEST... Reservations

Pia stamped her foot in the dirt, kicking up a cloud of dust, and with a flourish of her arm in the air, yelled:

"How *dare* she covet
<u>my</u> co-dependent
relationship!
She must die!"

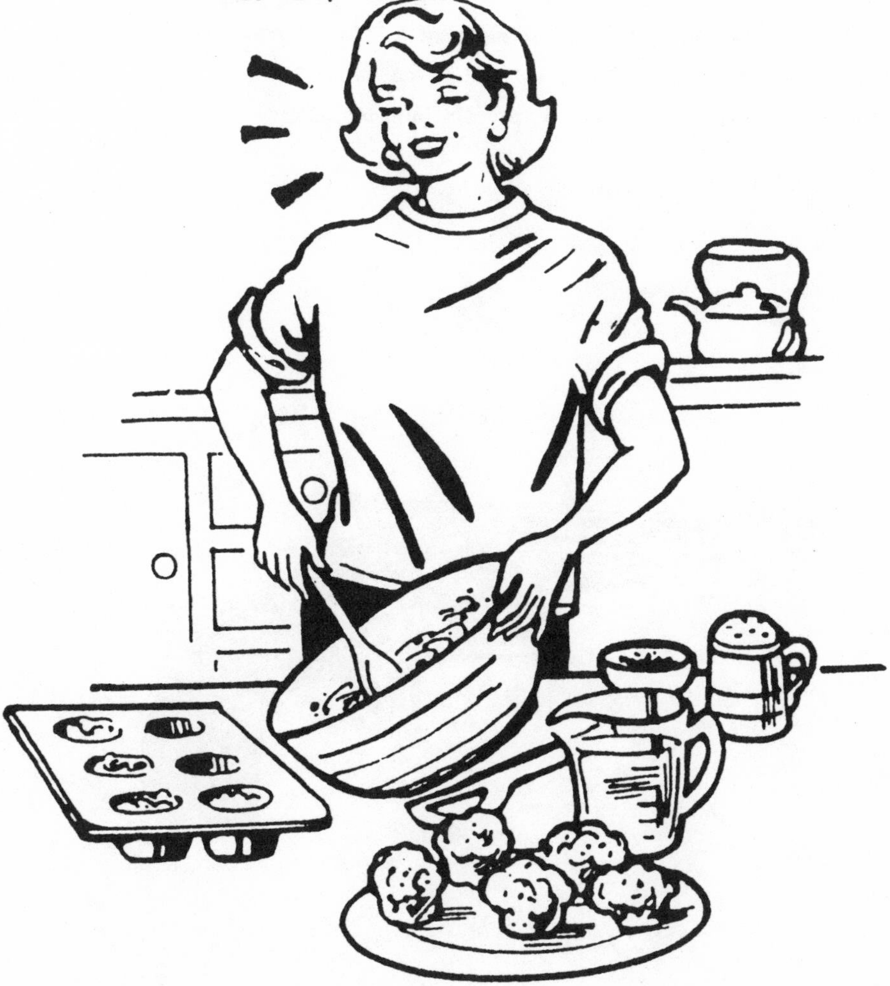

Chapter Two.

Pia knew that in order to get away with killing this flying bald woman in the name of honor, she would have to lure her to Argentina or Brazil. But it is not a matador's job to lure flying bald women to Latin America, so Pia gave up the idea of thrusting arrows into her neck as just compensation for defiling her woman. Everything else in her life was going too well for her to seriously contemplate going to jail on a prosaic murder charge.

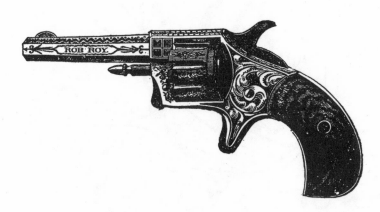

Chapter Three.

Irony.

Irony is not just something that happens in cleverly penned turn-of-the-century novels. No. Irony is thrown at us by Vertigo Gremlins laughing at us from the sidelines of life, and the mere anticipation of irony could humble us so much we'd go out of our way to help little old ladies across the street. Christ, we'd fucking wait for them.

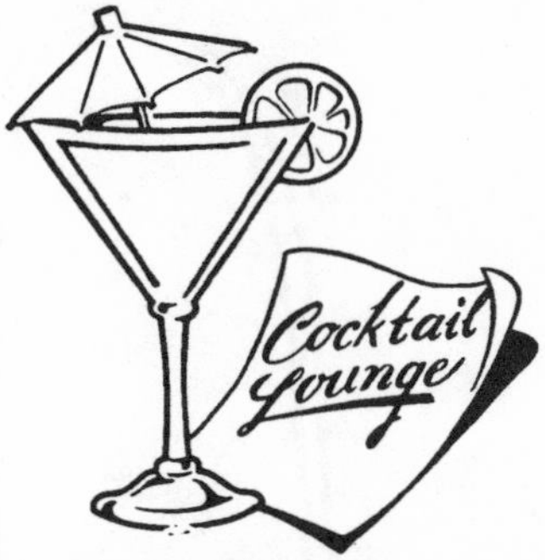
Cocktail
Lounge

All this to say that Pia's little matador heart was badly crushed like Mexican tin and she started waking up to a numbing glass of Spanish wine. After all, she wasn't the one with the drinking problem, was she? Then at some point she moved next to a liquor store and made Jack Kerouac look like a happy gym teacher. She smoked three packs a day, and in a matter of weeks she had to have the local butcher shop perform surgery on her cancerous throat (see what happens with no national health care?). By the time she crawled into an Alcoholics Anonymous meeting, she had to press one of those vibrating voice boxes on her throat to say, "Hi, my name is Pia and I'm an alcoholic."

You see, abusing oneself is often easier than getting up and changing the channel.

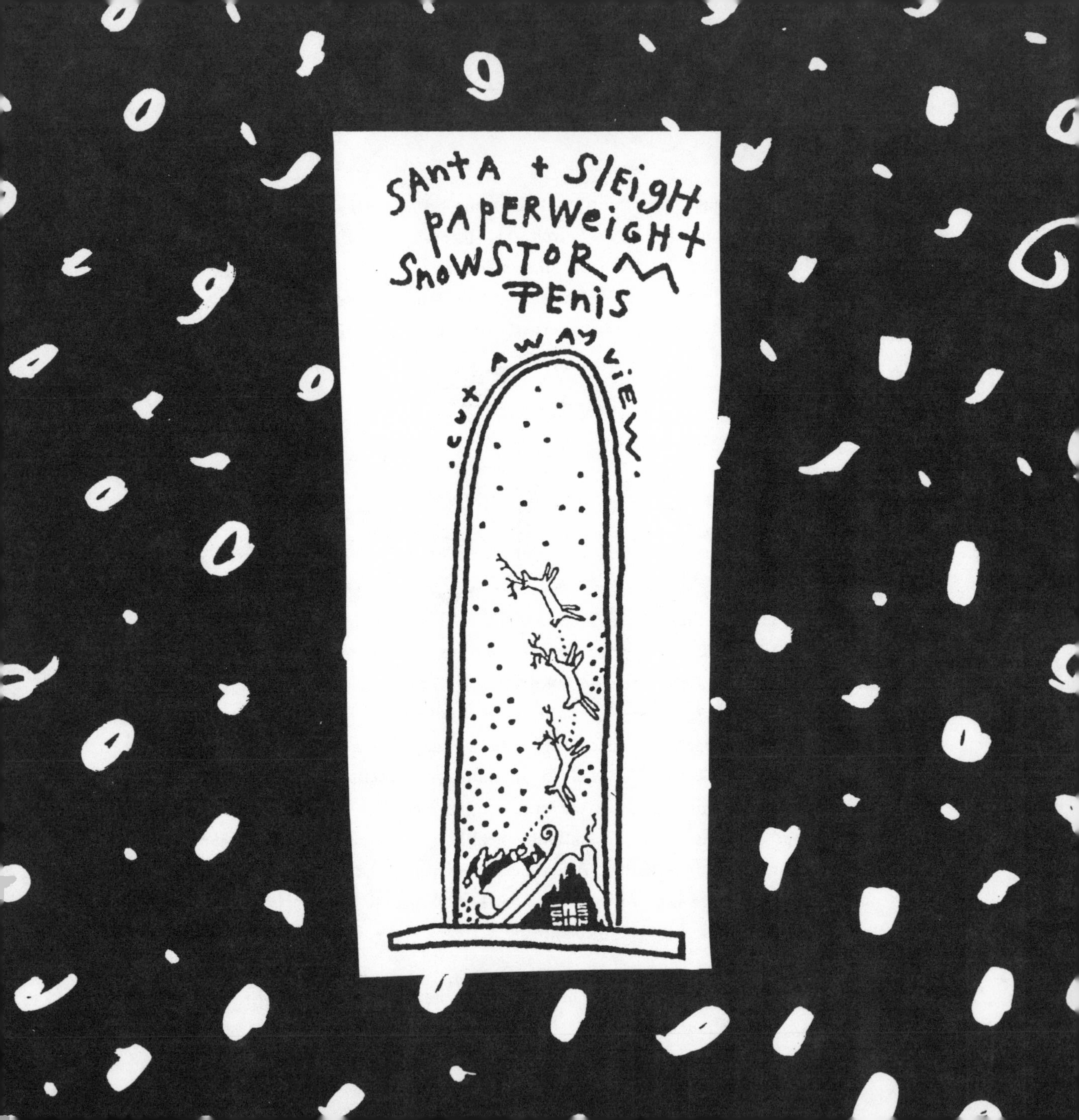
SANTA + SLEIGH
PAPERWEIGHT
SNOWSTORM
PENIS
CUT AWAY VIEW

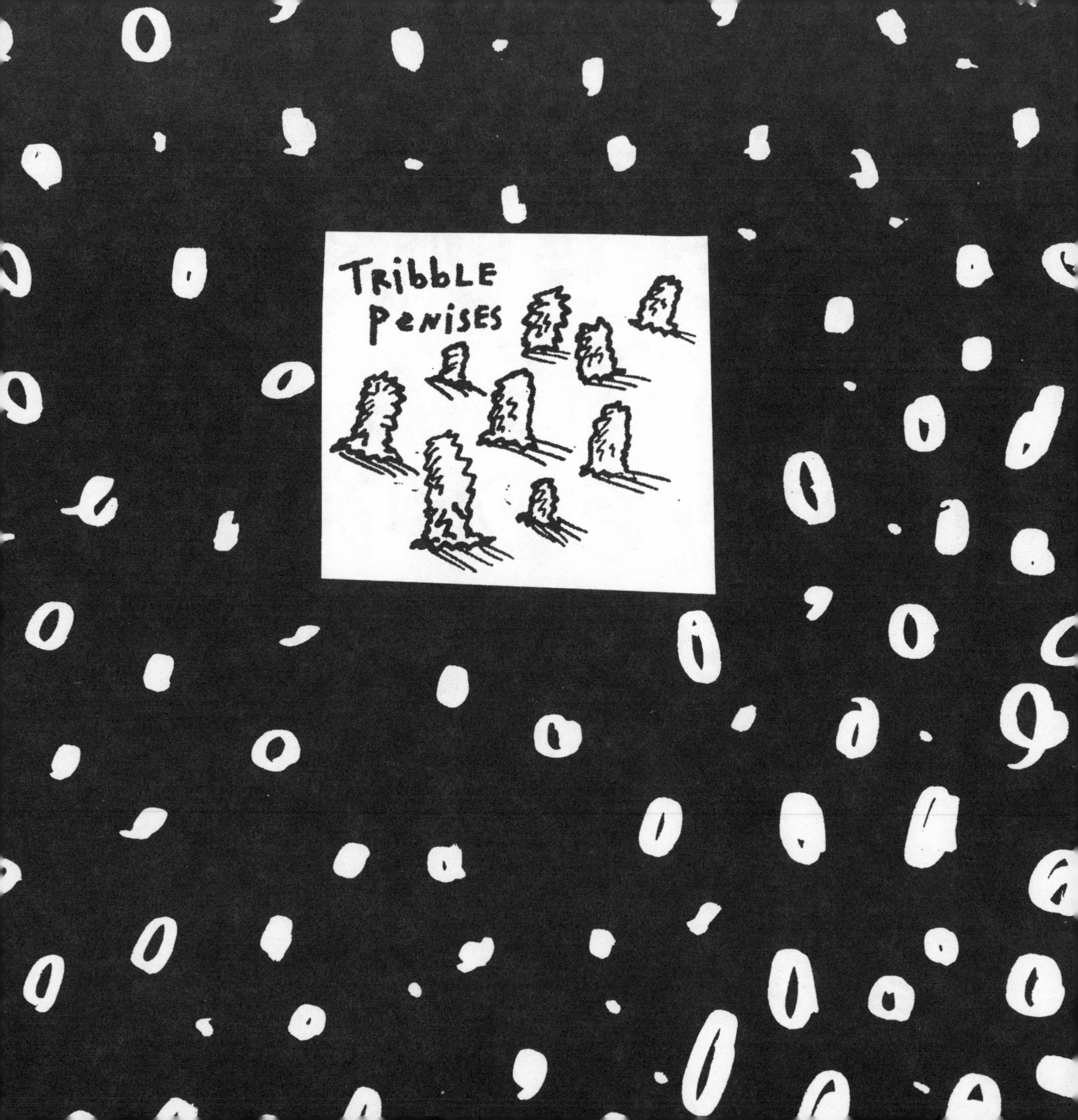
TRIBBLE
PENISES

HELL HATH NO FURY LIKE A CARTOONIST SCORNED

↓

BY A QUAKER GIRL WHO LIKES MAFIA MOVIES WAY TOO MUCH.

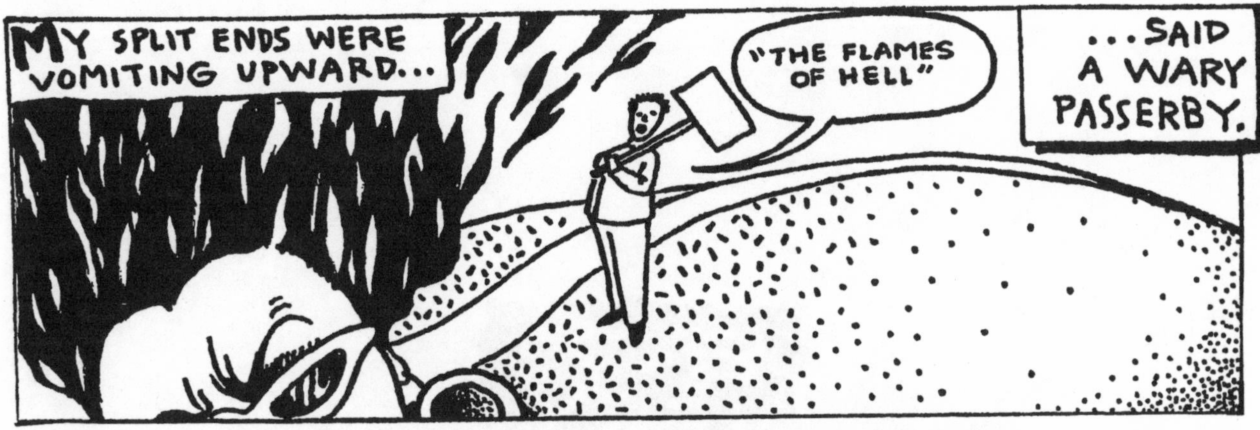
MY SPLIT ENDS WERE VOMITING UPWARD...
"THE FLAMES OF HELL"
...SAID A WARY PASSERBY.

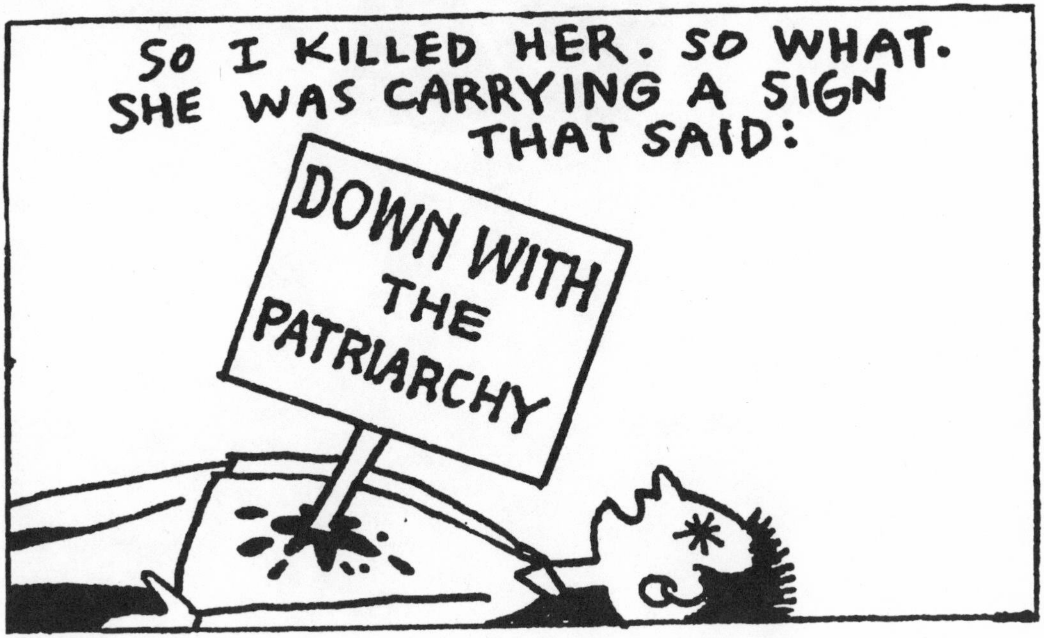
SO I KILLED HER. SO WHAT. SHE WAS CARRYING A SIGN THAT SAID:
DOWN WITH THE PATRIARCHY

SO
VERY
1972.

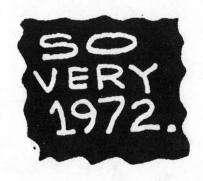

STOP WHINING, I SAID. SAVE YOUR MOTHER/YOURSELF. FEEL GUILTY FOR SAYING NO. NO MORE MILK BATHS IN EXCAVATED EXAMPLES OF CHILD ABUSE.

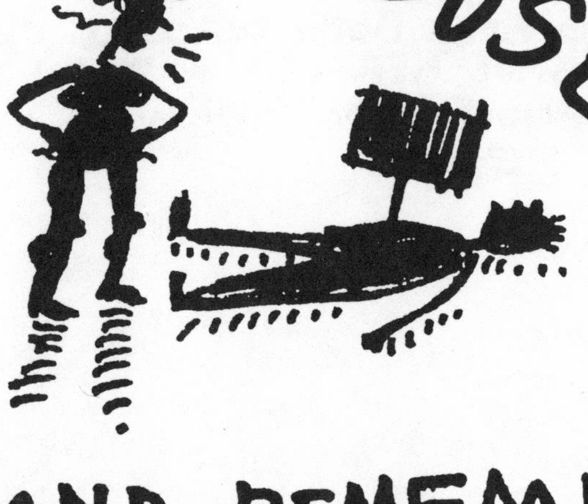

EAT MEAT AND REMEMBER BOSNIA.

BUT I DIGRESS. THIS IS MY LAST PORN MOVIE REVIEW. I DON'T HAVE A VCR TO USE ANYMORE. HOOTER MUJER PROMISED TO TELL THE TRUTH AND STOP CHEATING ON ME, BUT SHE SPENT A SECRET WEEKEND IN THE COUNTRY W/TENLEY.

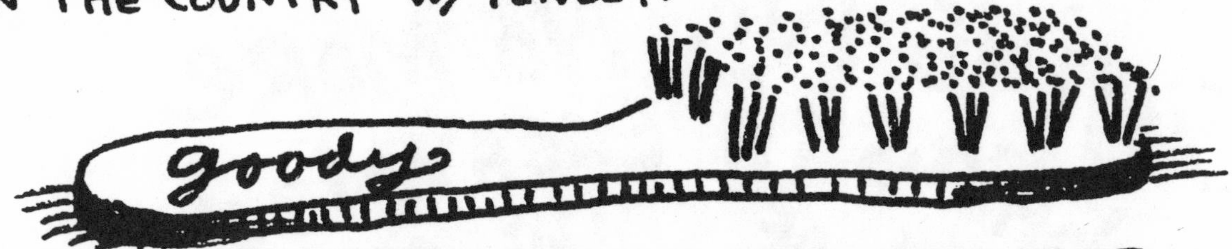
goody

I FOUND OUT BECAUSE TENLEY LEFT SOME BLUE BRUSH UP THERE, AND SINCE THE "ALL IS FAIR IN LOVE AND WAR" THING GOES BOTH WAYS, I CUT UP HOOTER'S DILDOES + GAVE HER VCR A BATH. IT DIDN'T LOOK DAMAGED ENOUGH ON MY WAY TO GIVE IT BACK TO HER...

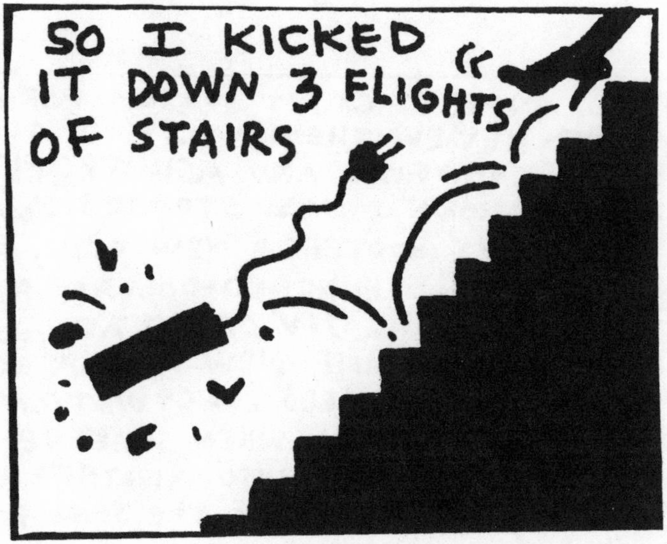
SO I KICKED IT DOWN 3 FLIGHTS OF STAIRS

NOW I CAN'T WATCH PORN MOVIES AND REVIEW THEM, UNLESS I SIT BY SOME CAMPFIRE AND ASK PEOPLE TO TELL ME PORN MOVIE STORIES. NOW I HAVE TO BUY HOOTER A NEW VCR, BUT SO WHAT. COUPLE-HUNDRED-DOLLAR RAGE IS SUCH A RUSH. YOU CAN'T ALWAYS LIVE IN FLAT-LINE NEW AGE PEACE + PASSIVITY. LIFE NEEDS PUNCTUATION NOW + THEN. ESPECIALLY WHEN SOMEONE TRIES TO TURN YOUR LOVE INTO ANOTHER FUCKING COUNTRY SONG WHERE THE SONG REMAINS THE SAME.

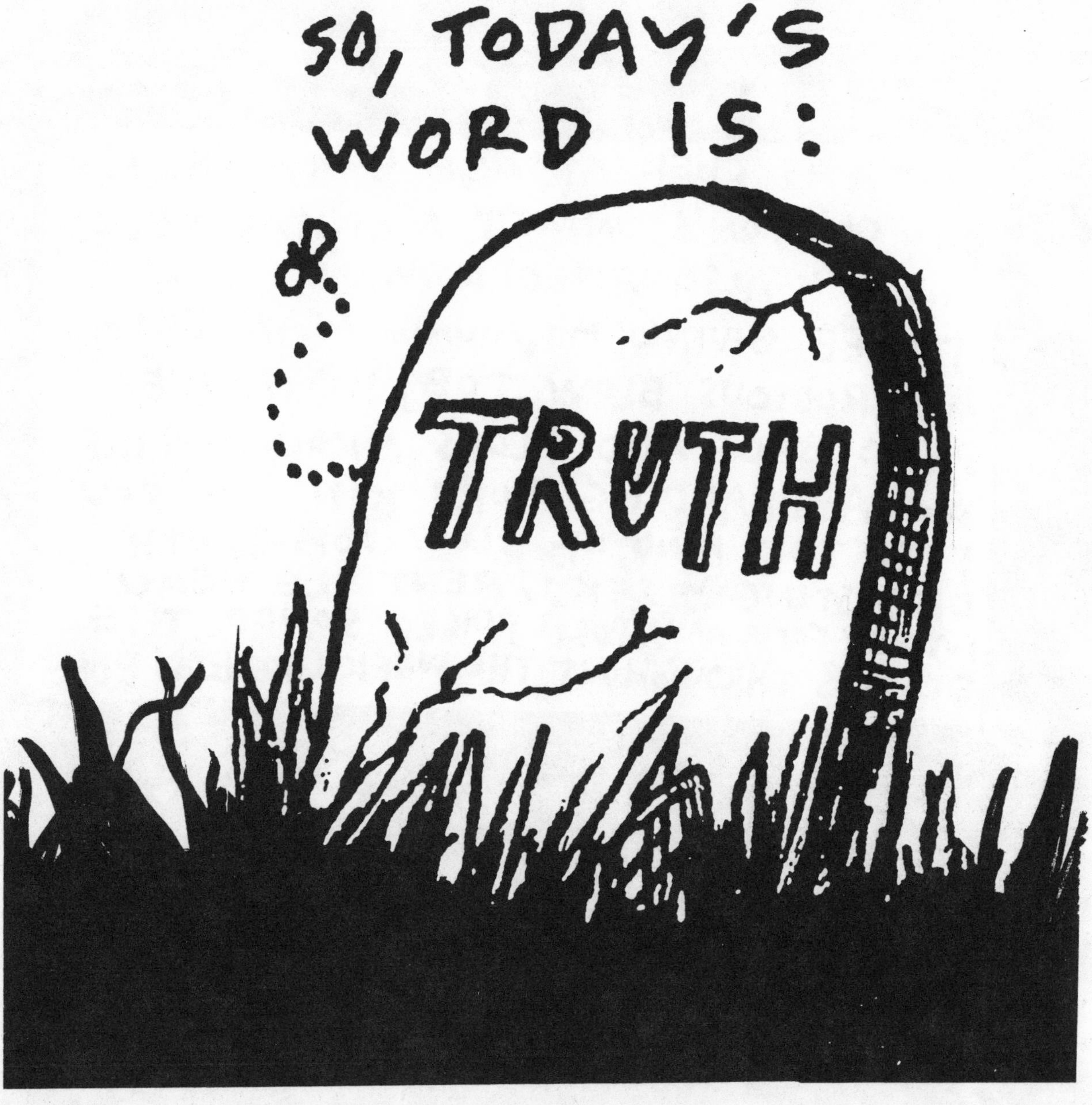
SO, TODAY'S
WORD IS:
TRUTH

TRUTH IS CHER AT AGE 5. TRUTH IS BILL CLINTON'S UNMET MARITAL NEEDS, AND IT'S ALSO AN OLD MAN IN A TOUPÉE GIVING A YOUNG MAN SUCH A FEROCIOUS BLOW JOB, HIS TOUPÉE PEELS BACK AND FLOPS AROUND LIKE AN APPLAUDING FORESKIN. IF YOU FIND THIS KIND OF BLOW JOB TRUTH DISGUSTINGLY SEXY, RENT "LE BEAU MEC" FROM ANY PORN PLACE. SAVOR THE SCENES THROUGHOUT THE WEEK LIKE BON BONS.

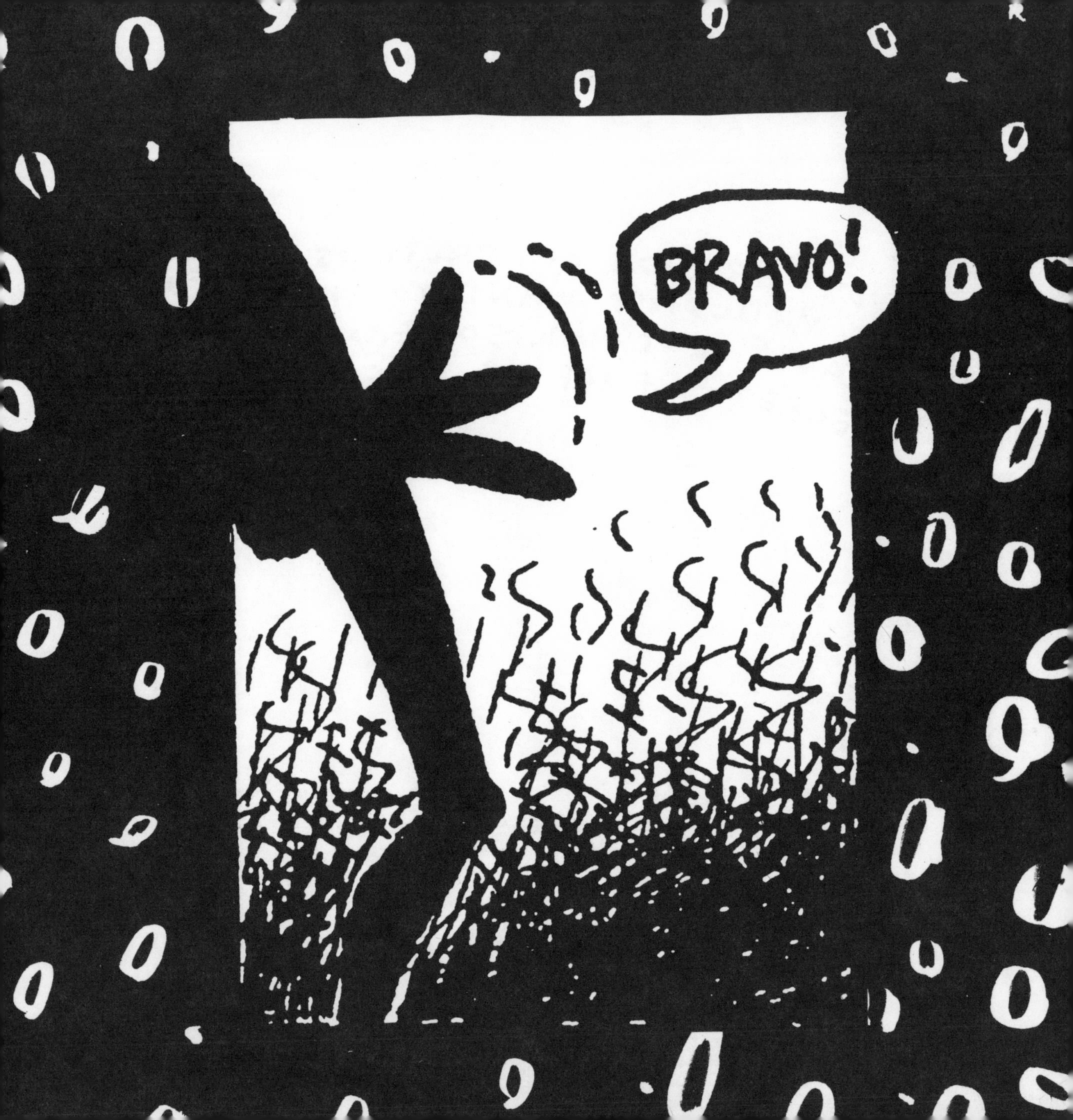
BRAVO!

THE OTHER SIDE OF TRUTH IS DISNEYWORLD, AND I WOULDN'T WANT TO LIVE THERE BECAUSE I THINK SOMEONE'S SECRETLY FUCKING THE CHILDREN.

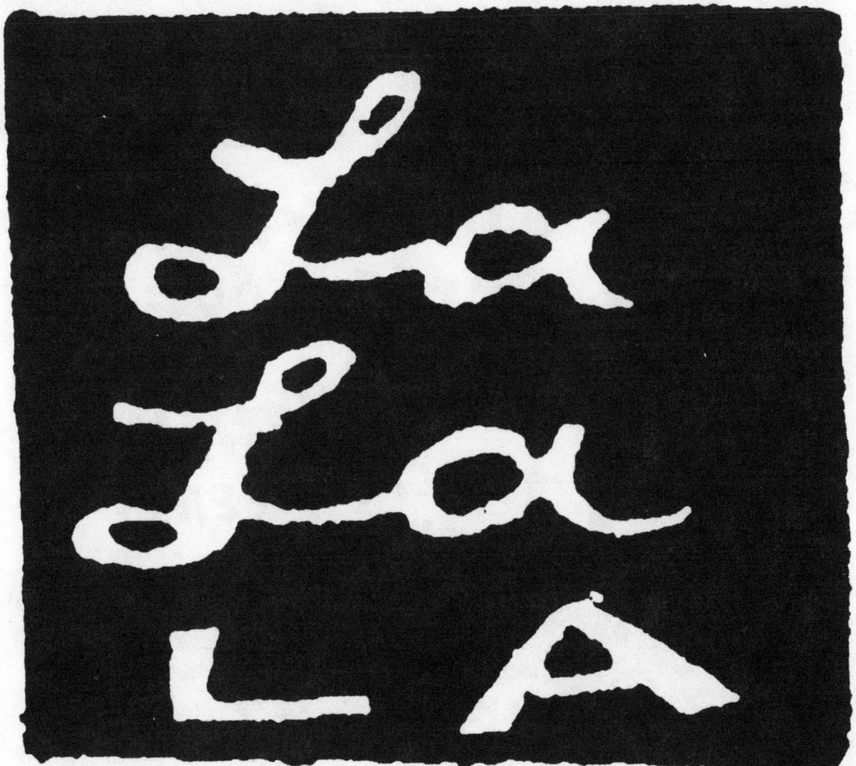
La
La
LA

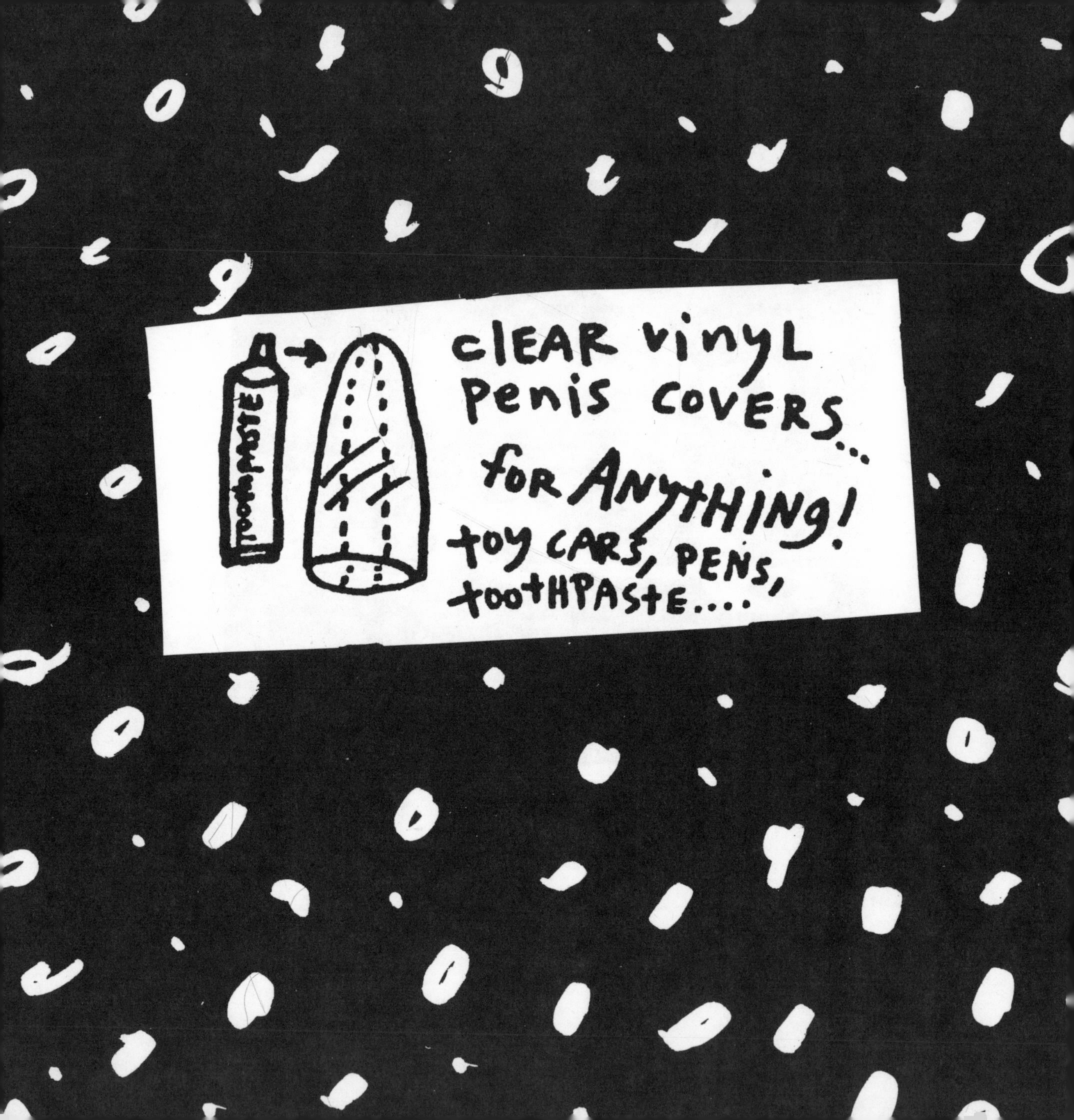
clEAR vinyL
penis COVERS...
for ANYTHING!
toy CARS, PENS,
toothPASTE....

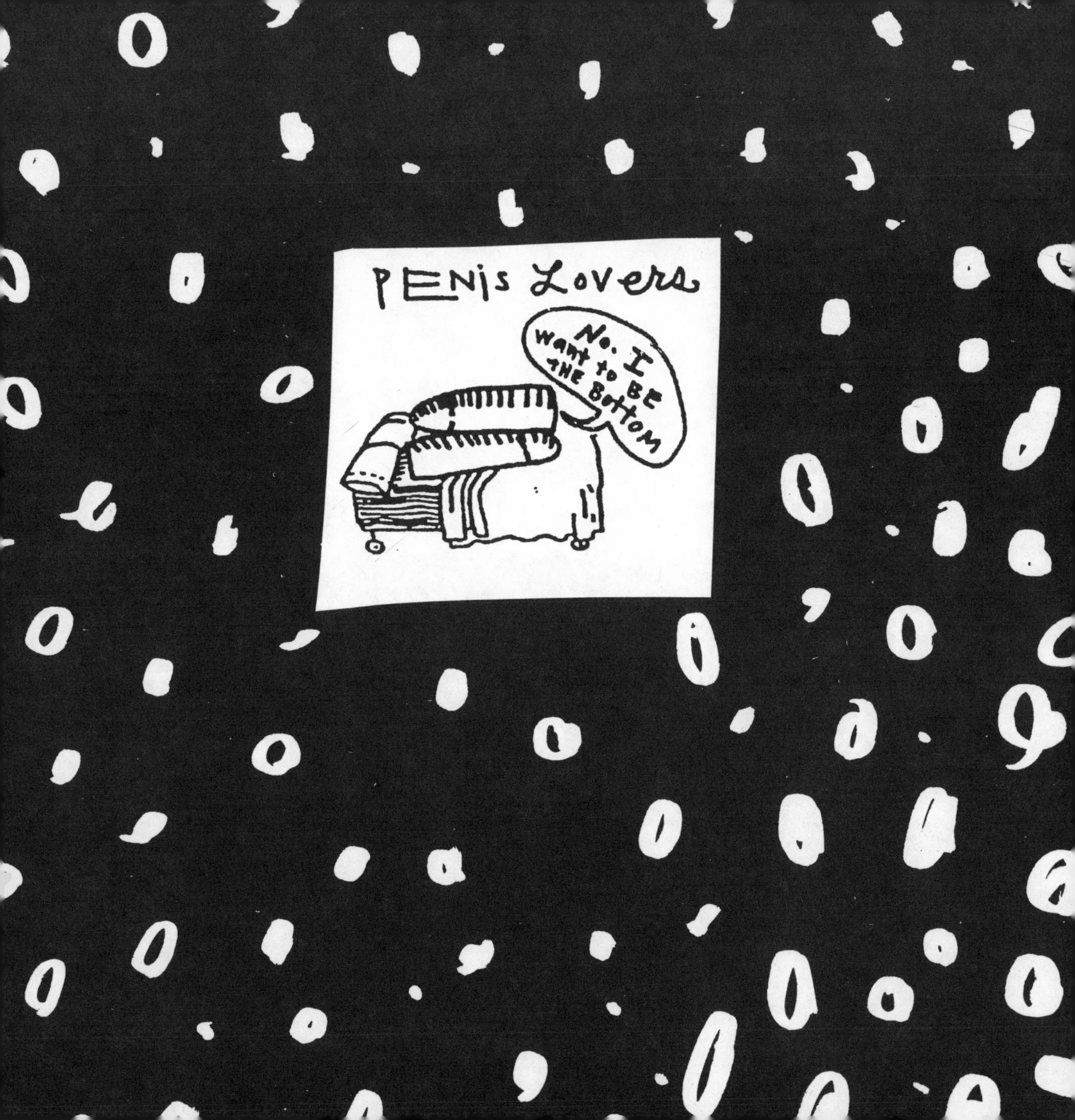
PENis Lovers
No. I want to BE THE BOttom

A FORAY into TEDIOUS NON·Monogamy

✱ Monogamy → SAFE, COMMITTED SPIRITUAL TUNNEL of Love WHERE GROWTH and stuff HAPPENS between 2 PEOPLE? OR a device thought up by iNSECURE people who need to live under the illusion they're the ABSOLUTE center of YOUR WORLd?

✱ NON-MONOGAMY → Really cool and SEXY in a Disco KIND of WAY? —OR A Major PAIN IN the ASS?

People who have more than one lover looked both scary and cool to me: Scary in a Stephen King kind of way, like they could actually hold back from giving their all to someone; and cool in a Fonzie kind of way, like they could actually hold back from giving their all to someone. Even after my girlfriend went cattin' around on me, and my trust and self-esteem were like a couple of Ford Festivas in a car crash, she still managed to look cool. I felt like a dork, and I even hate the word because dork is like a big penis without a chin waving hello to passing cars. Passing Ford Festivas.

so, forever chasing elusive coolness, I wanted to see what it was like having two girlfriends.

The Second Woman:

A slab of hair hung mysteriously over one eye. Her lips were pursed, her shoulders were hunched because her legs weren't nearly bow legged enough for that cowboy look. She squinted as if she were concentrating on something far deeper than the material world, for she was a painter in pain. Her paintings were like bad lesbian folk music paintings---they lacked emotional complexity--- but I tried to tell myself how daring and intense they were so I could go through with this Second Woman thing. I wanted this intense, squinting, painful cowboy to make me cool.

Intensity. That's what I wanted. A white girl even darker than me who took herself more seriously than a groin injury. We could walk down intense artsy fartsy paths together and imagine

history books written about our intense love and collaboration.
Plus, she didn't drink; she was in AA. After the longneck style
of my first girlfriend, sobriety became an aphrodisiac like
asparagus and brie cheese.

Well, I'm here to tell you, after three weeks, I was so bored, I
could've crammed paint brushes in my eye sockets. There's a
point, like maybe the sixth date, when intensity wears thin and
you hear a great big sucking sound which isn't the sound of jobs
going south. Nope. It's the sound of neediness, and she's looking
at YOU.

The other side of alcoholism isn't simply "not drinking," no--that's
somewhere in the middle--but it's Alcoholics Anonymous.   Good
program, good people, but at what point does constant
talking/thinking/taping phrases to your walls about drinking
substitute for actual drinking?

In her house, I scanned the spiritual mother earth goddess
creativity inner child books and listened to all of her bad
relationship stories.   I was thinking maybe it would be good for
her to get her mind off things.... become a triage nurse in Africa
and dig out some impacted people for awhile.

What happened to playing with legos and having idiosyncratic fun
with our dysfunctional parents and symbiotic sisters and throwing
our hands up in the air like we just didn't care?   We didn't point
so many fingers, we didn't have to be so fucking right, and we
didn't have as bad a time as we'd like to tell our therapist and
anyone who'll listen over burritos.   All these labels and all this
information isn't getting us anywhere.   It just reminds me that
being right only looks good on paper.

I like being a dork without a chin, waving to traffic.

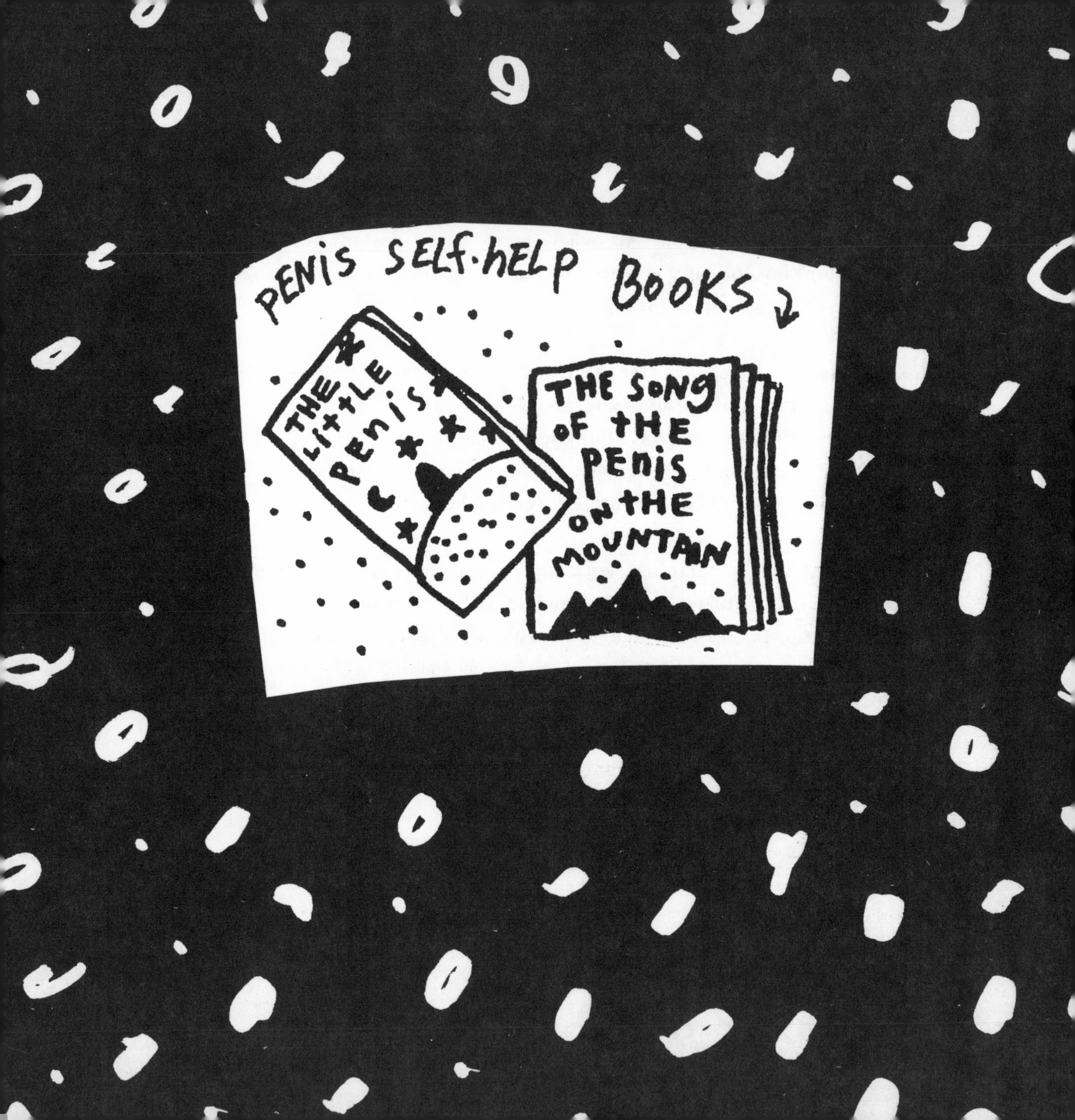
PENIS SELF-HELP BOOKS
THE Little PENIS
THE SONG OF THE PENIS ON THE MOUNTAIN

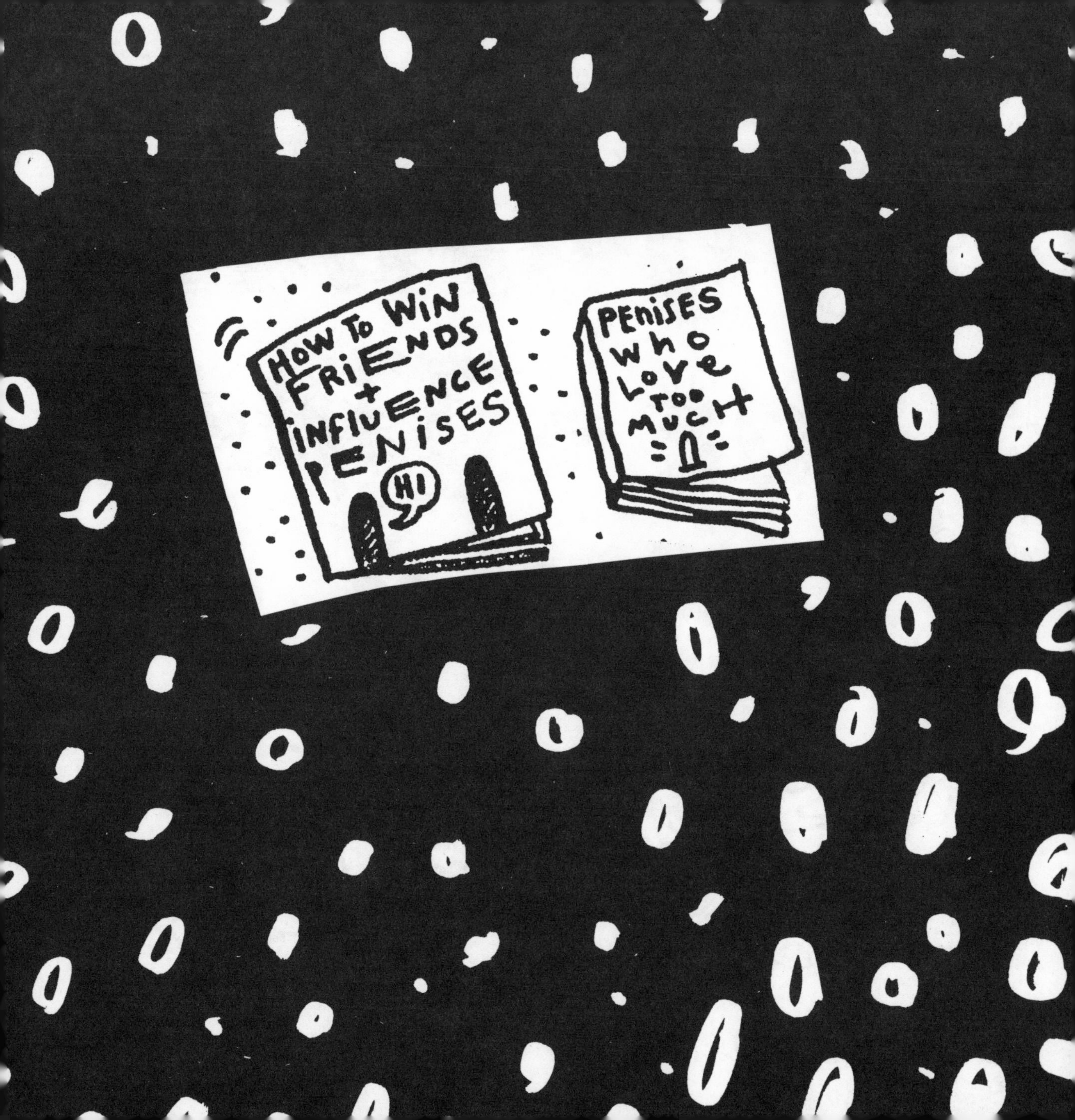
HOW TO WIN FRIENDS + INFLUENCE PENISES
HI
PENISES WHO LOVE TOO MUCH

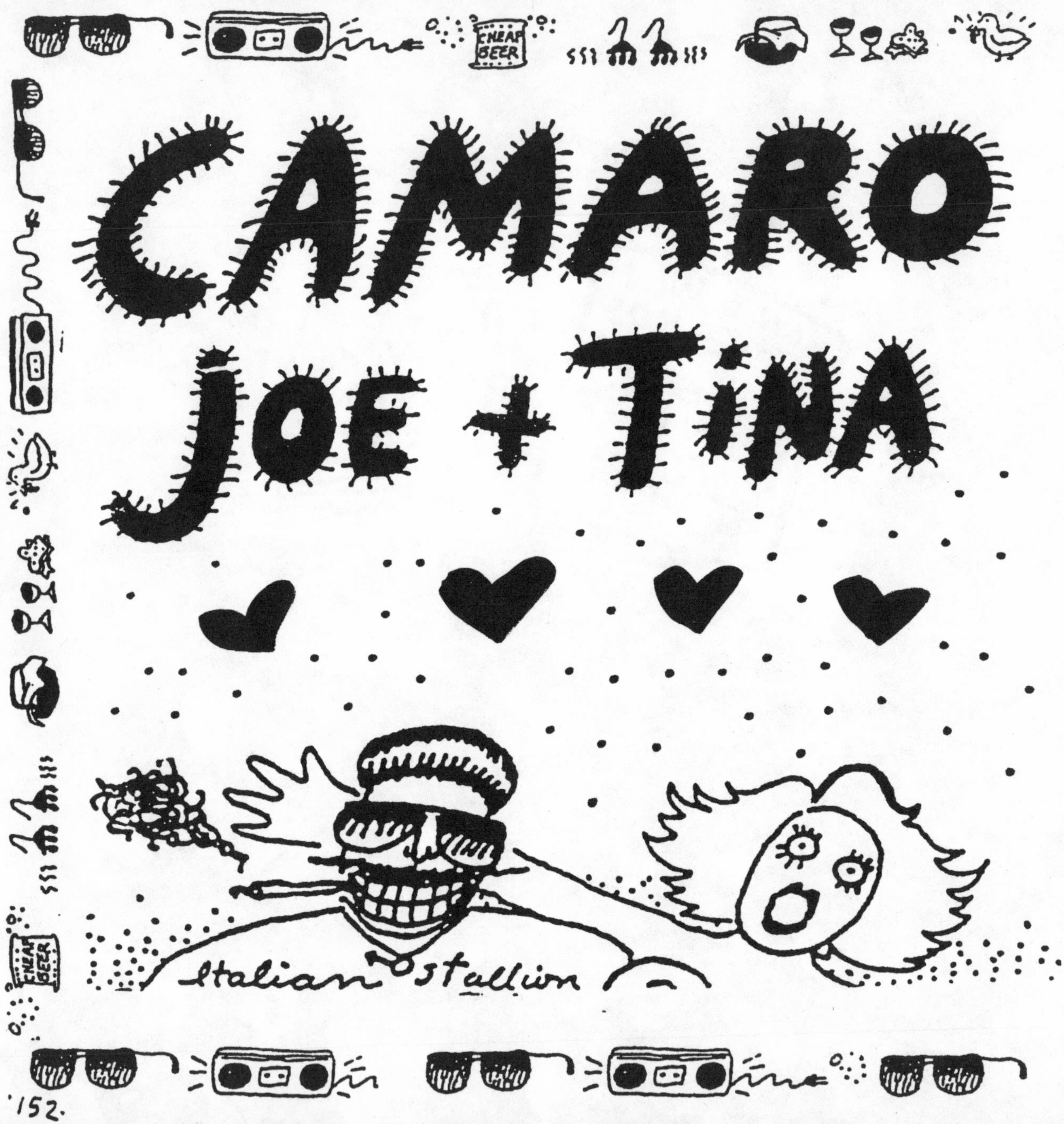
CHEAP BEER
CAMARO
JOE + TINA
Italian stallion

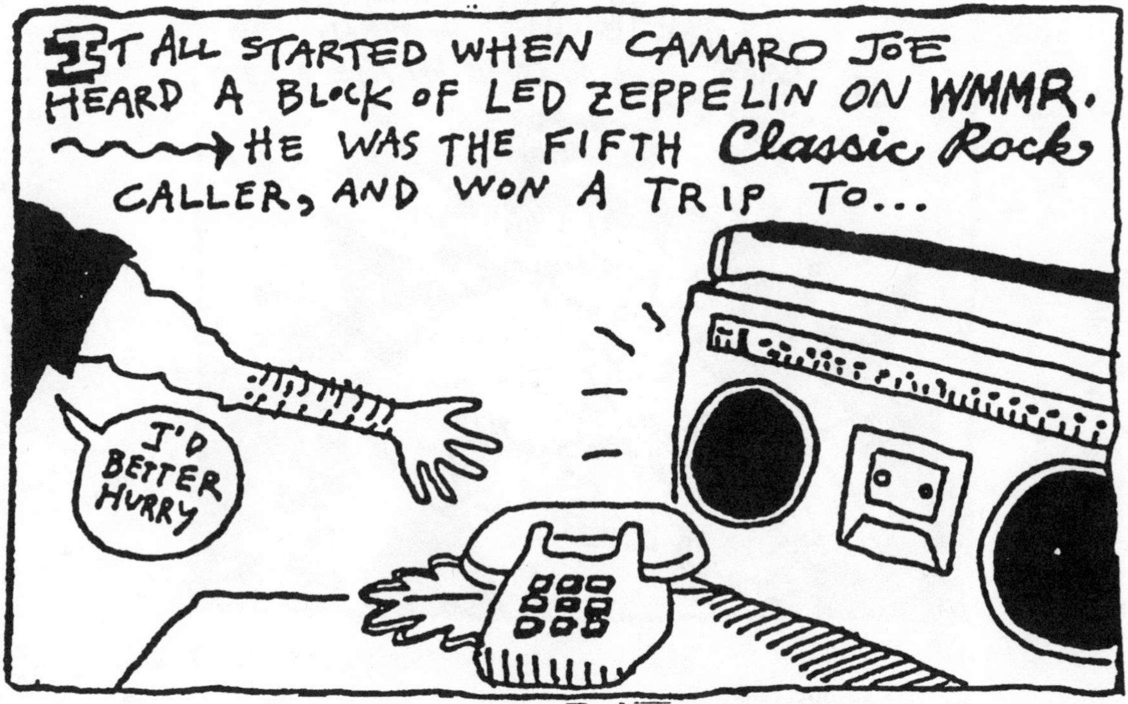
IT ALL STARTED WHEN CAMARO JOE HEARD A BLOCK OF LED ZEPPELIN ON WMMR. HE WAS THE FIFTH Classic Rock CALLER, AND WON A TRIP TO...
I'D BETTER HURRY

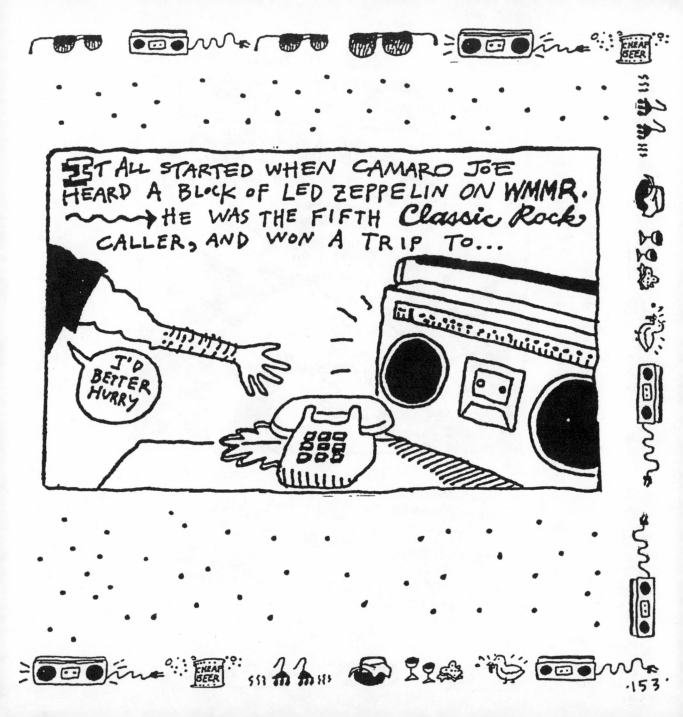

"...BAGHDAD! YEAH, AND I WANT YOU GUYS TO COME W/ ME!"
Italian Stallion

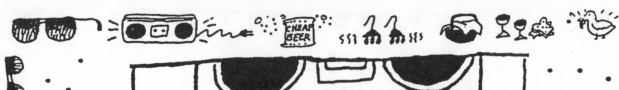

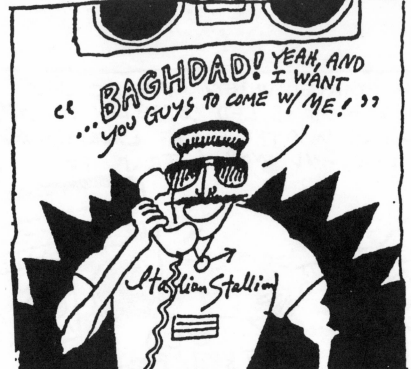

HE INVITED HIS FRIENDS, FIREBIRD TOM, IROC BOB and TRANS AM MUSTAPHA. →

THEY IMMEDIATELY HAD ALL THEIR CARS SHIPPED THERE, AND they TOOK A PLANE THAT AFTERNOON.

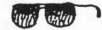

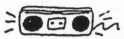

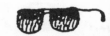

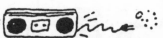

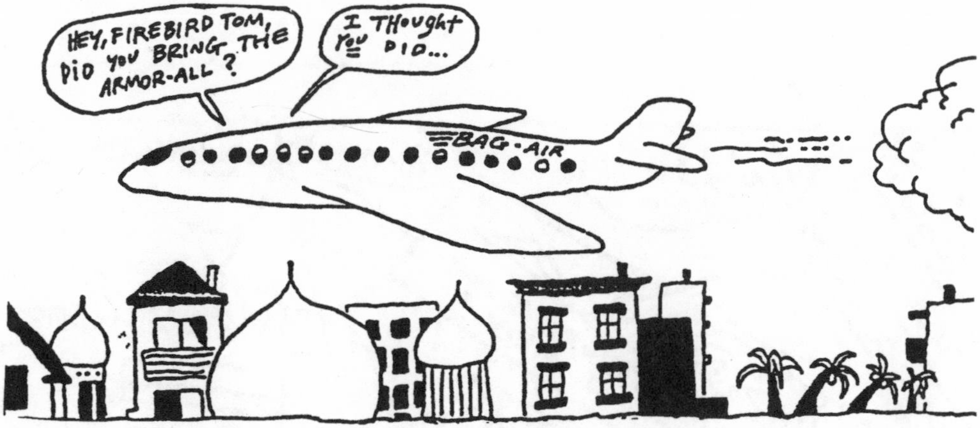
HEY, FIREBIRD TOM, DID YOU BRING THE ARMOR-ALL?
I THought YOU DID...
BAG-AIR

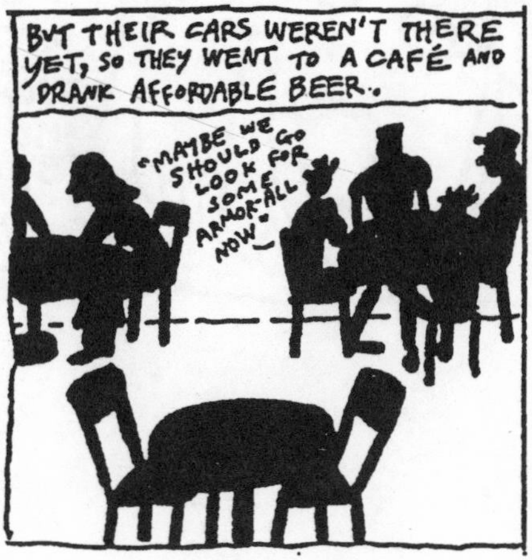
BUT THEIR CARS WEREN'T THERE YET, SO THEY WENT TO A CAFÉ AND DRANK AFFORDABLE BEER.
"MAYBE WE SHOULD GO LOOK FOR SOME ARMOR-ALL NOW"

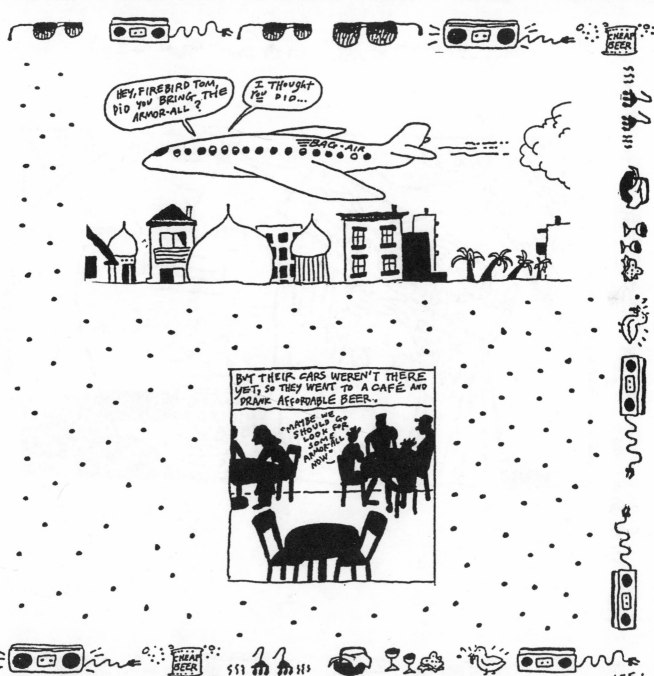

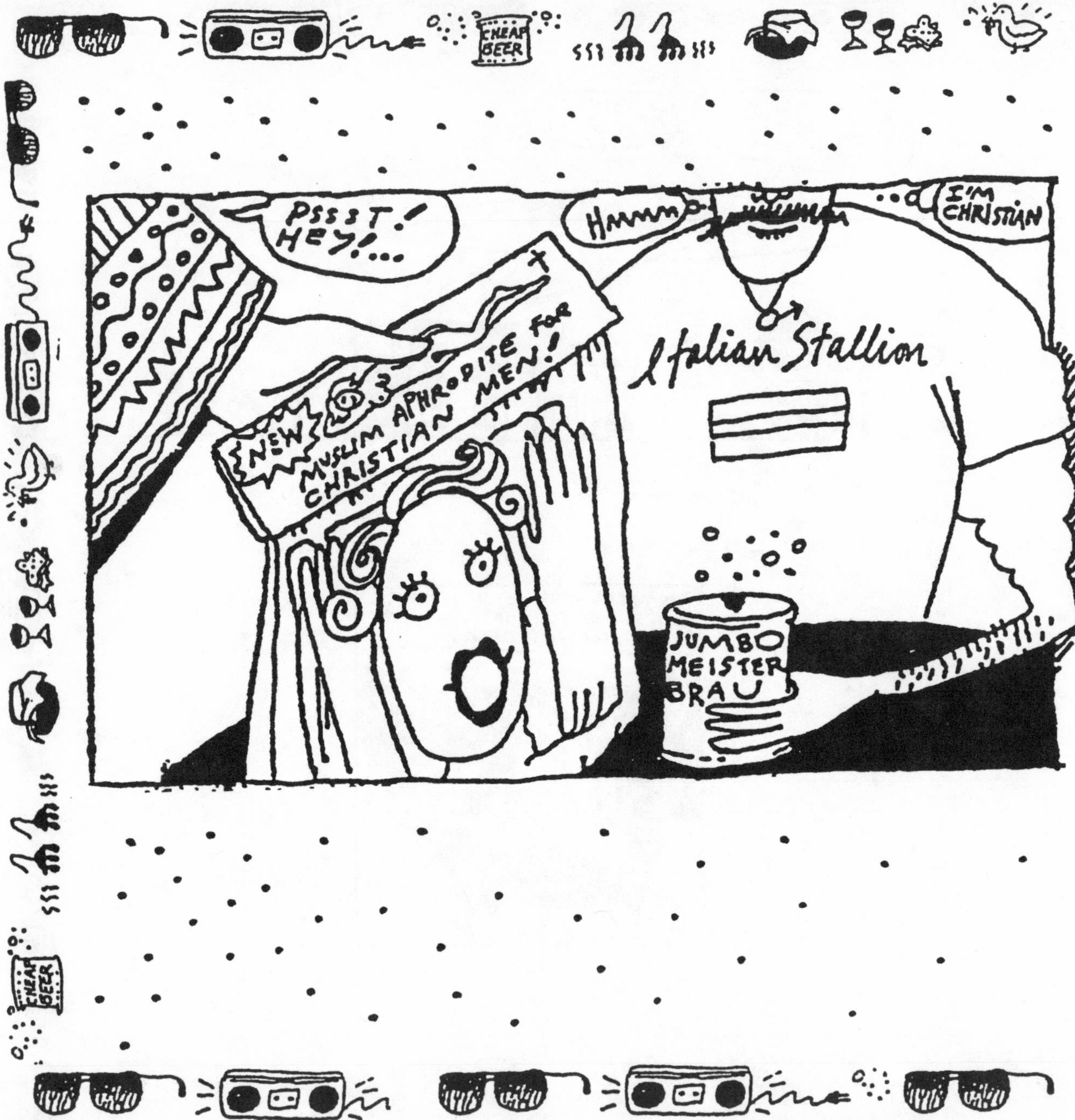
PSSST! HEY!...
Hmmm
I'M CHRISTIAN
NEW
MUSLIM APHRODITE FOR CHRISTIAN MEN!
Italian Stallion
JUMBO MEISTER BRAU
CHEAP BEER

A mysterious-looking MERCHANT WALKED UP to THEIR TABLE + OFFERED To SELL Camaro Joe A ∵MAGICAL∵ BLOW-UP DOLL: "Cheap. Real cheap. Less than **25** American dollars for you." All the guys laughed, AND CAMARO JoE PRETENDED To laugh, too. BUT → AS he HANDED OVER The MONEY to the guy, he fake-LAughed Again + SAID he was getting the doll As a joke Souvenir. / Later, when their cars FINALLY ARRIVED, The OTHERS WENT OUT To SIMONize theirs, BUT CAMARO JoE STAYED in His HOTEL RooM BLOWING UP **THE DOLL** . . . .

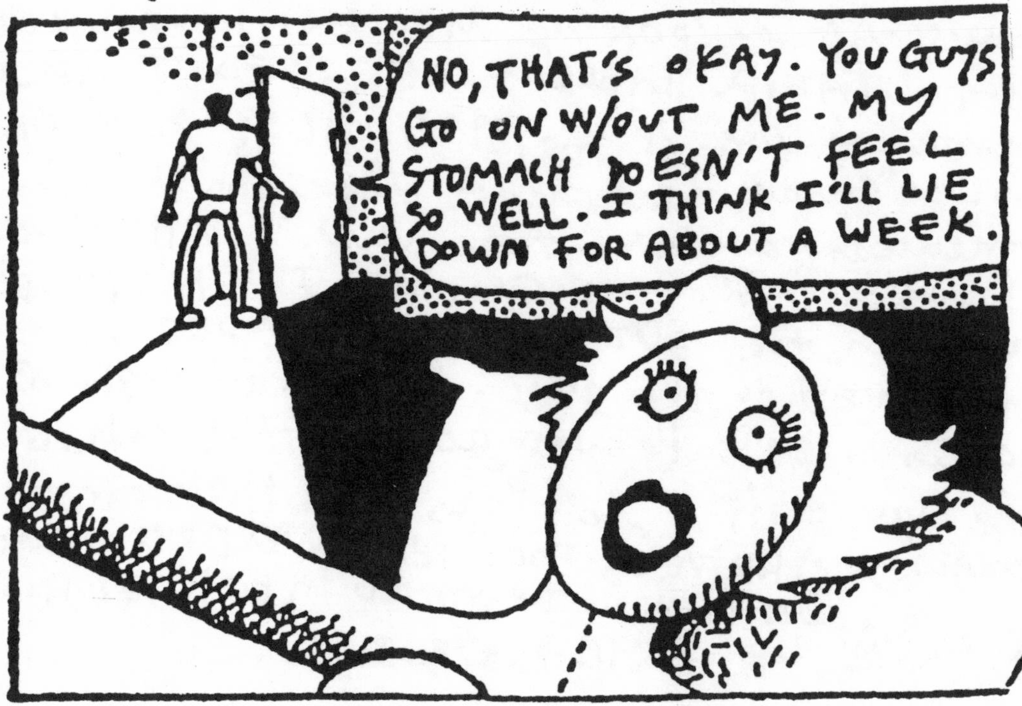
NO, THAT'S OKAY. YOU GUYS GO ON W/OUT ME. MY STOMACH DOESN'T FEEL SO WELL. I THINK I'LL LIE DOWN FOR ABOUT A WEEK.

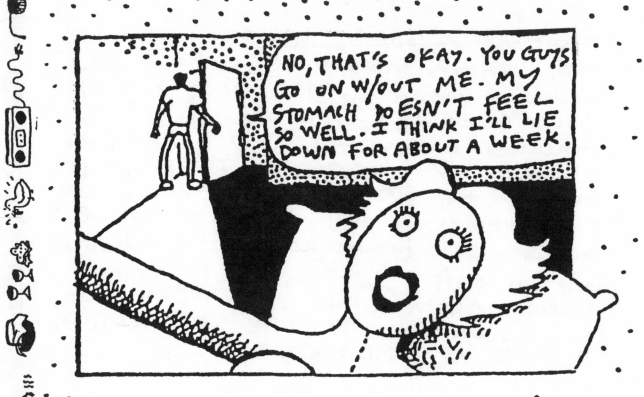

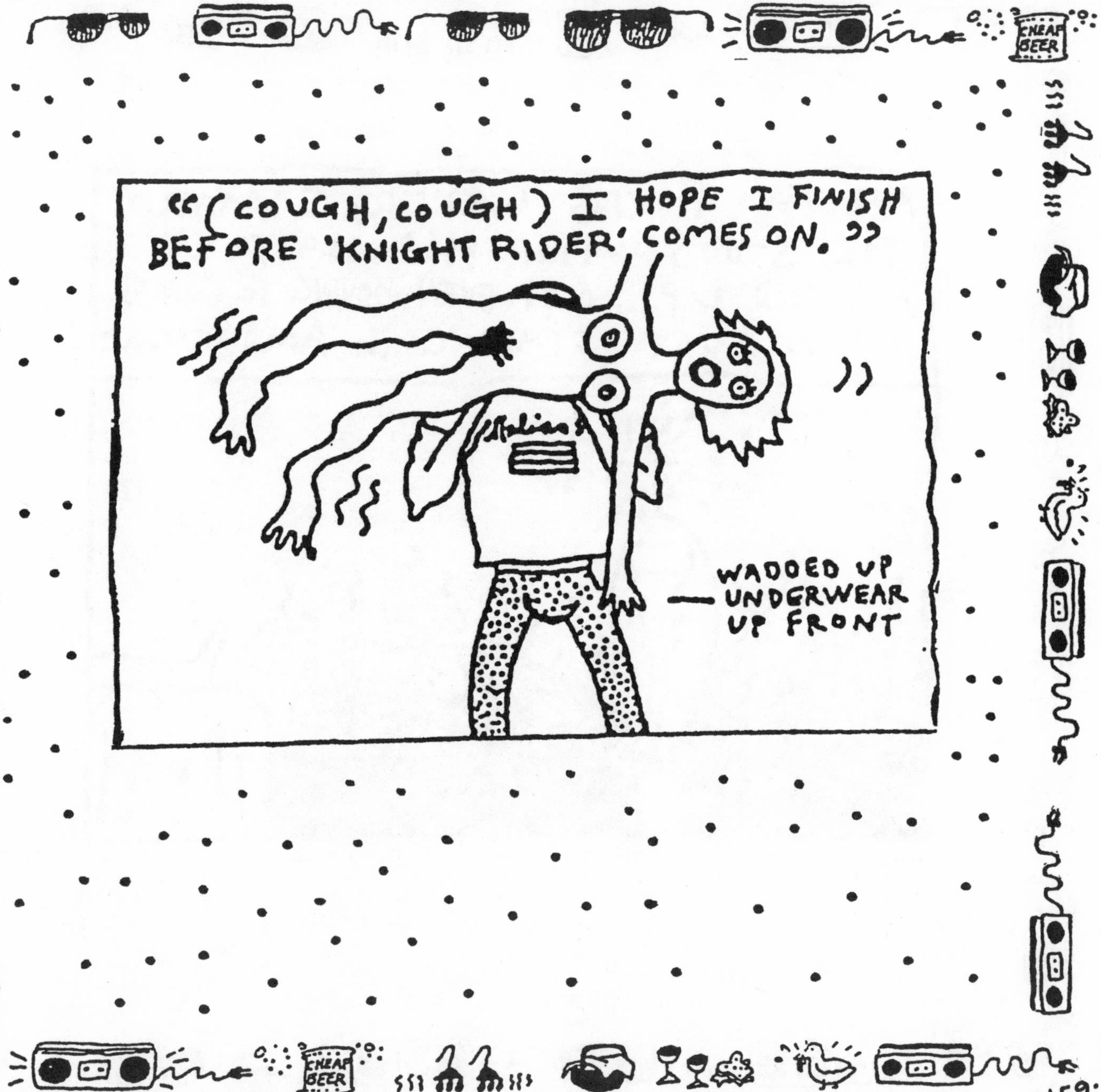
CHEAP BEER
"(COUGH, COUGH) I HOPE I FINISH BEFORE 'KNIGHT RIDER' COMES ON."
WADDED UP UNDERWEAR UP FRONT
CHEAP BEER

AND TWO HOURS LATER, CAMARO JOE STOOD WITH HIS HAIR MESSED UP.... NOT EVEN MOVING TO COMB IT.... JUST STARING in AMAZEMENT

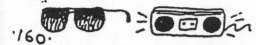

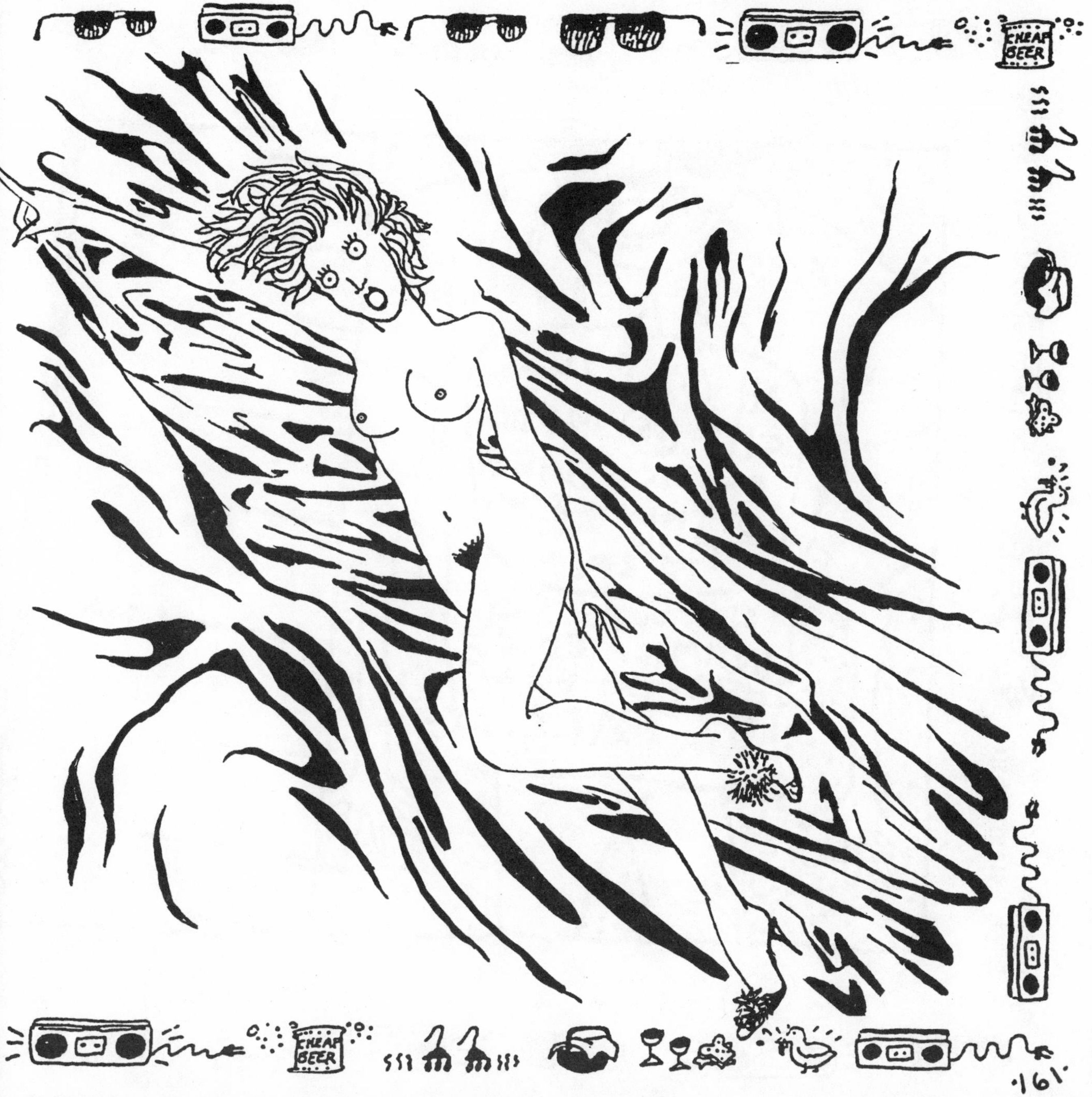
CHEAP BEER
CHEAP BEER

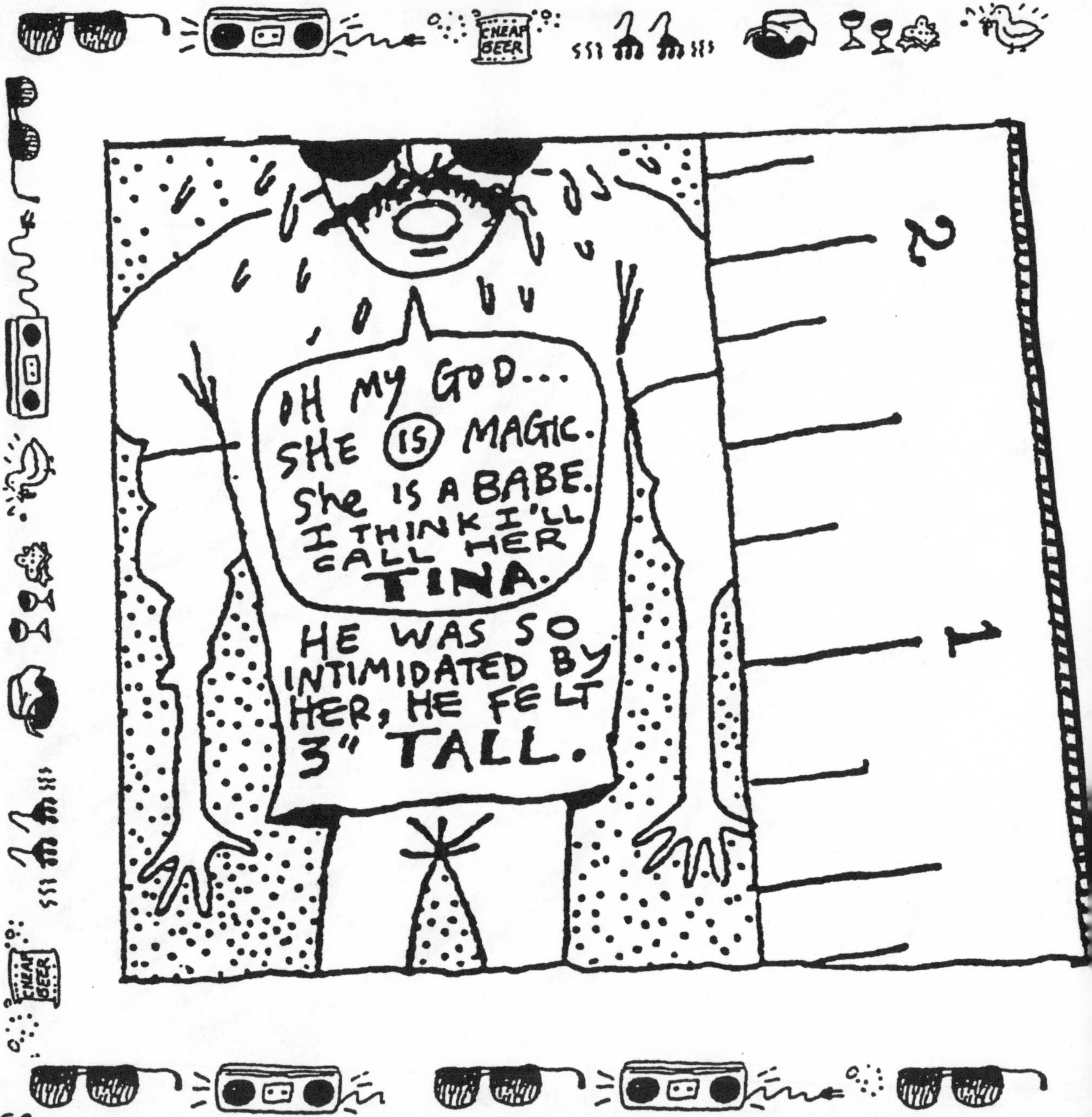
2
1
OH MY GOD...
SHE (IS) MAGIC.
She IS A BABE.
I THINK I'LL CALL HER
TINA.
HE WAS SO INTIMIDATED BY HER, HE FELT
3" TALL.
CHEAP BEER

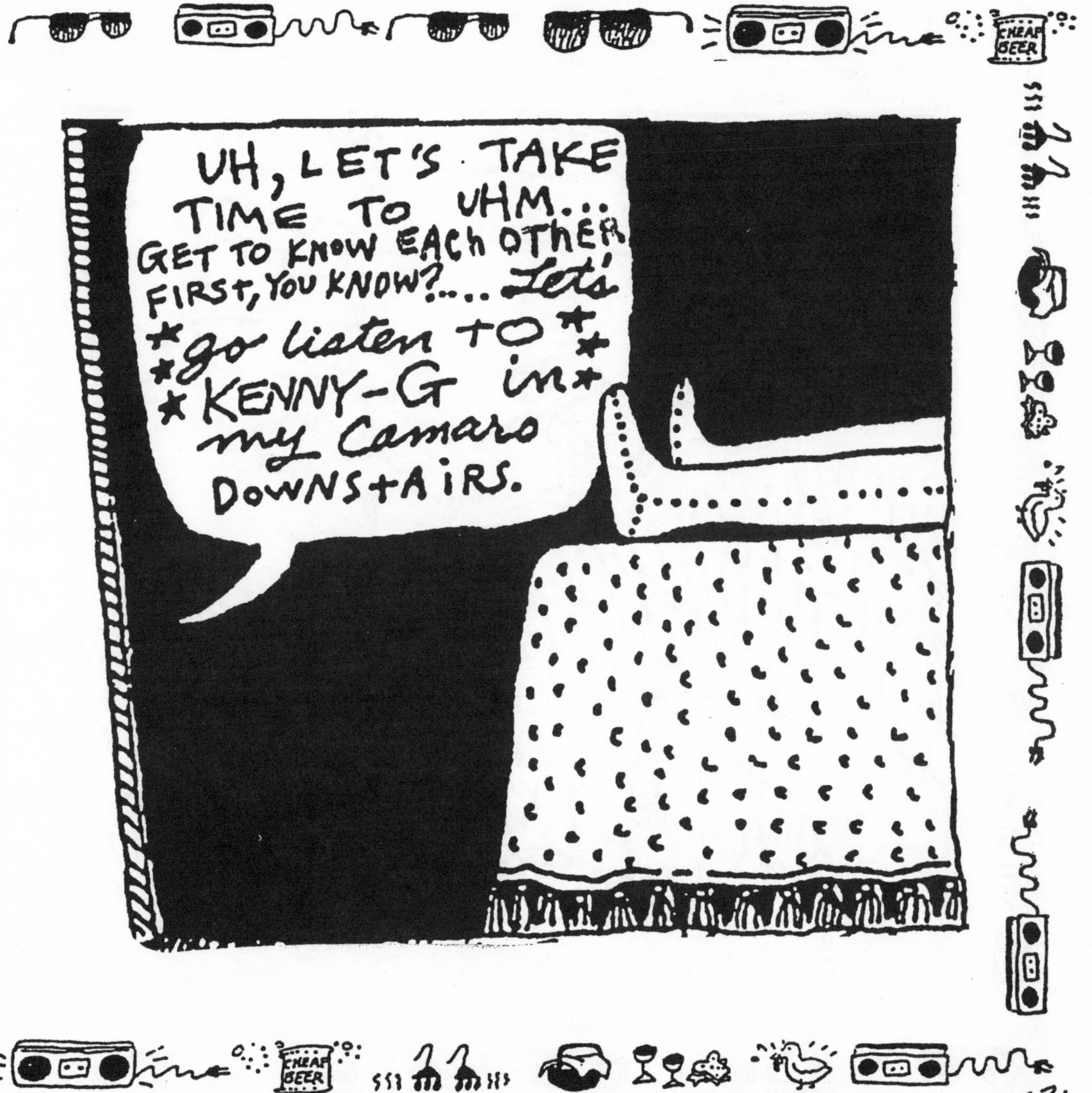
CHEAP BEER
UH, LET'S TAKE TIME TO UHM... GET TO KNOW EACH OTHER FIRST, YOU KNOW?.... Let's go listen TO KENNY-G in my Camaro DOWNSTAIRS.
CHEAP BEER

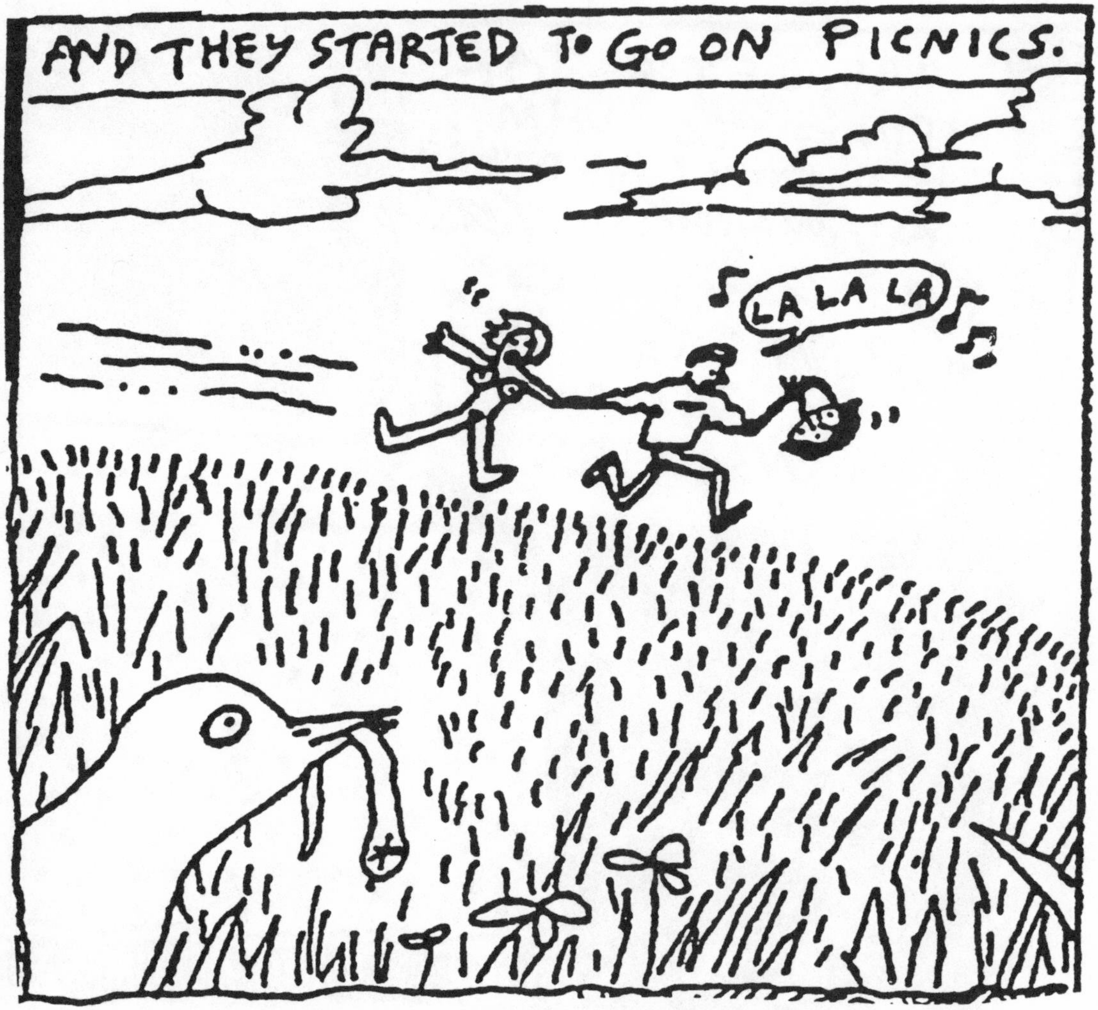
AND THEY STARTED TO GO ON PICNICS.
LA LA LA

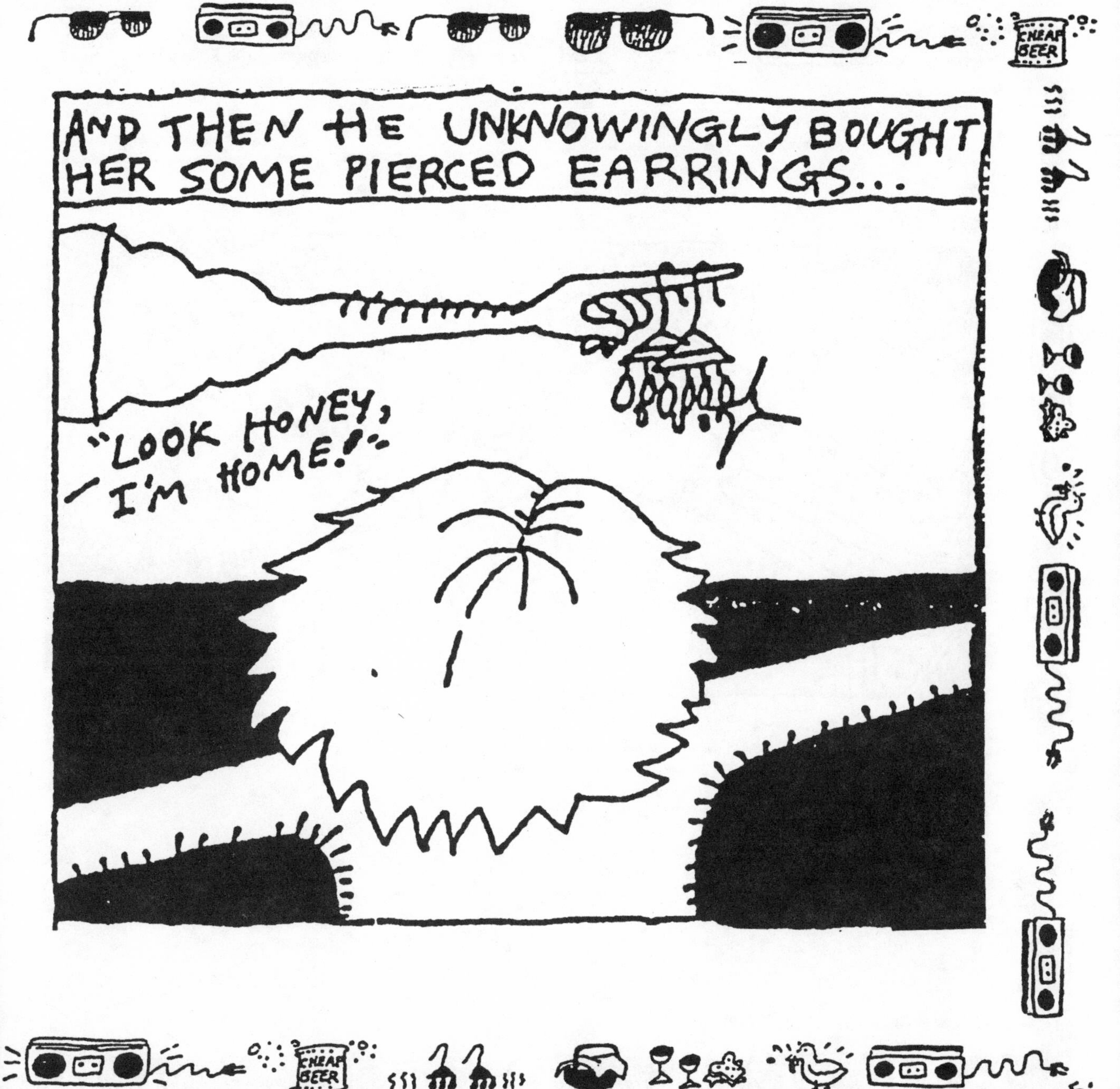
CHEAP BEER
AND THEN HE UNKNOWINGLY BOUGHT HER SOME PIERCED EARRINGS...
"LOOK HONEY, I'M HOME!"
CHEAP BEER

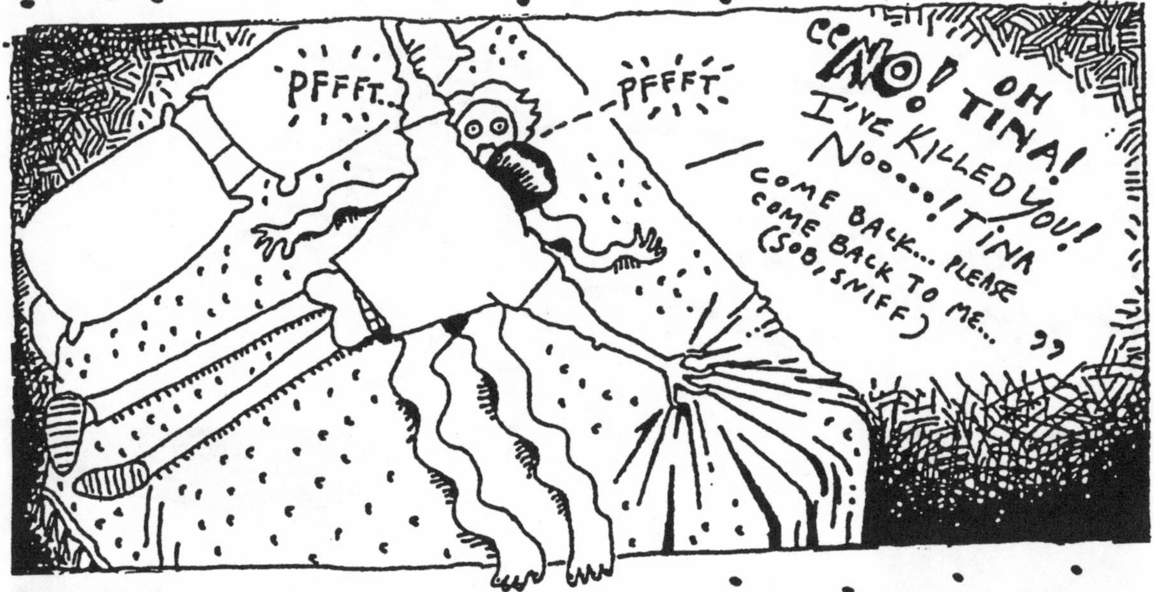
PFFFT.
PFFFT
"NO! OH TINA! I'VE KILLED YOU!
NOOOOO...! TINA
COME BACK... PLEASE
COME BACK TO ME... (SOB, SNIFF)"

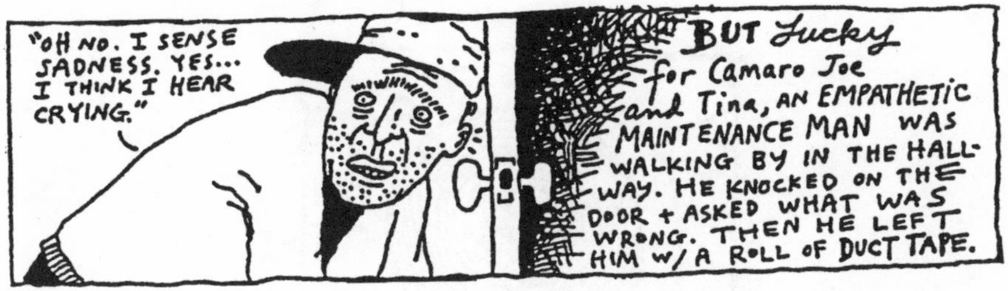
"OH NO. I SENSE SADNESS. YES... I THINK I HEAR CRYING."
BUT Lucky for Camaro Joe and Tina, AN EMPATHETIC MAINTENANCE MAN WAS WALKING BY IN THE HALLWAY. HE KNOCKED ON THE DOOR + ASKED WHAT WAS WRONG. THEN HE LEFT HIM W/ A ROLL OF DUCT TAPE.

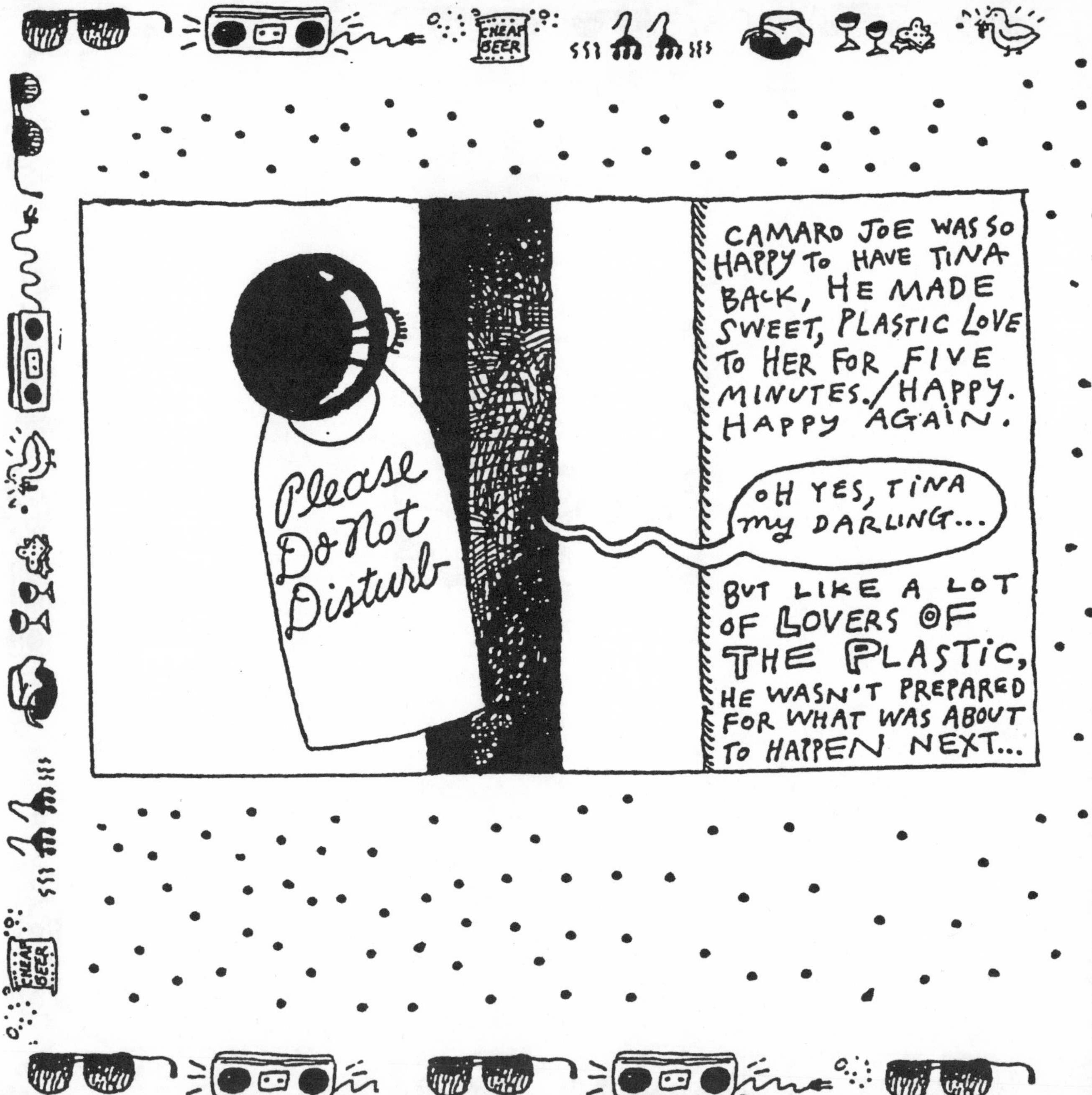
CAMARO JOE WAS SO HAPPY TO HAVE TINA BACK, HE MADE SWEET, PLASTIC LOVE TO HER FOR FIVE MINUTES./HAPPY. HAPPY AGAIN.
Please Do Not Disturb
OH YES, TINA my DARLING...
BUT LIKE A LOT OF LOVERS OF THE PLASTIC, HE WASN'T PREPARED FOR WHAT WAS ABOUT TO HAPPEN NEXT...
CHEAP BEER

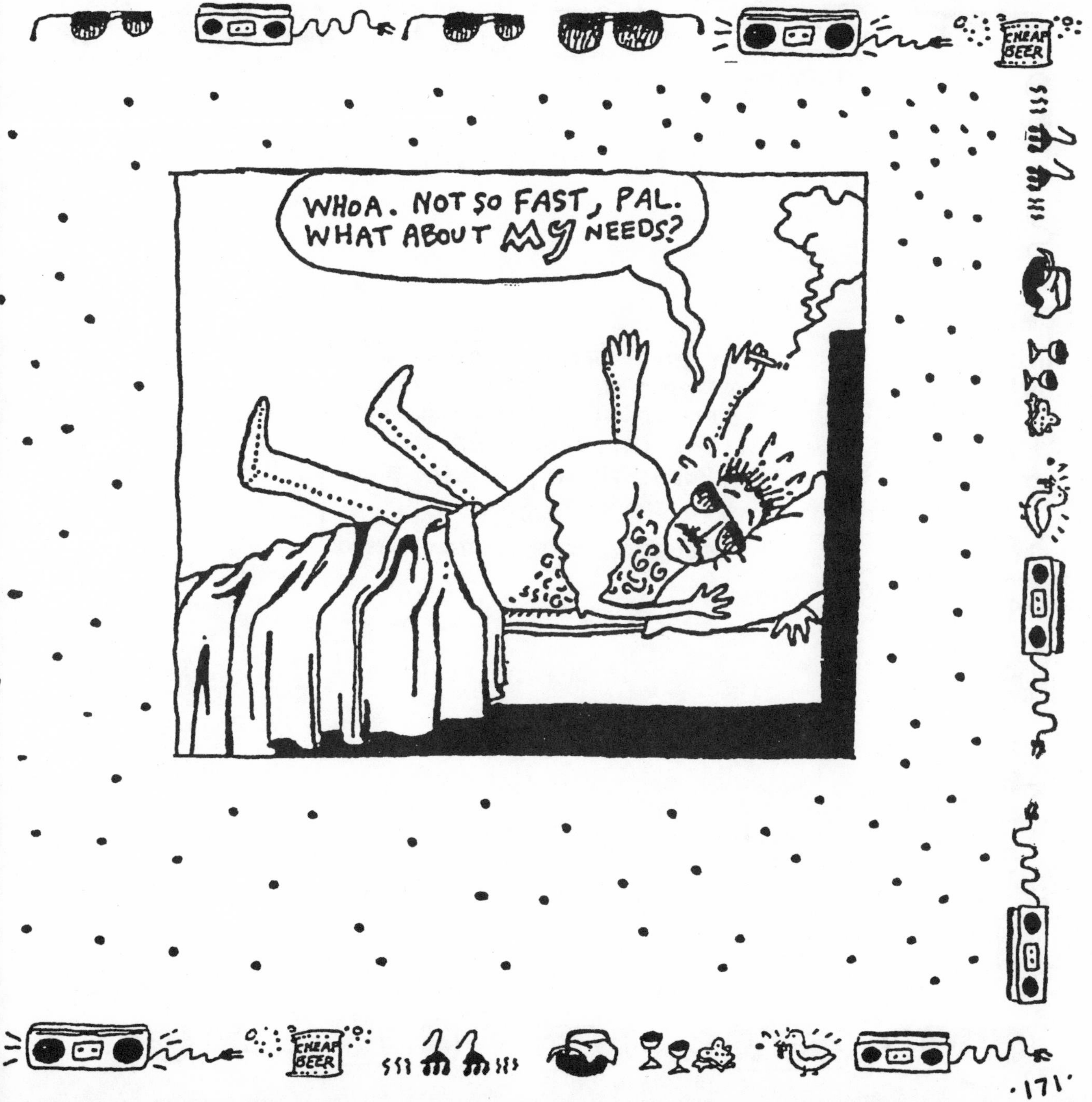
WHOA. NOT SO FAST, PAL.
WHAT ABOUT MY NEEDS?
CHEAP BEER
CHEAP BEER

CAMARO JOE IMMEDIATELY
ZIPPED HIS PANTS BACK UP +
FORCED HIS "ITALIAN STALLION"
T-SHIRT BACK OVER HIS
BODY. THEN HE RAN BACK
TO THE CAFÉ + SAID ...

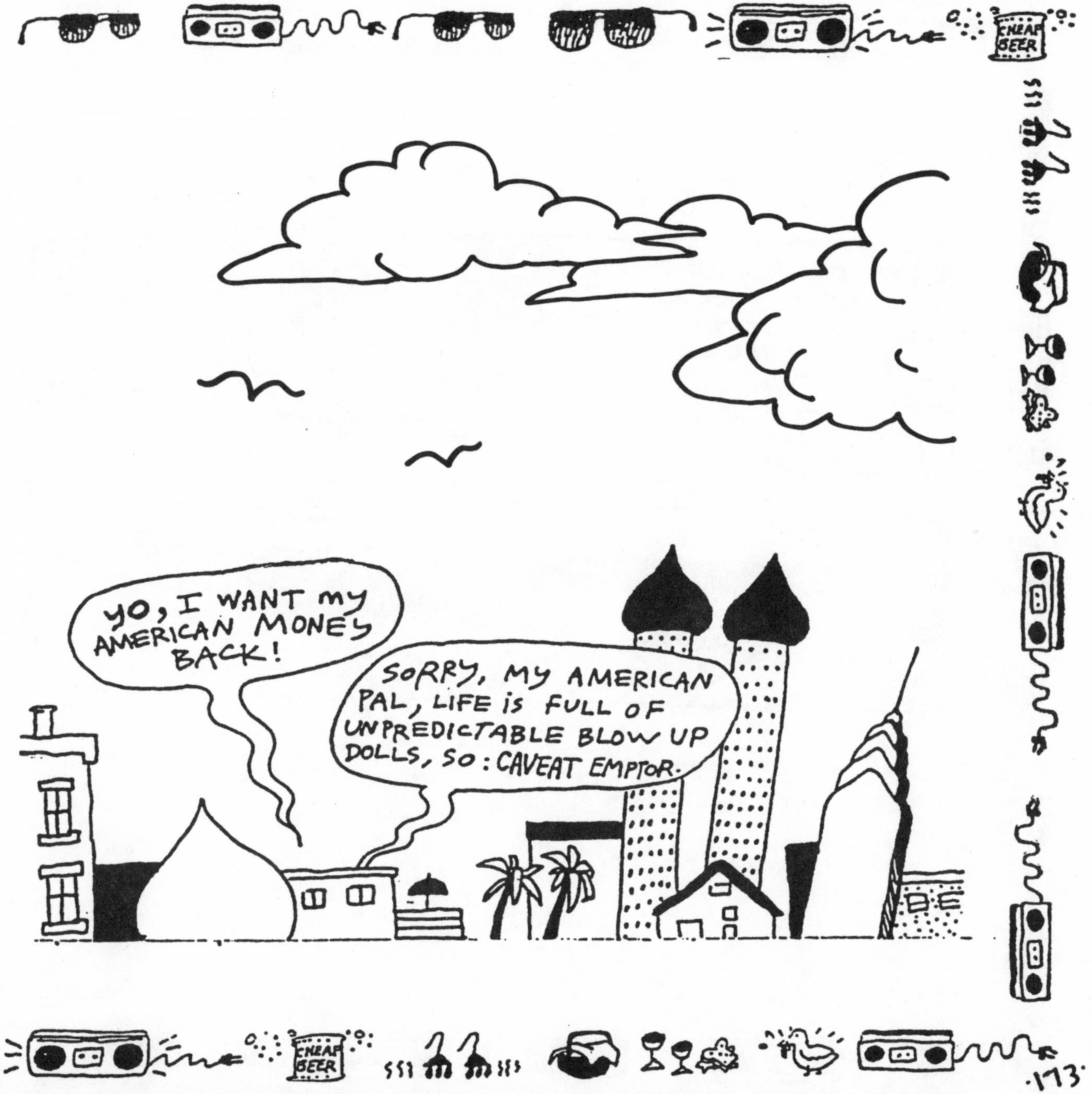
CHEAP BEER
YO, I WANT MY AMERICAN MONEY BACK!
SORRY, MY AMERICAN PAL, LIFE IS FULL OF UNPREDICTABLE BLOW UP DOLLS, SO: CAVEAT EMPTOR.
CHEAP BEER
CHEAP BEER

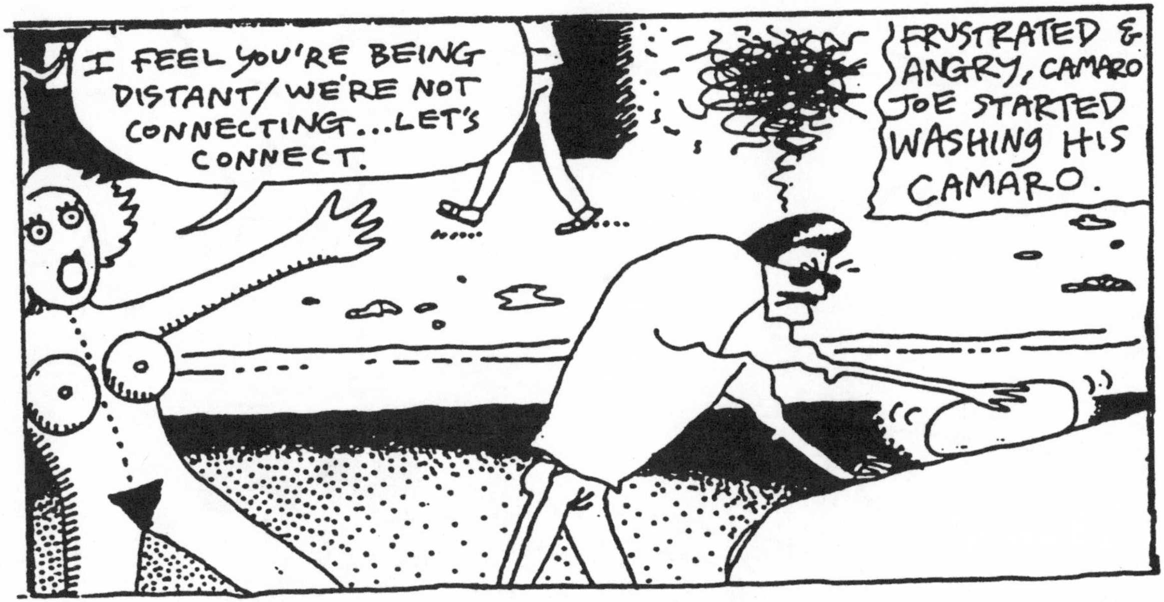
I FEEL YOU'RE BEING DISTANT/ WE'RE NOT CONNECTING...LET'S CONNECT.
FRUSTRATED & ANGRY, CAMARO JOE STARTED WASHING HIS CAMARO.

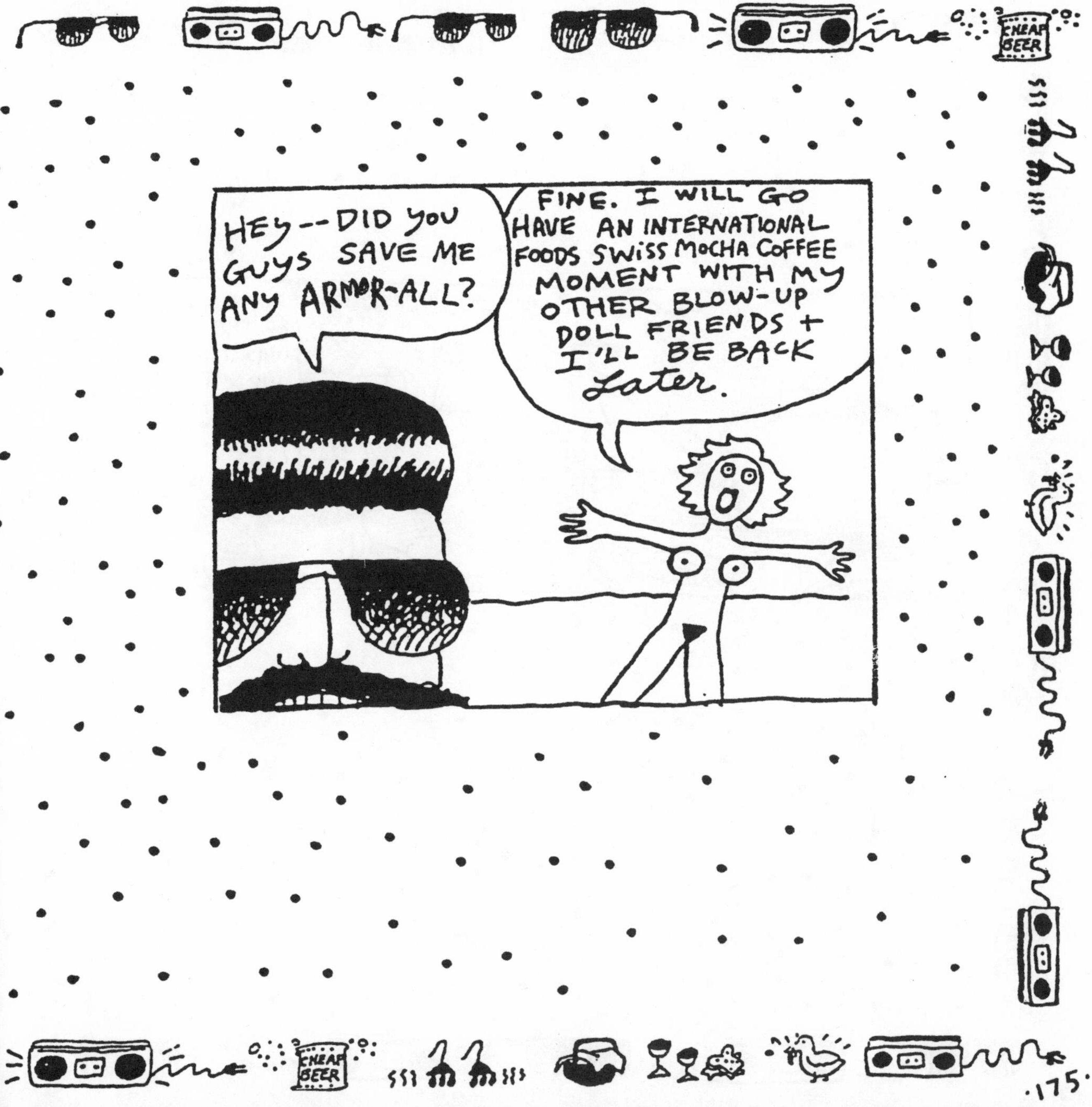
HEY--DID YOU GUYS SAVE ME ANY ARMOR-ALL?
FINE. I WILL GO HAVE AN INTERNATIONAL FOODS SWISS MOCHA COFFEE MOMENT WITH MY OTHER BLOW-UP DOLL FRIENDS + I'LL BE BACK Later.
CHEAP BEER
CHEAP BEER

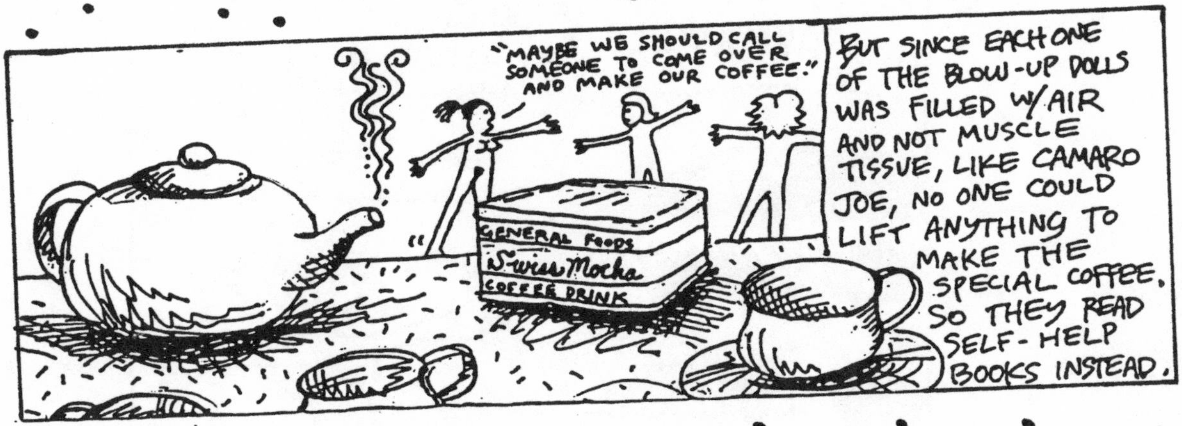
"MAYBE WE SHOULD CALL SOMEONE TO COME OVER AND MAKE OUR COFFEE."
GENERAL FOODS
Swiss Mocha
COFFEE DRINK
BUT SINCE EACH ONE OF THE BLOW-UP DOLLS WAS FILLED W/ AIR AND NOT MUSCLE TISSUE, LIKE CAMARO JOE, NO ONE COULD LIFT ANYTHING TO MAKE THE SPECIAL COFFEE. SO THEY READ SELF-HELP BOOKS INSTEAD.

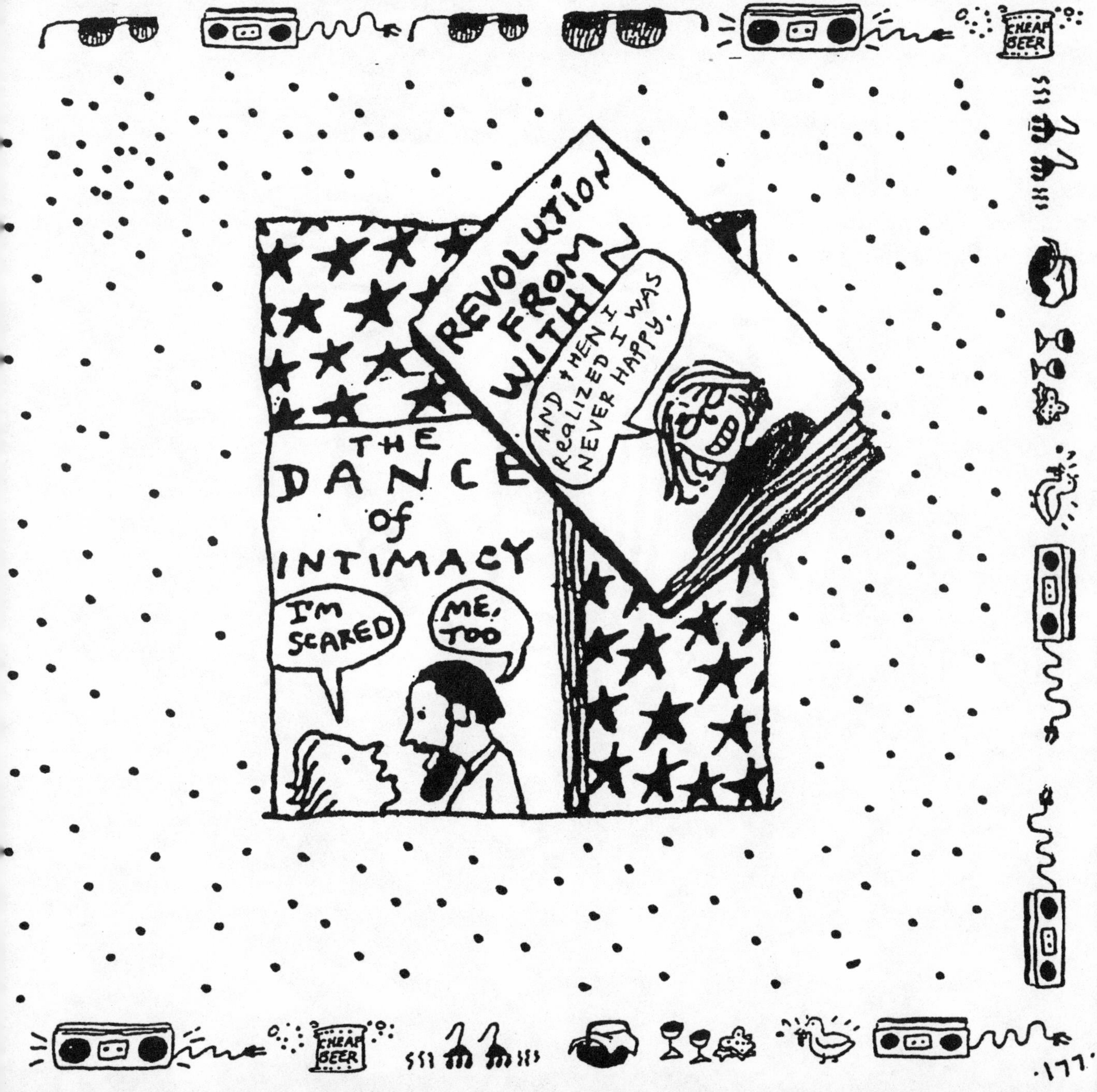
CHEAP BEER
REVOLUTION FROM WITHIN
AND THEN I REALIZED I WAS NEVER HAPPY.
THE DANCE of INTIMACY
I'M SCARED
ME, TOO
CHEAP BEER

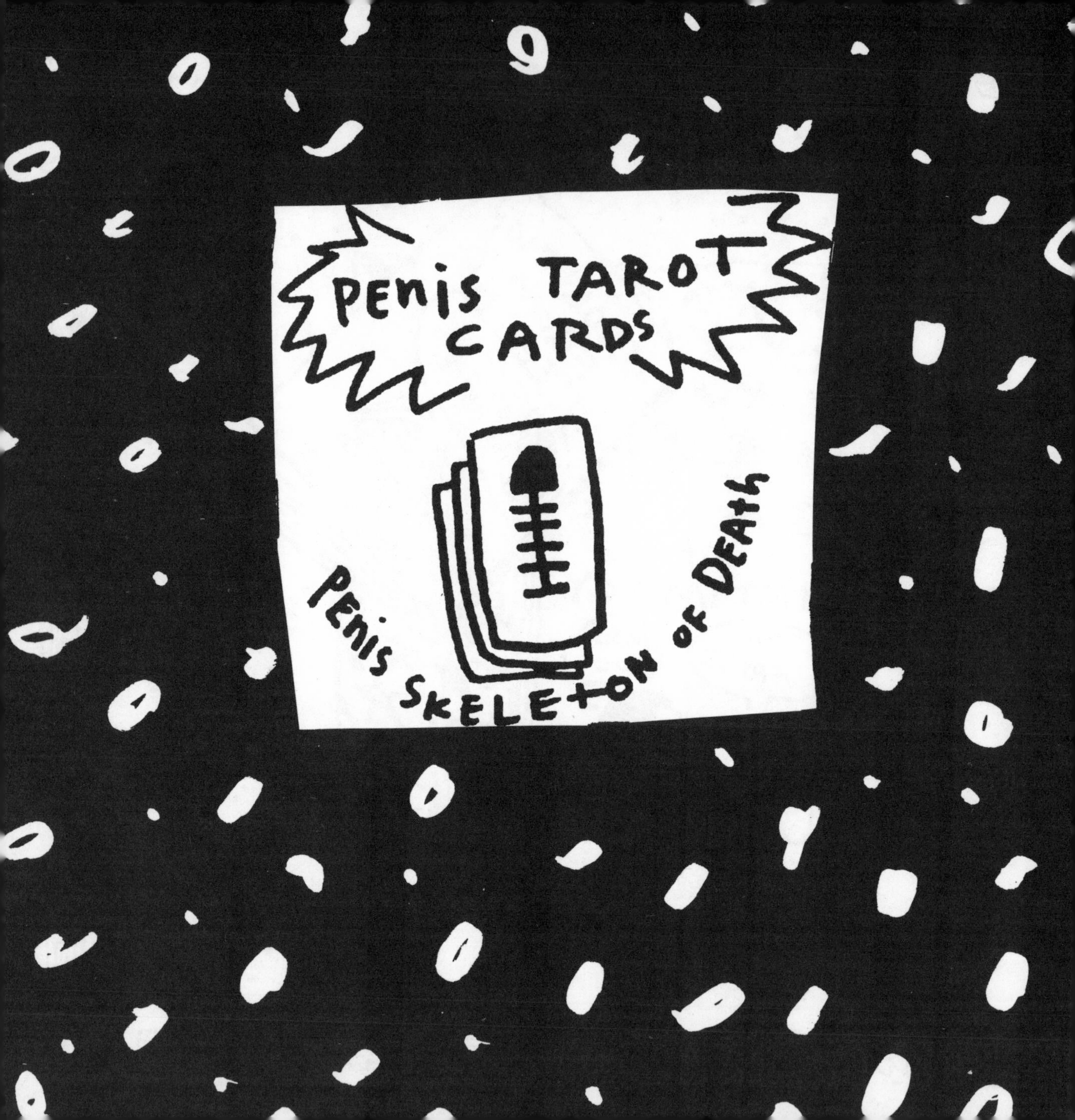
PENIS TAROT CARDS
PENIS SKELETON OF DEATH

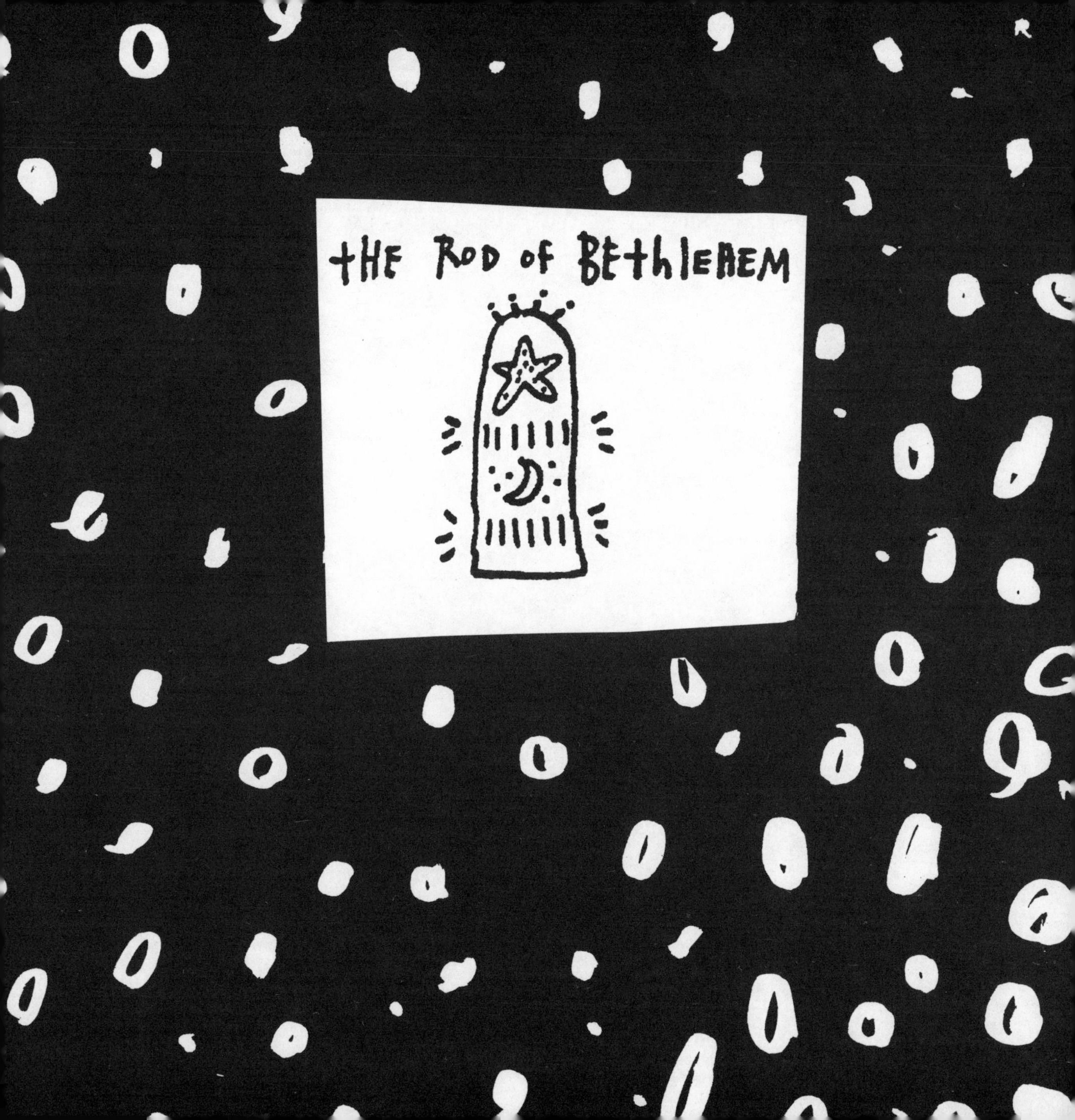
THE ROD OF BETHLEHEM

View Master Flashbacks.

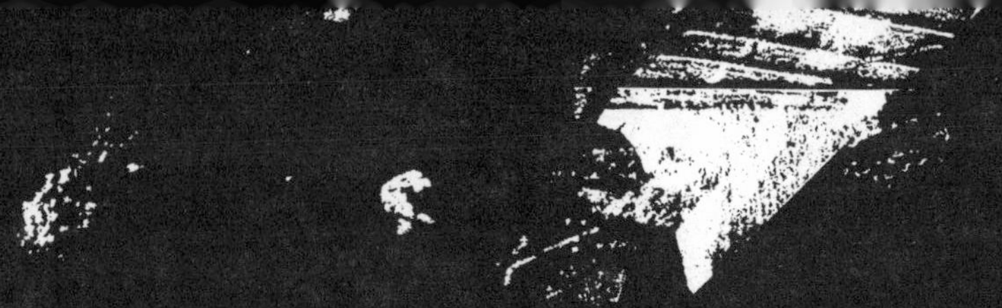

I was looking through my new view master. It was the new red kind with rounded corners.

So smooth./So sensual./So *red.*

I inserted a "WINNIE THE POOH" slide and held it up to my face :

I saw a big oak tree with a door, and through the door I could see the edges of a wooden spiral staircase, and an old trunk off to one side.

Hmmm... A staircase that went up and a closed trunk... Maybe, just *maybe* there was porridge in the trunk. I wanted in there. I wanted so badly to walk up that perfect balsa staircase and into the three-dimensionality of this immaculate view master claymation world.

There was never any view master trash, nor any view-master pain.

I craved this world , and immediately felt my stomach lurch and my soul shrivel like a very sick raisin.

Maybe Rudolph and the Heat Miser would be there, patiently waiting for me on a styrofoam ice berg, and we could glide over to the island of misfit toys, and give the gay Charlie-in-the-box a t-shirt with a pink triangle on it. It won't say "silence equals death" because there isn't any AIDS in this secretion-free world.

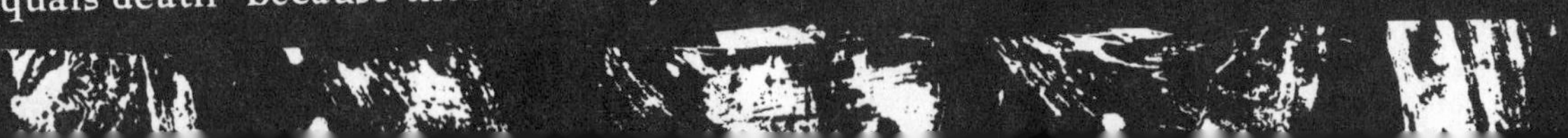

I will be Christopher Robbin's lover, and blow in his claymation ear. (whoosh)

I will say to him: "Hey----I want/need/love you, and I'm going to rape your mouth and ram my playdough tongue down your dusty throat."

He will love me for dominating him and sigh in my arms. I will carry him up the balsa wood staircase, and we will make love on the miniature patchwork quilt/

Afterwards, we will eat hot porridge from the magic porridge trunk. Later, we will have *sex* in the magic porridge trunk because

(a), it is fun, and

(b), because we are unlubricated:

we are clay.

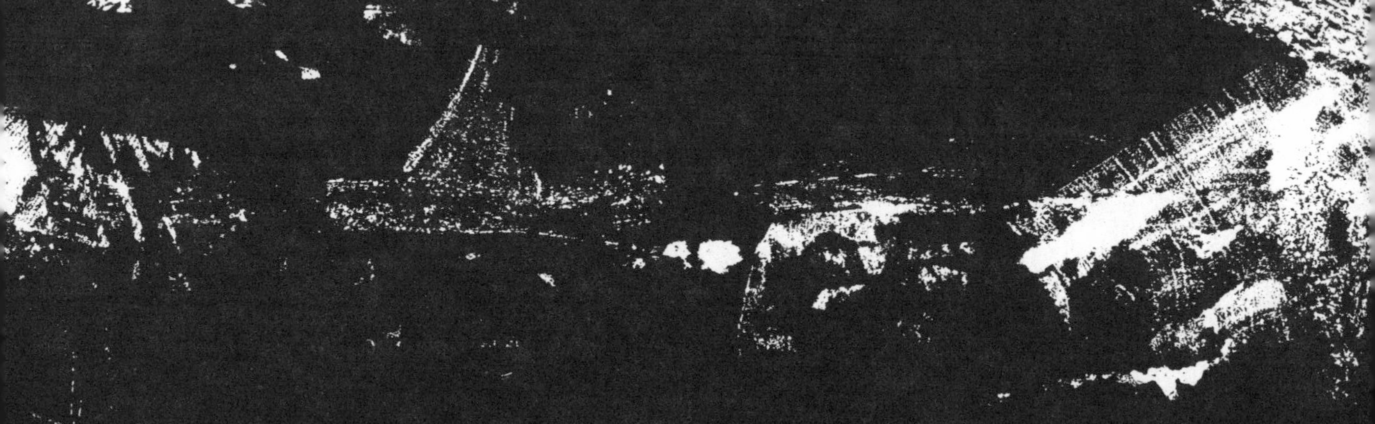

But in my twenty-five year old heart, I knew there was no way to safely enter the view master land of claymation. And this impossibility nearly caused me to toss my head back, shriek and throw my body--with its bodice-ripping honey brown thighs--down my ghetto pine stairs.

But I didn't. / No. /Instead I kicked out the lights and had a memory dream called "Half breed that's all I ever heard....Half breed, oh how I love to hate the word"

I was in second grade and jumping on the bed while singing along to cher's "Halfbreed" song on my plastic-blue record player. I sounded exactly like cher, and I was proud. I was also proud as I put on my mustard brown construction paper headband with its magenta feather.

I jumped off the bed and said:

"Yes, Cher, I feel your halfbreed Indian pain. All you have to do is call me and I will be your halfbreed friend."

But just then, an evil, evil person came into the room and said: "Hey, you! You Puerto Rican girl in the Andy Warhol wig----Cher isn't even part Indian. And you wanna know something else? There isn't even any Santa Claus and Jackson Browne beats up women!"

Bam! A pen stabbed right into the heart of my newfound identity-crisis/soul-mate thing. I cried as I slowly dropped my headband in the trash and shelved "Cher's greatest hits" forever.

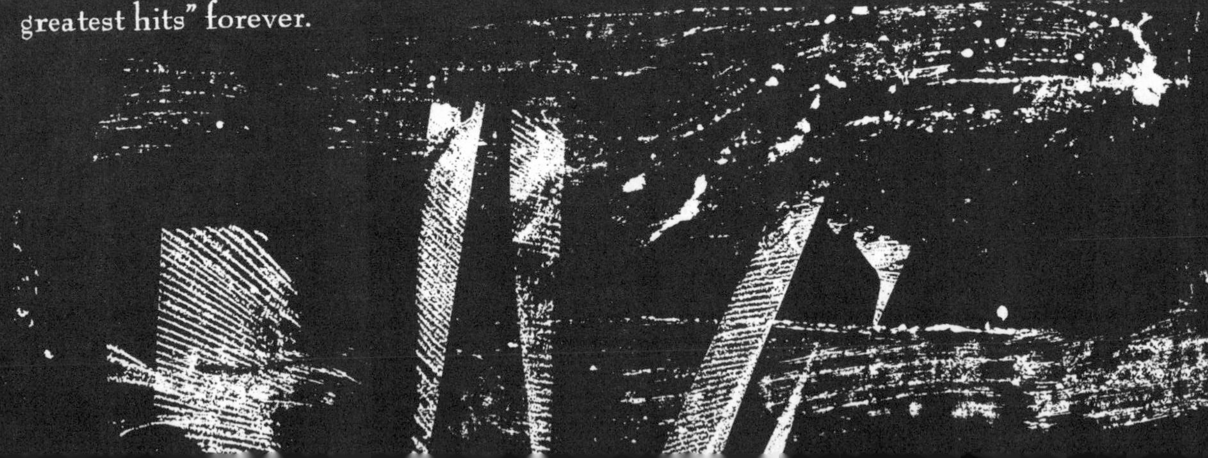

While picking up the shards of my confused and shattered world, I decided to become black because someone once said I was--and didn't I feel a pang of horror as I walked into my Jewish friend's house once and saw this old black cleaning lady in uniform-white, walking out the door/ shyly diverting her eyes and demurely crossing her arms in front of her/ tiny black patent leather purse?

Yes.

Then I was black. Black until I screamed and refused to eat the soul food placed before me. Black until the black girls told me I thought I was something because of my hair.

Oh, how I wanted the planet-sized afro of "Get Christy Love," the almost pornographic police detective with hot pants and go-go boots. The white lipstick of semen against her black skin, and underneath views of karate kicks to the foe. Yow/ I feel my seventies nipples harden and my Freudian penis envy rising.

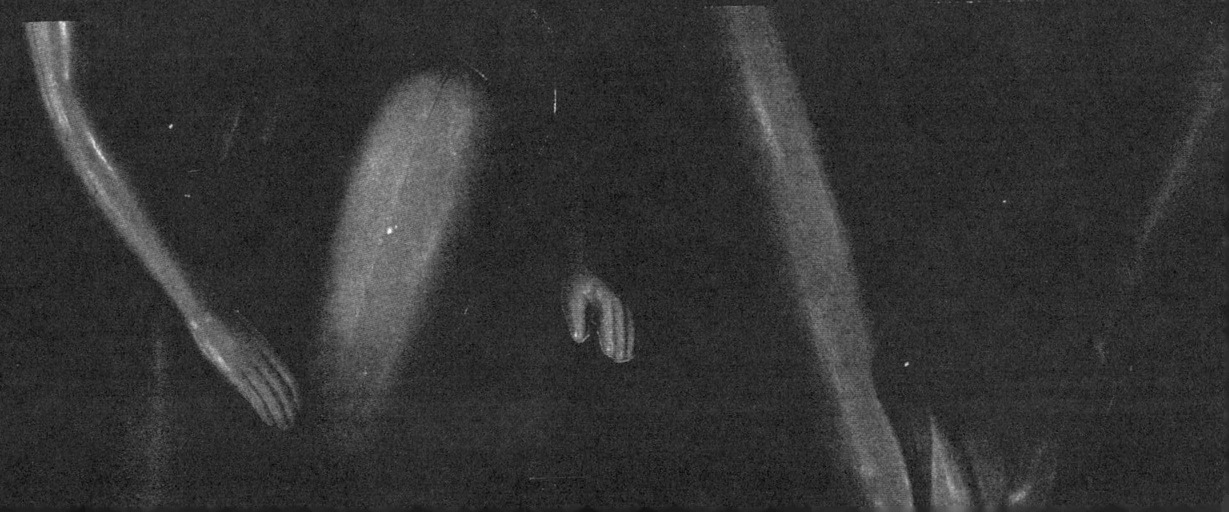

Sandra May

Erika Lopez is the author of the graphic novel Flaming Iguanas. She divides her time between San Francisco and Philadelphia.